Teaching
Religious Knowledge

Teaching
Religious Knowledge

A BOOK OF METHOD
FOR TEACHERS

BERNARD R. YOUNGMAN
L.C.P., F.R.S.A.

*Headmaster, Hoveton County Secondary School. Sometime
Senior Lecturer in Education and Head of the Religious
Knowledge Department, City of Coventry (Men's)
Training College*

With a Foreword by
Dr. BASIL YEAXLEE
C.B.E., M.A., B.Litt.

*Fellow of the British Psychological Society. Sometime Reader
in Educational Psychology in the University of Oxford*

UNIVERSITY OF LONDON PRESS LTD
WARWICK SQUARE, LONDON E.C.4

To
MY WIFE

Third Edition Copyright © 1958
by BERNARD R. YOUNGMAN

First Edition	.	1953
Second Edition	.	1956
Third Edition	.	1958
Third Impression	.	1963

Printed & Bound in England for the UNIVERSITY OF LONDON PRESS LTD
by HAZELL WATSON & VINEY LTD, Aylesbury, Bucks

FOREWORD

To teach in accordance with an Agreed Syllabus demands considerable knowledge and skill as well as conviction. It has become a cliché that if Scripture is to be taught universally it should be at least as well taught as any other subject. The eager desire of so many teachers to make the most of their privilege and opportunity finds frequent expression in the demand for books and lectures on method, though they tend to discount the advice of the theorist. Mr. Youngman may well command their confidence, because he possesses both clear insight into principle and mature experience of the ways in which practical effect can be given to it. In earlier years he taught in Primary and what were then all-age schools. Now he is in daily contact, as Headmaster of a County Secondary School, with boys and girls between eleven and sixteen. As formerly a Training College lecturer he is familiar with many types of school other than his own. The needs and potentialities of both younger and older pupils are well presented in these vigorous, incisive, imaginative chapters. He brings forth out of his treasury things new and old. It would be a singularly insensitive, not to say self-satisfied, teacher who failed to derive stimulus and detailed suggestions from a book into which so much enthusiasm and such discipline of judgment have gone, and which can be commended with both pleasure and assurance.

BASIL A. YEAXLEE

PREFACE TO THIRD EDITION

A few necessary amendments have been made, especially in Chapter XXI, and the Bibliography has been brought up to date. It is gratifying to note the special attention now being given to the revision of Agreed Syllabuses. It is to be hoped that all L.E.A.s will make it a matter of urgency to provide Agreed Syllabuses suitably geared to the Secondary Modern School and distinctive from those for the Grammar and Technical Schools. I would commend to my readers the present need for closer Day and Sunday School teacher relationships, so that together we may base our religious training of the young on sound principle and practice and with understanding of one another's problems.

Bernard R. Youngman

PREFACE TO SECOND EDITION

A Second Edition gives me the opportunity to revise and correct the existing text and to bring in up-to-date information.

Further, in response to suggestions and requests, I have added a chapter on the approach to Teaching Philosophy in schools, which I hope may serve my colleagues whose fortune it is to deal with more advanced classes. This is one of the less well-defined courses recommended by the Agreed Syllabuses, and I have endeavoured to outline practical applications. I trust that more than a few brave spirits with the upper forms of progressive Secondary Modern Schools will find here and there a suggestion that will enable them to embark upon a worth-while venture; I hope, too, that these approaches may serve usefully my colleagues in Grammar and Independent Schools where advanced courses are already undertaken.

For technical reasons this chapter (XX) is placed at the end of Part II of the book.

Bernard R. Youngman

PREFACE TO FIRST EDITION

THIS is meant to be a friendly book, in which one teacher is endeavouring to share with others some of the approaches, experiences and methods found useful and practical during his several years in all types of schools with all types of children.

The style, therefore, is intentionally informal, and perhaps my older and more experienced readers will forgive the occasional lapses into chats to students.

Part I may serve as a reminder of the changing attitude towards Religious Education during the past years, and of the impact made by the 1944 Act upon this branch of our curriculum.

Part II is avowedly practical. But we must bear in mind that knowledge of techniques and methods is not enough. Our duty in the school is to "preach Christ," according to the revelation of His life and work given in the Bible. "These things were written that ye might believe"—that is the source of our faith; "I know in WHOM I have believed"—that is the core. The teacher must have roots in himself if his work is to be anything more than mechanical application of method to material. Like the shepherd of old he must lead —and he must know where he is going; he must find pasture—and must have been there before.

I owe much to many people for help and guidance in the writing of this book—my patient pupils, my willing students, other authors who have so obviously shared the similar experiences, my friends and critics who have read all or parts of the manuscript. In Dr. Basil Yeaxlee I have a friend and mentor beyond price; I cannot assess the richness of his kindly understanding and practical advice, but I do happily and humbly acknowledge their untold worth in the shaping of my work. I owe thanks, too, to members of my Staff—Mrs. P. Greenaway, Religious Knowledge specialist, Mr. R. Edwards, Art Master, and Mr. S. Read for his excellent photographs; to Mr. W. L. Jenkins, of Trelawny S.M. School, for quotations and examples of work; to Mr. H. Workman, of Montacute, for exchange of ideas and methods; to Mr. R. H. Mumford, whose idea it was that the

8

book should be written; to Mr. H. E. Brown for seeing the manu-script safely through the many stages of production.

I have tried to acknowledge all quotations and ideas where I am cognisant of their sources, but must make a general acknowledgment of all others used without my consciously remembering their origin.

Finally, may I hope that I have provided help for those who need it in a job that needs doing so well that the ignorance and indifference now prevalent may be boldly challenged—and perhaps to some extent dispelled?

BERNARD R. YOUNGMAN

CONTENTS

PART III—SOURCES OF INFORMATION
AND GUIDANCE

PART I

EXAMINING THE PROBLEM

CHAPTER I

INTRODUCING THE BOOK—AND
THE PROBLEM

DON'T skip the Introduction. It's like the front door of the house, and is usually the best way in.

Let us look at two lads, separated by nearly two thousand years of time. Towards the end of the first century A.D., Paul wrote to one named Timothy words that have come down to us as a crystallising of the Christian faith: "From a child thou hast known the holy scriptures which are able to make thee wise unto salvation through faith which is in Christ Jesus." Timothy had been brought up in a Christian home by Christian parents, nurtured in beliefs that meant something to him all his days; his background, training and faith were secure.

In 1948, a student in training as a teacher was confronted with a class of 14 + boys for a Scripture lesson. He decided to find out their background. Here is his report verbatim: "I elicited the information that the Bible is divided into Old and New Testaments. When the boys were asked the names of some books, the sum total consisted of Genesis, Psalms, Matthew, Mark, Luke, John (a natural sequence from a local limerick!) and . . . 'Is there a book called Micah in the New Testament, sir?' On being asked to tell the gist of any one story they could remember from the Bible, only one lad volunteered an answer, and he stammered falteringly about a man, whose name he did not know, going near to a bush and taking his shoes off. At the next lesson I started on a more general note, and after reminding the boys that they had a number of books for various purposes, asked, 'What sort of book is the Bible? What does it tell us about?' A glimmer came to the eyes of a single lad who replied hesitantly, 'Please, sir, it's a geography book.' Not wishing to dampen this faint spark, I said, 'Yes, it does tell us about geography in a way. Which country does it tell us about in particular?' 'Israel,' said the boy. 'And where is the country of Israel?' 'Please, sir, in Jerusalem.' "

And this, in the Year of Our Lord, 1948—four years after the Education Act that "put religion on the map!" A far cry, indeed, from Timothy to Tommy Smith, even allowing for the fact that Timothy had Paul for his teacher.

Do you recall the "Top of the Form" programmes on the radio? Just a short time ago, one of the rounds in the battle of knowledge was on Scripture. It was a signal and dismal failure. It is not possible to give the questions verbatim, but here they are in essence:

> Who fed on locusts and wild honey?
> What was Paul's name before he was converted?
> Who refused to leave her mother-in-law?
> What occupation did Peter follow?
> Who was the oldest man mentioned in the Bible?
> Under whom were the people of Israel exiled?
> What is the name given to the Latin form of the Bible?
> Name any one modern version of the Bible.

Of these eight questions the teams of children answered *two*— Saul and Babylon. Yet, were the questions difficult or unfamiliar? Surely they were quite fair and representative of at least a simple knowledge of Biblical matters; the result was not only sad, it was woefully indicative of that lack of knowledge of the Holy Scriptures which we find so distressingly obvious in our schools.

Examples to the contrary may be produced, but reports and discussions at Conferences, Courses and Research Committees reveal that this is still typical of the state of religious training in far too many schools; it is pathetic and it is challenging.

No one in the profession, or outside it, doubts the existence of the problem of Religious Knowledge teaching. That it demands attention is obvious. The real issue is—How best to solve the problem? This is the question I am trying to answer, by offering a wide variety of detailed methods by means of which our children may be helped to a practical understanding of the Holy Scriptures. Perhaps one may hope that some new approach will reveal to them a reason for life itself.

CHAPTER II

SHALL I TEACH IT?

Considering the subject; a plea for training; essentials for the teacher; the challenge to the Christian teacher.

THIS book is intended to help both specialist and class teacher asked to take Scripture at least with his own class.

We need first to consider the minimum essentials of this branch of teaching. Few teachers can claim scholastic qualifications in Religious Knowledge, but we must admit at the outset that, specialist or not, the Religious Knowledge teacher must equip himself beyond mere faith and conviction. His own philosophy, however sound, can be transferred to his pupils only through methods that are practical, attractive and educationally right.

On the whole, the present position of non-specialists concerned with the teaching of the subject appears to be this. More than ever do they want to teach Religious Knowledge, but more than ever before do they feel that despite conviction and good intention they lack knowledge of the Bible itself and the Faith they profess. It is possible for children, especially older children, to ask questions that can be answered only by a teacher who possesses both—and it is surely a dreadful thing to fall into the hands of adolescence! Teachers who by training and qualification can claim to be specialists may have both and yet find their work monotonous and unrewarding as they pursue the few well-worn methods of the past.

Hence, we must stress the need for knowledge of the subject supported by wide reading, personal conviction and sense of vocation. Without these, even as specialists, we cannot make any method attractive.

We might admit here, too, a plea for some kind of adequate training in Biblical studies and simple theology. Conferences, Courses and Schools in Religious Knowledge are becoming increasingly well known and well attended. It remains for Local Education Authorities to release their teachers and enable them to get this necessary training easily and without financial hardships, in term time as well as in holidays. Diplomas and certificates of appropriate standing are available and will be made more and more suitable for the practising teacher. The State insists upon the inclusion of Religious Knowledge in the curriculum; it should take steps to see that well-qualified teachers are provided to teach it. As the Secondary Education Report of the Advisory Council on Education in Scotland says, "Devoutness and good intentions are no substitute for adequate scholarship." In this report, too, stress is laid upon the need for a course in Methodology and Scripture teaching.

We cannot all be specialists, but we have libraries, lectures, courses and conferences. And, humbly, we can learn much in the seeking with our children. For certainly, as the Archbishop of York said recently at a North of England Education Conference, "there is little hope of the recovery by the nation of Christian faith unless it is taught to the children in the schools"—and it is we who have to do that teaching.

The Christian faith has been spoken of as being tried and found wanting; today, it too often doesn't get tried because it isn't wanted! And perhaps it isn't wanted because it isn't known. Let us be frank. Our children do not know the Faith, or the Bible, as once these were known. It is the Bible that provides the way of life we need to give to them. As the Spens Report says, "The traditional form which that [religious] interpretation [of life] has taken in this country is Christian, and the principal justification for giving a place in the curriculum to the study of the Scriptures is that the Bible is the classic book of Christianity and forms the basis of the structure of Christian faith and worship."

It has already been said that the essentials for the good teacher of the subject are knowledge and background reading, personal conviction and sense of vocation. These are interdependent, and though we may look at each separately, they are of necessity complementary. We must put first an accurate knowledge of the Bible. Time and study will make it a full one. Further reading will extend and develop that knowledge. We are going to discuss methods—i.e. How to teach; but we must know What to teach. It is so easy to teach in a lesson something the children will have to unlearn in years to come. Many of them may pass through painful spiritual experience of doubt and scepticism because of ill-informed teaching. This is something we must avoid at all costs and, as far as is in our power, prevent. This can only be done by making a reasonably sound critical approach to our own reading and study. The Bible is our text-book, and discerning scholarship has revealed more and more the God-man relationship that is the basis of Christian living.

Much of this knowledge and background study (as in all subjects) is for the teacher only. A good teacher must know more than he needs to teach; it gives him a sense of perspective if nothing else. Yet, the mere passing on of Biblical background is not enough; and this is where our second point—personal conviction—comes in.

If you want to teach Religious Knowledge, and feeling badly equipped go to the trouble of getting your material and background right, the strength of your own faith will temper the desire to impart just facts. What happens is this. As one studies, accepts, rejects and finds that through the wood marked with trees one *can* see a path, one realises that the Old and New Testaments are a unity. The Bible is about God and His revelation to men "at sundry times and in divers manners." He has spoken "from the beginning," and the records, so carefully analysed, annotated, documented, edited by the critics, make that Message clearer simply because interpretation has been aided by clarification. The Bible, "transformed from a file of books into a line of men," is in some ways a library of biographies and autobiographies of men who were spiritually moved to speak and to listen; they peopled "the strange new world of God within the Bible." They lived in their eras as a people of God; it is the teacher's faith that in the twentieth century men should live as people of God. That is precisely where his personal conviction meets its test. For, what signs of any Christian conviction do his children see in their world? It is impersonal, war-ridden; agnostic, unbelieving, afraid; it is ruled by a "help-yourself" and "whip-it-quick" code. It is so much occupied with living by bread alone that it knows not how to live. It does not hear, and if it does it does not heed, the challenge of the Bible, whose treasure is so different from the treasure of men. How easy, then, for the teacher to concentrate on the academics of his subject and to strengthen a worldly agnosticism in his pupils. How hard for him to couple his knowledge to his faith, and pit both against the willing ignorance of modern man. Yet, that is uncompromisingly his task. It is his duty to expound today the ageless message of God as found in the Bible in such a way that they will listen, and listening will understand, and understanding will practise the precepts of God to the confounding of men:

> Man is lord of the Universe;
> He knows much better,
> He does much worse!

It is not a light duty. Our own faith needs to be mightily clear and strong.

So, to our third point—sense of vocation. Whatever the cynics may say of the reasons why men and women take up our profession, experience indicates that a glorious majority have chosen teaching with a fine sense of vocation. After every war we plan to make the world a better place, a Christian brotherhood. England is always to be the New Jerusalem. The cynics say, "What a hope!" The teachers say, "Here am I. Send me." Like the prophets of old, they seek to inspire their children to be good citizens. Teachers of Religious Knowledge have this special task—to present the Word of God to the children with the guidance of the Spirit of God, that by knowledge hand in hand with faith the building of the New Jerusalem may be better than they know, and that it may be a place where there is a positive faith in a living God.

Let us make no bones about it. The teacher of Religious Knowledge must be a Christian teacher. He must consecrate and dedicate his abilities, his talents and his personality to the service of God. His work is equal to that of the minister of the Gospel. The disciples said, "Show us." Our children say, "Show us God. Show us Jesus. Then we shall understand."

Whatever the particular approach in the classroom, whatever the special lesson or the intrinsic benefit, what matters in the long run is that the teacher should bring home the fundamental themes of the Bible described and developed in the Old Testament, fulfilled and glorified in the New—life, death, the past, present, time and eternity, sin and forgiveness, judgment and mercy, right and wrong, evil and good. The teacher's task is rightly to present these, developing—perhaps even beginning—a Christian tradition whose essence "lies in the insistence upon the reality of God as the determining factor in man's understanding of his life."

All this seems a counsel of perfection that none of us can ever attain. There is no doubt that none of us can afford to wait until we have striven and to some extent attained. Our task is plain—to equip ourselves, to strengthen ourselves, to offer ourselves. For it is more than a vocation, it is a mission.

You may have read *How Heathen is Britain?* by B. G. Sandhurst (Collins). It is a startling analysis of religious education prior to the 1939–45 war, and well worth attention. In a letter to *Religion in Education*, Sandhurst says that what is wrong with the results of Christian education—"the drift to paganism among the young"—is "that there is an extraordinary lack of integration or correlation between religious instruction and life." After analysing the position he goes on, "The readiness to learn about their faith is a new and great opportunity. *It lays on every Christian schoolmaster a serious responsibility*." As Dr. Yeaxlee so sanely comments, "The challenge must be met in the schools . . . not because so many boys and girls never go to church or hear about religion at home, but because Jesus Christ is either the Truth—about God and about Man—or He was the incarnation of that lie in the soul about which Plato wrote. If He is the Truth there is a vital connection between the Christian faith and every form of truth in which we set out to educate children—historical, scientific, economic, political, moral—or there are no such things as a consistent universe and consistent thinking."

The challenge comes to all teachers of Religious Knowledge. If you are uncertain of the field, visit any Youth Club, talk to adolescents; the result is too often disquieting. Then come back to the challenge, and prepare once more to bring the precepts of the Christian faith into the daily lives of the children. Teaching Religious Knowledge is uphill work, but it is not an impossible task. You will need knowledge and study, personal conviction, sense of vocation. You will need to be very sincere, extremely tolerant and infinitely patient. You will also need a great determination, a tremendous sense of humour and a hide like that of a rhinoceros!

CHAPTER III

A BACKWARD LOOK

Scripture lessons "then"; facing the problem.

Much of the failure for which our schools are blamed is no doubt due to the "bad old days" when Scripture was "taken" from 9.10 to 9.30 every morning, with nine-tenths of the time occupied with hymn practices, play rehearsals, medicals, collecting of moneys for savings and the like. It is small wonder that as a result Scripture was regarded as of little or no importance, and that two—and often three—large classes might be lumped together so as to give time off for marking. It certainly could not be classed with Mathematics or English; in fact, these subjects often benefited from time stolen from the Scripture period preceding them. The subject was never tested; children read round the class, or were set to learn psalms of prodigious length without any understanding of their meaning.

Some of us were more fortunate, and gladly acknowledge our debt to conscientious teachers who demurred at giving up their precious twenty minutes so that stock and books might be checked. We remember with gratitude their Scripture lessons; our lives are the better for them.

The author of *How Heathen is Britain?* tells us that 83 per cent. of his men learned nothing in their Scripture lessons. Even if his experience is exceptional, it is none the less significant—and sad. Many say their lessons were "quite useless," "parrot-wise," consisting of "Bible reading only." For many "no attempt was made to bring out the man-God and nation-God relationships wherein lies the principal value of the Old Testament." And again, "The facts of the tremendous revolution that Christ brought about were never discussed. It seemed as if the subject of Christ's teaching and life was labelled 'Please do not touch—highly explosive!'" The majority of lessons appear to have been Old Testament stories. If the life and teaching of Jesus were tackled, it was mostly in a chronological rather than either a practical or a spiritual way. "The great bulk of our schoolmasters have forgotten the real object of religious education—the production of a sound and reasoned knowledge of our Lord's divine personality and of God's purpose in creating us."

It would not be fair to leave this heavy charge solely on the shoulders of teachers of the past. There has been a war. Thousands of children lost their basic training in all the time-table subjects. We have been hard put to it sometimes to understand their lack of knowledge, tending to forget the hours they spent in shelters and the lessons they never had. But well before 1944, educationists were showing signs of concern, and as sponsor of the Act, Mr. Butler saw the pathetic picture of religious training prior to that time, and the need for definite action to put things on a new and sound footing. The setting up of L.E.A. Conferences to prepare syllabuses—Agreed Syllabuses—was only one of the many steps taken in the right direction. The compulsory teaching of Scripture, whether termed Religious Knowledge, Religious Instruction, Divinity or just Scripture, was another.

One might have hoped that by now many of the recommendations of the Act were forced upon the notice of the heads of all schools. Yet there are still many schools where Religious Knowledge remains on the time-table from 9.10 to 9.30, still at the mercy of marauding interruptions in new guises—milk deliveries, collecting of numbers for school meals and National Savings. It is reported of one county that of nearly four hundred schools only fifteen "have changed and utilised the freedom given by the Act to distribute religious instruction periods throughout the day." For most of them, the first period remains the favourite time. The corollary is obvious—that most if not all teachers have, willy-nilly, to take part in the teaching of the subject, which the Act by its conscience clause for teachers is meant to obviate.

The Act made it compulsory to open school with an act of worship. In many schools there remains much to do to make the Morning Service of real spiritual value to the community.[1]

And classes are still herded together for the Scripture lesson. Students have been known to ask for lesson material for the following classes: 88 boys of 10+, 103 of 8+, 73 of 10+ mixed, 75 of 10+ mixed, 80 of 9+ mixed—these last three in the same school.

[1] See Chapter XVII on "School Worship."

Lest it should be thought that Primary Schools only are open to criticism, it should also be noted that in one and the same Secondary Modern School, Paul was "taken" in mixed classes of the following age ranges: 12, 13+, 12+ and 13+, A and B streams. To say the least, there was something rotten in the state of the syllabus.

On the other hand, we may look gladly on a shining band of schools which have made the required changes and are remarkable for their fine influence and for the permeation of the whole life of the school community with a Christian spirit. Scripture lessons are looked forward to because they mean something to teacher and children alike, for the Cinderella of the time-table has been placed where she belongs in her true dress: Morning Worship in these schools is an outward sign of the invisible bonds of the Christian spirit.

That this is so is clear proof of what may be done by hard work, sincerity, trust and example. We, too, can attain that level.

CHAPTER IV

A FORWARD LOOK

Principles applied; reviewing the class; the Bible as text-book; methods and material; correlation; testing; the new challenge.

WHAT are the possibilities of the future?

Success in any branch of the curriculum depends to a large extent upon the sensible application of educational and psychological principles. Religious education can succeed only if it is treated like any other subject. Theory has a distressing habit of collapsing in the classroom, but it is less likely to do so if we remember the guidance of general methodology. We have to bear in mind, first, the interests and abilities of the class; second, the demands of the subject; third, our own dispositions, knowledge, failings; fourth, the influence of environment upon children. These facts indicate that we must know our children and display an intelligent knowledge of what we are going to teach, that we need to plan and devise carefully our visual aids and make our lessons live with clear aims and sensible applications. These lessons may well prove a success and make the subject a favourite; we dare not consider the alternative.

Two forty-minute periods "on the time-table" should provide eighty minutes of interesting experience; the temptation to preach will be ever present, especially for the teacher who means well, but it is a danger that may create a distaste for the very lesson we want to be attractive. Nothing more quickly dulls interest for children than a classroom sermon; boredom results and, eventually, antipathy. Association of ideas may cause the transfer of that dislike from the teacher to the whole subject, and even to the thought of religion altogether.

We should try not to be disappointed with our class too soon. Perhaps they do not need a teacher so much as a leader. We do well to recall our own childhood—our impulses, fears, beliefs, courage. These children are not lost in original sin—nor are they angels. But they are extremely willing to follow the right leader. So aim at winning their confidence. If they see that their teacher is trying to do his best, that he is not preaching at them, that he dis-likes anything in the nature of pi behaviour, that he gives them the chance to question, discuss, even object . . . they will respond. It is so vitally important to harness the natural instincts, and these are never stronger than where thoughts of God, sin, life and death are concerned. There are powerful impulses, too, that impel children to form gangs and secret societies; these, rightly controlled, will encourage the same children to form groups and committees for voluntary service of all kinds—duties that are the seeds of altruism and the beginnings of Christian action towards one's neighbour.

Appreciation of these facts will help you to keep your own know-ledge up to date and your faith vital. Teach your subject as if you really enjoy it; if you don't, give it up. But if you believe sincerely that the Bible is an unfolding of God's purpose, that it is the story of challenge to men through the ages right up to the present moment, your teaching is bound to be practical and will succeed.

Always among the initial problems any lesson brings is the type and state of the text-book in use. Class Bibles need close examination as to suitability. Opinions differ as to the best version, but the fact remains that we must make the Bible familiar and liked. It is not surprising that children regard this book of theirs, with its tiny print and sombre binding, as potentially dull and uninteresting. Perhaps one day some publisher will be able and bold enough to put on the market a School Bible as cheaply and as attractively produced as many of the more familiar books of adventure. Is not the Bible the greatest adventure-book of all?

As children get older, and especially if they are used only to an annotated version or a selection of extracts, they should be introduced to the Authorised Version; and wherever possible they should be encouraged to bring their own, there being much in the pride of possession. Exclusive use of the Authorised Version is somewhat of a danger. The flowing beauty of Elizabethan speech often cloaks the twentieth-century meaning and brings unnecessary difficulties to children. There is ample time and place in Literature lessons to enjoy the poetry of the Bible. Meanwhile, the Authorised Version, the Revised Version, and modern versions like those of Moffatt, Knox, Phillips and the New English Bible, should rub shoulders on the classroom shelves. The Bible in Basic English should be used more often than it is; children welcome its clarity and simplicity.

The practical aspect of teaching turns to a large extent upon choice of suggested methods. We must get rid of any existing old methods like reading-round-the-class, verse-by-verse exposition, meaningless repetition; and retain any of the old methods that do conform to our principles. Inspiration lies in the things around us. Very often a snatch of wireless news, a newspaper headline, a war map, a rumour, will provide an opening. A new approach always helps; thus the escape of a Borstal boy may introduce the Prodigal Son, or a report of the work of the Red Cross may lead to the Good Samaritan. But it is as well to remember that too many new things pall, and there is always room for some good old-fashioned teaching. However, the events of the day are always grist to the mill and tend to place the subject in the ordinary every-day life of the children.

Methods should be varied with judgment. You will not want to attempt all those suggested in this book, but should not be afraid to experiment. We learn by making mistakes, but if the lessons are well prepared the mistakes will not be too serious. Try not to pander to a class by overdoing a favourite type of lesson. Always plan for class expression of some kind, and vary both application and activity to avoid monotony. Expression work should extend beyond the classroom when and where possible with practical service.

We must not overlook yet another aspect of the lesson. Despite the fact that subject specialisation often makes for isolation, special-isation in Religious Knowledge may be the very means of integrat-ing the curriculum by conscious and deliberate intent. Every lesson in the subject opens the doors of correlation with some other subject —geography, history, art, music, crafts, science. Many lessons may well begin from another subject—the Crusades in History, evolution in Science, a hymn in Music, some model in Craft. Such correlation even tends to enhance the subject for the children. At times it may seem that the religious aspect of the lesson is in danger of being swamped by correlation. There is little fear of this, however, if the aim of the lesson is clear. Illustration, visual aids, correlation—these are adjuncts, means to a desired end, and the end is the *aim* of the lesson. With that clear and kept clear, no teacher can stray far. There is another reason for keeping the lesson aim clear and simple. Students have been known to state their aim in a Literature lesson as "To inculcate a love of poetry" or "To appreciate the world of poetry" when what they meant was, "Enjoying Masefield's 'Cargoes.'" It is so easy to take such a wide view that there is no aim at all. There is, however, something extremely attractive in the probably apocryphal story of the student who prepared his lesson aim as: "To please God—at least!"

In all lessons, whether approaching the class by group or individual methods, encourage co-operation in the bringing of visual aids of all kinds. Stimulate discussion. Airing views in a Mathematics lesson may be both unnecessary and "not the thing." But children like sound reasons for less objective arguments, and they have a right to ask questions about matters that are not so clear as that 2 and 2 make 4. In Religious Knowledge it should be very much "the thing" to question and discuss.

There must be room for revision. Ask lots of questions. The greatest Teacher of all was the greatest questioner, too. Make notes of blunders, vagueness, lack of knowledge. Plan future work so as to clarify these; what the children know may be grievously small, but you have to build on that.

Revision automatically leads to testing. Children argue that what isn't worth testing isn't worth learning, and expect tests in Mathematics and Geography; why should there be none in Religious Knowledge? We are trying to make it a normal subject on the time-table, and to get rid of the idea that it is something special or different. Of course, it *is* special and it *is* different, but not in this way. There should be oral and written tests of all kinds, at suitable intervals. School reports should bear numerical results and class positions as for other subjects. A 10 per cent. in Mathematics may be outweighed by 80 per cent. in Religious Knowledge, and who can estimate the psychological value of that?

Suggestions for the building up of a most necessary library are given in the chapter on "Aids and Activities"; this part of our work in strengthening the subject should be constantly in mind.

You may feel as you browse through these suggestions and later the methods presented in this book, that the approach is too secular and not deep enough spiritually. Cold print looks like that. Some things must be said in setting and facing the challenge before the Christian teacher; some attempt at saying these has been made. But the Religious Knowledge lesson must be a normal lesson—with a difference. The teacher may adopt or adapt a method; it is his job to make these bones live by his knowledge of his subject, his personal conviction and his sense of doing happily a worth-while piece of work. It is this approach that gives his lesson the aura of being different, that makes his children feel that although Mathematics and English may help them to get a livelihood, there is something in Religious Knowledge that helps them to live.

It is difficult to put into words the eventual seeping of this spirit into the life of the school. Much of it is gathered up into the School Service, house competitions and the sense of playing the game; courtesy, quiet behaviour, willingness, readiness—all these indicate it. It is part of the school tradition. A school may have a tradition without it; it is certain to have a better one with it.

Let us sum up. You and I are trying to help our children to understand the world they live in, to assess the value of their own personalities, and to become Christ-followers. We want to give them a vision of the greatness of the best that has been said and done, and, above all, practical experience of living in a community that might be the epitome of the longed-for world community. We are trying to impart a faith by means of which religion becomes the soul of a "culture, rich, creative, integrating," in which children and their parents render willingly, freely, wholeheartedly, their Christian service. We want our boys and girls to become those who shall "maintain the fabric of the world, and the work of whose hands is their prayer." That is the ultimate aim; our lessons and methods are to that end. In every Religious Knowledge lesson we are trying to bring the Kingdom of God nearer realisation; it is an exhilarating thought. We are endeavouring to make our children once more as was said by John Green of seventeenth-century England—"the people of a book, and that book—the Bible!"

The class teacher wonders as he plans and prepares, teaches and guides, whether it is ever worth while. Except for occasional happy tests results (when he wonders whether the test was too easy), there are so few signs of success. Teachers of experience do not look for results; the things worth measuring cannot be measured. The Medical Officer may measure height, but the teacher can rarely discover increase of spiritual stature in his children. The older members of the profession look around and see men and women they once taught. Happy they who find in these some sign of their life-work; happy indeed, for in these is their reward.

CHAPTER V

THE SYLLABUS

The Agreed Syllabuses and the teacher's freedom; drawing up the class syllabus; plans for Junior classes; plans for Senior classes; plans for C and D streams; the root of the matter—doctrine.

ONE of the finest results of the 1944 Act in the realm of Religious Knowledge has been the steady flow of Agreed Syllabuses; it is also good to see that many of these are being revised in the light of experience gained through use.

Never in the history of education has the religious aspect been so splendidly considered. Teachers throughout the country have what they have needed for years, and openly acknowledge the debt owed to the far-sighted compilers of these guides. The most bewildered teacher now has his path made plain for him; yet, strangely enough, he is none too happy about it. He says it is too full, this syllabus, and the approach too academic, too intellectual. It is more suited to Grammar School children than to his own, and although better than nothing . . . Let us answer him. Until such time as special Secondary Modern School syllabuses are prepared, as no doubt they will be, the remedy is in his own hands. Of course no one syllabus is fitted as it stands to any one school or group; there is no such thing as standardised religion. The teacher must accept the approach as a tribute to his own mentality, take the material offered and mould it to suit his own children wherever they happen to be. After all, given the full syllabus, the least he can do is to work out his own scheme within that framework; balanced selection is vitally important, and no conscientious teacher is willing to leave that to someone else.

Freedom to work within the outline of the Agreed Syllabus is a matter for great anxiety with some teachers. The breadth of the scheme frightens them; they forget the impossibility, let alone the undesirability, of attempting it all. As A. C. Toyne so neatly observes in his *Religious Teaching in School*, "If we attempted to cover all the syllabus, the school-leaving age would be 70!" On the other hand, teachers must take care not to spend a disproportionate time on any one part of the syllabus suggested.

This is not the place to comment upon or review the various syllabuses. But it is as well to emphasise the rich variety, the independence, the sanity, and often the originality, of them all. No two are alike, yet all have fundamental aims which are left to the teacher to attain. Here, again, is freedom. No one can lay down categorically either method of approach or speed of working, and the compilers of the syllabuses go out of their way to make this freedom very obvious. Having indicated that their aim in setting-up the syllabus is to present Christianity as a way of life, with the Bible as text-book and inspiration, their suggestion—not instruction—is that the course might be followed out in some such sequence as this:

(a) Providing direct instruction in the Christian religion as having an historical foundation.

(b) Interpreting the historical facts revealed in the Bible stories.

(c) Deciding whether these are true.

(d) Applying them to life as Christian ethics.

Or, simply—what happened, what did it mean, what do we believe about it, what does it mean for us today?

This is extremely straightforward for all types of school and denominations.[1]

The syllabuses are most careful to assure the teacher that he need not be tied in any way to content or method.

Thus:

London: "It cannot be overstressed that the syllabus is planned to be suggestive rather than compulsory."

Northern Ireland: "Neither course is rigid and there is a wide variety of choice within each syllabus."

West Riding: "It is not expected that the teacher should adhere strictly to the syllabus. It is for guidance only. . . ." And, ". . . the

[1] In case any teacher is anxious that what he eventually tries to teach is indeed a Christian Faith acceptable to all "churches," there is a definite statement issued by the Christian Education Movement with the approval of the Joint Conference of Anglican and Free Churchmen. This statement—"A Common Basis for Christian Teaching in Schools"—is a clear and forceful nine-point enunciation of what Christianity affirms, and you are left in no doubt as to what that faith is. See *Teaching the Christian Faith*, Appendix (I.C.E.).

function of the syllabus is to guide and to suggest and at the same time to leave the teacher freedom to adapt it. Select so that in instruction due weight is given to the social implications of the Christian faith."

Cumberland: "Teachers should have the maximum amount of freedom within a given framework for the drawing up of their own schemes of work."

What all syllabuses say in effect, is: "Here is an outline, here is the material, here is guidance to help you to formulate clearly what you are setting out to do in your lessons. Choose from the syllabus what your children can absorb and what you yourself feel capable of teaching. Don't attempt to do it all, but make sure that what you do you do well." They might all add: "Of course, we do expect from a teacher of Religious Knowledge a measure of conscientious approach to his teaching."

It is this freedom that teachers both welcome and fear. They don't want to be fettered, but they are never sure what to select and what to teach. Shall they put this in, shall they leave that out? Why? Or, why not? What kind of guiding factors are there for helping them to select both content and method?

Let us, however, be quite clear on three important practical issues, related to the classroom, subject and children:

1. How long is the lesson, and how many lessons per week are provided? The total amount of time for the subject controls the expected amount of work.

2. How long is the course? We may plan very hopefully for a four-year course, but a little mental arithmetic will show that in actual fact a considerable number of children in both Primary and Post-primary Schools do *not* complete four years, often by a long way; a few others may be with us for five.

3. What are the children like mentally? Are they the brighter A stream, or do they belong to the sadly labelled D's? The implication is that the same syllabus will not do for both types; nor, indeed, for those B and C children in between. Some measure of slower working or a simpler approach must be kept in mind when the scheme for a class of duller children is being drawn up.

Now, having to some extent put our problem into clearer perspective by reminding ourselves of the type of children for whom we are catering and the amount of time allotted to cover a given course, let us hark back to the doubts already expressed, and consider how best to select material for the children we now have in mind, for these are real queries in the minds of many teachers.

In doing this it may help to consider four questions, not necessarily in sequential order, but rather complementary to each other.

(a) *Does the material selected contain in itself the element of continuity?* That is, if it is a Primary scheme does it make for a straightforward beginning and a smooth continuation in the Post-primary scheme; and if it is a Post-primary scheme, does it follow on naturally from the groundwork of the Primary scheme? This implies knowledge of the complete syllabus recommended, and to appreciate the importance of these considerations it is necessary to read the *whole* of the syllabus from which the material for any scheme is selected. It is only in this way that you realise that the particular course to be covered is, in fact, but a part of a larger ideal —the guiding of the child from the infant class to the leavers' form, and perhaps beyond. Unless this is clear, you do not see your responsibility in the right light or in the right perspective; merely to read the contents of one section is to put on blinkers that blind you to your real responsibilities.

(b) *Does the material selected lend itself to a variety of teaching methods?* It is so easy to choose subject-matter that can be taught by one or two familiar methods, like story-telling or dramatisation, which eventually dull the appeal of content and lesson. If the material stultifies teaching method and prevents the lessons from being adventurous and exciting, there is need for wider selection. Draw from other syllabuses that offer a wider scope for a particular course. In any case, don't stick slavishly to the one Agreed Syllabus. Each Local Education Authority probably expects to find its own syllabus being used in its own area, at least as a basis; although I was surprised to find in Southampton, for instance, that the syllabus hails from Durham! Get several syllabuses from the local library; if possible, buy them. They all have something to give besides mere content. There are chapters on worship, methods, aids, Biblical criticism, historical study, the Church, comparative study of religion, subjects for discussion; some are local in content, some introduce a theological and philosophical element in the top classes. All of them are extremely practical and very much aware that the syllabus is a servant and not a master.

With this second question in mind, it is less likely that you will succumb to the temptation to make casual selection from the syllabus and hope for the best!

(c) *Does the material selected form a course that really presents Christianity as a way of life?* This phrase tends to become very glib; it is so often mentioned in all syllabuses and in most lectures and text-books. The danger of misinterpreting it, and even losing it in a welter of Bible study, is quite a real one. We have to be very careful that we do not concentrate on presenting the Bible as the source *par excellence* of inspiration and yet miss its relevance for today. Children can so quickly get the notion that Christianity is something belonging to two thousand years ago. Any scheme must take this possibility into account and, to the exclusion if need be of some Bible material, must contain lives and stories from the continuous stream of Christianity; children have to be shown that Christianity as a way of life is something that has inspired the lives of men and women all through the ages, and that it is an intensely historical as well as a vital aspect of religion. They have to be shown how writers and musicians, poets and artists, reformers and scholars and martyrs, have taken this way because to them it was— and is—the only Way.

From time to time, therefore, you will realise the need to apply class teaching to present-day problems and to find answers to everyday questions, building up for the children a sense of rightness in Christian ethics and Christian living. This cannot be done without being prepared to re-shape and re-direct the scheme when the need arises; not arbitrarily, but with reason. It may have to be modified or expanded or completely revised; if the basic aim of the course or year is not forgotten, this is to the good, provided you are quite sure *why* the alterations are being made.

(d) *Does the material selected give a scheme that presents the Bible?* This is the other side of the same coin. A danger arises when our third point is pressed too far. It is possible to concentrate so much on biographies and historical events that the Biblical stories and incidents get left out or pushed into the background. Never forget that the Bible is *the* text-book, that its message is irrefutable, that unless we give it to the children at school the chances are that they will never know it as the treasure-trove of the Christian's adventure.

Each scheme has to maintain a happy balance between these necessities; perhaps by far the best way of relating them is always to use the Bible story first, and then to draw upon relevant events throughout history as illustrations of the Bible message. Particularly in the upper sections of the school, where a good deal of discussion and research work in projects, etc., may tend to concentrate on social and personal difficulties, should we beware of shelving the Bible. Here especially we should come back to the Word again and again to prove, illustrate and illumine the very things found problematical in life today.

Now, a word about the arrangement of the material for the teaching. There was a time when the Old Testament and New Testament lessons were given on alternate days of the week, with learning-by-heart on Fridays. How we switched from Moses to Jesus, from Egypt to Italy—and back again, if we were lucky—until we were never quite sure who was what or where. The miracle is that we retained any sequence at all. We all know the old tag about children mixing Saul the King with Saul of Tarsus, but there was a student specialising in Religious Knowledge who admitted that he had read the whole of Samuel but couldn't find the Conversion of Saul anywhere! How much of that vagueness was due to the confusing Scripture lessons of his early years?

Whatever else happens, this system of teaching should go. With the introduction of two definite periods on the time-table, the tendency to adopt such a scheme is lessening. There must be avoidance of confusion, clearness of aim and purpose, consecutiveness; this will never be done by alternating daily or even weekly the teaching of the Old and New Testaments. In any case, there seems little virtue in running two sets of visual aids for parallel sets of work.

Let us examine examples of the approaches that can be made to the preparing of a scheme from the material and guidance given in the Agreed Syllabuses, trying to recall all we have said about the need for balanced selection of content.

Syllabus for Juniors

Juniors are interested in *real* things—people, events, occasions.

The syllabus prepared for them must be full of action and vitality, without abstractions and unreality. The underlying aim is to present to them the revelation of God, culminating in the coming and the work of Jesus, and it must be done in such a way that the children see in the people of the story the kind of folk God wants and the kind of folk they can copy. The content of the scheme will inevitably be covered again in the Post-primary School, but the foundation of a simple yet strong belief in the things of God must be laid here. Let us look at possible schemes. Here is one based on the idea of terminal subjects:

7–8 YEARS

Term

1. God the Father	Abraham, Isaac, Joseph . . . Jesus, martyrs of the ages.
2. God's call to individuals	To Abraham, Joseph, Samuel, David. . . .
3. God's help	Other stories in these lives.

8–9 YEARS

1. God made the world	Stories of His purpose, Abraham, Jesus, great lives.
2. God needs help	Moses, Disciples, Paul, missionaries, to present day.
3. God gives help	Ditto, further stories to show.

9–10 YEARS

1. God's men and women	Prophets, Jesus, great lives.
2. God's leaders	Abraham, Moses, Jesus.
3. God's Kingdom	Jesus and His stories.

10–11 YEARS

1. God shows Himself	To prophets, in Jesus, to all who work for Him.
2. God calls nations	Abraham, Samuel, David . . . to present day.
3. God watches over His people	Disciples, preachers, the spread of Christianity.

This scheme is based on the *Sunderland Syllabus*, but may be applied to any other.

Such a scheme as this underlines the nearness of God and the relevance of His presence, not only in days gone by, but in life today. It has the advantage of covering several parts of the Bible, and of passing through the centuries many times. As the children come to a familiar part, they will link what they knew beforehand with what they are learning afresh, and this tying-up of knowledge is an important factor in their training.

If a more definitely logical sequence is preferred, there is a broader treatment of the material on these lines:

7–8 YEARS

Life of Jesus—His work (based on Mark).
Stories from the Old Testament.

8–9 YEARS

Journeys and Teaching of Jesus; the kind of Person He **was**.
More stories from the Old Testament.

9–10 YEARS

Heroes of the Bible. Old and New Testaments.
How men and women followed Jesus.

10–11 YEARS

Teaching of Jesus—about us.
                   —about prayer.
                   —about worship.
More men and women who followed Him.

The *L.C.C. Agreed Syllabus* will give details of this adapted scheme. You may prefer to spend the whole year on the life and work of Jesus and the following year on Old Testament stories, but it might be a pity to ignore the Old Testament altogether for a whole year and then leave out the stories of Jesus for another. The apparent abstractness of the 10–11-year work in this scheme is only apparent. It is intended that the fundamentals of prayer and worship and God's care for individuals should be taught through the stories of the Bible and relevant incidents in the lives of great men and women through the ages.

Here is yet a third scheme, on the guidance of the *West Riding*

Syllabus. It seems to fall into the three-term plan, but need not unless it is so desired.

7–8 YEARS

Jesus the Son of God.
God who made the World.
God and the Prophets.

8–9 YEARS

God and Man (Old Testament).
God and Man (New Testament).
Prayer and Worship.

9–10 YEARS

Stories from the Old Testament.
Stories from the New Testament.
Stories from the lives of saints, martyrs, missionaries.

10–11 YEARS

God's Call (Old Testament).
Jesus the King.
The Church begun; its spread.

Some teachers may yet prefer a "concentric" type of syllabus. In this, there is a general theme running right through the whole scheme, and each year it is illustrated by a selection of stories that broadens and deepens the conception implied in the theme as the children move from the first to the final stage of their education in any particular school. The obvious advantage of such a plan is that it tends to lay a firmer foundation for Post-primary studies than some other schemes, in that "the children receive an impression of the Bible story as a whole, rather than a detailed knowledge of some particular period." This is exceptionally well done in the *Cumberland and Westmorland Syllabus,* where the theme suggested is the record of how:

(a) man drew nearer to God through the progressive revelation of God;

(b) this process continues, as seen throughout the ages in noble and useful lives;

(c) our Bible reached its present form.

This type of plan may be the answer to many of their problems that some teachers will welcome; it is certainly a great advance on many already put forward.

But in all schemes the content is the same; it is only the matter of order and arrangement that one has to decide. It may not be necessary to provide a special scheme for the very dull children of the school. They need the same stories and the same teaching about God and Jesus. But of course they do need a special line of approach in method, and will probably have fewer stories and events put before them. Of the four schemes quoted, the first is easily modified, and the last most clearly adaptable, to what are known as the C and D streams of the Primary School.

Syllabus for Seniors

The progress of the Seniors depends greatly upon the soundness of the foundation laid in the Primary School. They are capable of more detailed study; their increasing critical powers lead them to seek a merging of story into history, they want to see the Old Testament ideas transformed and transmuted by Jesus, and made relevant to the twentieth century; in a word, they want to see the *point* of what they have been told in the Primary School.

The syllabus, then, may be adapted to the view that the best approach is one that deals with "a term for a subject, three subjects per year." The inherent value of such a scheme is the unity of each term's work within the full framework of the year, which is itself a definite part of a four-year course. It will be noted that in each year the children are introduced to all three aspects of the Bible story and Christianity; the scheme is planned so that the third term of each year leads on to the first term of the next. Some people may object that this scheme is piecemeal, but one must admit that two periods per week for up to fourteen weeks is hardly a small amount of time devoted to each aspect.

Here is the plan in some detail:

1ST YEAR

Term

1. New Testament — Life of Christ (based on Mark).
2. Christian Church — Story in Acts to Chapter viii.
3. Old Testament — Revision of early stories; history up to the Exile.

2ND YEAR

1. Old Testament — Exile to "The World Christ Knew."

Term

| 2. New Testament | Teachings of Christ; Synoptics. |
| 3. Christian Church | Acts ix to the end. |

3RD YEAR

1. Christian Church	Spread of Christianity to Middle Ages.
2. Old Testament	The Old Covenant; Religion developing into worship of the One God, Jahweh.
3. New Testament	The New Covenant; Personal and Corporate Religion.

4TH YEAR

1. The Bible	Old Testament, Apocrypha, New Testament, in the Story of the Bible.
2. Christian Church	Reformation to the present day.
3. Old and New Testaments	Jesus the Messiah; Jesus for the Jews; Jesus for all men.

5TH YEAR

| Selected themes | Bible literature; letters of Paul; great religions; personal and social problems; creeds; questions. |

The material for this scheme is best set out in the *1949 Cambridgeshire Syllabus,* but further references and content will be found in other syllabuses.

Many teachers prefer a scheme in which a yearly topic is followed. The weakness of such a syllabus is that the children are deprived of either Old or New Testament for a whole year at a time. In its continuity it does provide a logical sequence, but to the exclusion of the fact that children do learn bits and pieces from here and there, rather than an ordered series of facts. This is a weakness of which we must take stock. Also, in a non-specialist school, a teacher may not be too keen on teaching the same topic year in and year out. It may lead to haphazard and casual teaching. But one must also admit that hundreds of Mathematics teachers do just that in their chosen subject or class.

Here is a suggested scheme on the yearly topic plan:

1st Year

Life and teaching of Jesus   Based on Mark.

2nd Year

History of the Hebrews   Beginnings to "The World Christ Knew."

3rd Year

Growth of the Church   Beginning from Acts, through Church History.

4th Year

The story of the Bible.

5th Year

Selected topics.

There must be some arbitrary division to fit each term, otherwise there is a likelihood of getting to the end of the year with the topic barely touched. It is unlikely that the subject-matter will be covered with time to spare.

What many teachers feel desirable is a scheme that will be both logical and psychological. This is not easy, but perhaps this next suggestion will to some extent meet the case. Again, it is a yearly topic scheme, but it is planned in such a way as to include content from both Old and New Testaments each term and year, as well as to link with present-day events to make the study relevant to the twentieth century. The approach follows the biographical study of lives illustrating the main topic, with the retention of chronological sequence. There is a definite "unity in diversity" in this scheme that appeals, especially as each year gives a form of revision to the year that is gone, through the eyes of a different set of people or through a new series of events. Here is such a scheme:

1st Year

Men of God   From Abraham to Schweitzer.

2nd Year

The Kingdom of God   (a) Israel.
                                   (b) Jesus and His Kingdom.
                                   (c) Spread of the Kingdom.

3RD YEAR

People of God

(*a*) Prophets.
(*b*) Disciples.
(*c*) Missionaries.

4TH YEAR

Revelation of God

(*a*) Old Testament progress.
(*b*) New Testament fulfilment.
(*c*) Church today.

5TH YEAR
God and Ourselves.

Where the main headings lend themselves to division into three sub-headings, one may be tempted to take each as a term's work; such a plan might not be entirely wise, but it would ensure that that part of the scheme was, indeed, done. The main drawback to this syllabus is the wideness of choice of content. There is always a danger of trying to do too much, and teachers are strangely loth to be accused of doing too little. This means that the plan needs very careful study and weighting in the selection of incidents and lives to illustrate the theme in hand. Here, again, there is plenty to be found in any of the Agreed Syllabuses.

This leads us to consider the type of scheme that is avowedly concentric. It has been examined as a Junior School syllabus, and once again the best example is that given in the *Cumberland and Westmorland Agreed Syllabus*. A theme is decided upon, and this is covered in four stages (not necessarily years), each aspect of the general theme being dealt with in related first, second and third terms of each year. The basic idea is that the children are given a wide general view of the Bible as opposed to a detailed study of particular periods, the presumption being that it is better they should have an impression of the whole rather than a specific knowledge of part. Here is an outline of the plan:

> FIRST TERM: "How men have learned what God is like."
> *1st Year:* The power that calls out men of God.
> *2nd Year:* What men learn by living together.
> *3rd Year:* Evidence about God.

SECOND TERM: "What did God do in Jesus Christ?"
  1st Year: He came on earth to live.
  2nd Year: He showed men how to live together.
  3rd Year: He worked for His Kingdom.

THIRD TERM: "How does God's Spirit work among men?"
  1st Year: Through the Bible (its story and message).
  2nd Year: Through daily life.
  3rd Year: Through the Church.

The fourth stage gathers into the relevant school terms the thoughts engendered and crystallised by this scheme of study, so that the children leave with a definite approach to the tenets of the Christian faith. These are shown in this way:

FIRST TERM: "What Christians believe."
SECOND TERM: "The work of the Spirit."
THIRD TERM: "How does God's Spirit work among men?"

Thus, at whatever term the children leave after their fifteenth birthday, they will have covered the Bible story broadly, and will have been given an appreciation of what it means to be a practising Christian in a very clear statement of beliefs. This is a commendable consideration.

One thing we must avoid at all costs in our work is an academic approach, for the majority of our pupils are by no means bookish by nature or training. If we do but remember that the Junior curriculum is to be "thought of in terms of activity," we shall not err in the Primary Schools. Juniors need to be shown the lives of men and women of the Old and New Testaments, and through the ages to the present day, in such a way that they feel these folk are worth knowing and worth copying. So do the Seniors, but, in addition, the older children have a growing critical faculty that must be given expression; they want to see the relation of religion to life, especially as it affects theirs. There must be a sense of reality in the story of the Bible as it unfolds and reveals God; they want to see the relevance of His word and work in meeting the problems of adolescence in particular and adult life in general. "Life is real, life is earnest" to these boys and girls, and our teaching must be at all times practical.

The length of stay of children in the fifth year—for some, even in the fourth—depends upon the date of their fifteenth birthday. Few stay for the whole year, although there are encouraging signs that more will stay on until they are sixteen as school curricula, accommodation and general facilities improve. This means that individual attention to the problems of the immediate future will loom large in the final year of the syllabus. Some kind of summarising of the work done in the previous years should be attempted, preferably through Projects and guided Search Work. Once the necessary material has been prepared, it may be possible to arrange for the work to be done on the lines of the Dalton Plan. This is the time to meet agnosticism, and to prepare the adolescent for the strange new world of office, shop and factory—and pay-packet!

C and D Streams

In no school is it possible to follow out a syllabus intended for bright children with those of poorer mentality. The difference may not be so marked in the Primary School, where the method will be story-telling and biographical to a large extent. But with Seniors there must be a special scheme; a watered-down A stream syllabus is doomed to disaster. It must be very simple, attractive in content, and one lending itself to much practical work and aids of all kinds. Do not fall into the error of thinking that a Junior course will suit dull Seniors; they are not so dull as all that, and they quickly resent any form of talking down.

One approach to a likely scheme is to have in mind what is intended for the year the class happens to be in, and then to modify according to their known ability. This will mean that anything resembling Biblical criticism or requiring average reasoning ability will be excluded. Apart from the simplest exercises in Bible work, you will be unable to base any of the work on individual plans; many of these children will be unable to read, and that in itself is the greatest hindrance to progress. Much of your time may even be taken up with the preparing of simplified versions of Bible extracts, so that, though slowly and even painstakingly, they may be introduced to the Bible itself.

The syllabus will centre in the life-stories of great people—of the Bible and through the ages. There will be ample scope for including well-known stories and incidents from these same sources, always linking the Bible story with those of today.

This gives the choice between a simplified version of the main syllabus for other classes (and a simplified version isn't the same as one watered-down), or an entirely new one based on biography; or it may be possible to merge the two.

Here is one scheme:

1ST YEAR

Life and teaching of Jesus   Selected incidents; parables.

2ND YEAR

Spreading the news   Incidents in the lives of Peter, John, Paul.

3RD YEAR

The story of the Hebrews   Abraham, Joseph. . . .

4TH YEAR

How we got our Bible   Stories of early writers, martyrs, printers; modern versions.

5TH YEAR

Our jobs   When we leave school; importance of vocation, fellowship, service.

Our third example of a syllabus for Seniors lends itself extremely well to modification to suit the streams of lower mentality; it is in essence sequential, moving from the Old to the New Testament, and onwards to the present day. Furthermore, it gives each year the revision so much needed for all children, never more so than for the children we are now considering.

Let me remind you again of the concentric type of syllabus; this is especially adaptable to the needs of children of lower mentality.

Here is another scheme based on the four questions underlying all Agreed Syllabuses (p. 31); the headings are suggested in the *Hertfordshire Syllabus*, but the material may be found in any other.

THEME: THE CHRISTIAN RELIGION

1ST YEAR. *What happened?*

1st term.	Birth, Boyhood, Early Ministry of Christ.
2nd term.	Preaching, Healing, Delivering.
3rd term.	The End—and the Beginning.

2ND YEAR. *What did it mean?*

1st term.	Historical setting—God the Almighty.
2nd term.	Prophecy—about the Messiah—the Son.
3rd term.	The World Christ Knew: God the Father.

3RD YEAR. *What do we believe about it?*

1st term.	Immediate influence: Spreading the Gospel.
2nd term.	Impact on Great Lives.
3rd term.	Inception of Great Movements.

4TH YEAR. *What does it mean for us today?*

1st term.	Conduct: Christ's teaching about—God, Man, Living, the Church.
2nd term.	Problems—Social and Personal.
3rd term.	The Bible—the Heritage of Man.

This is a four-year scheme so arranged that successive groups of leavers receive "rounding-off" terms. We must be realists and accept the fact that, as the law now stands, most of our pupils leave before the end of the fourth year, especially those of lower mental ability. But as extended courses in other subjects—academic and technical—are developed, encouraging would-be leavers to stay on, there will be the need for the longer Religious Knowledge courses envisaged in the Agreed Syllabuses.

The better we know the type of children we are dealing with, the less likely are we to plan too great an amount of work. We need to be careful not to fall between the two stools of spending too much time on one section and speeding over a wide syllabus. With Juniors there will be much story-telling and much practical work; with Seniors the main difficulty will be to get them to talk, to be open and frank about the lives of these people and what they stand for. Practical expression is essential—pictures, drawings, pin-men illustrations. Incidents and stories should be mimed and acted as suggested in the relevant chapters of this book, and variety of approach made so that children do not get tired of any one method.

Many schemes are based entirely upon biography. These do not lend themselves to yearly lay-out, and if you have sole charge of a class of children of very low mental calibre over a long period—say the whole four years—it is probably wiser to keep to a biographical or concentric scheme that can be adapted to the progress made by the class.

In the final year there should be talks on aspects of post-school life, jobs, worship, citizenship, with examples from both Bible and daily life. The *Lancashire Simplified Syllabus* is advised for this work.

Note on Memory Work

In all syllabuses there should be noted special passages for the children to learn by heart. The tendency is for teachers to do this, and then to forget to see that it is carried out. See that the children do learn the pieces recommended or selected from the many given in the Agreed Syllabus being used.

The Root of the Matter

This chapter on the syllabus remains incomplete unless we summarise just what it is we are endeavouring to teach our children by its means. We have gone to a great deal of trouble to sort out our principles of approach, and in the next part of the book we are going to study practical applications of these principles. We may well ask, therefore—To What End?

A former Secretary of the National Union of Teachers once said that "a syllabus of religious instruction without doctrine is a contradiction in terms." This sums up the position. Our syllabuses are devised for the sole purpose of imparting doctrine—teaching religion, if you will. Our syllabuses undoubtedly cover background, history and ethics, but it still remains for us to teach Religion.

Teachers jib at the word "doctrine." To some it implies strict beliefs of some particular Church, often Anglican beliefs that Nonconformists cannot accept; to others the word savours of ritual and mysteriously unorthodox—and often orthodox—views.

This is a point taken up by the Institute of Christian Education booklet *Teaching the Christian Faith*, in which it is carefully indicated that when doctrine is confused with denomination, uncertainty and vagueness of purpose are created for the teacher. Differences of interpretation there must be, but these differences "cut right across denominational frontiers." Further, "there exists a solid body of agreed faith which is common to all the denominations. It is this agreed faith which we wish to see taught in school and home and church." (See footnote on p. 31.)

Teachers are reminded of the Cowper-Temple clause of 1870, reaffirmed in 1944, which forbids the teaching in State schools of any doctrine "distinctive of a particular denomination." Thus it is that in their arduous task of compiling the various Agreed Syllabuses, committees and panels have endeavoured to present a common core of Christian teaching—the story of God's revelation to man, consummated in the Person and Life of Jesus; in short, the truths that help us to love Him "with heart and soul and mind and strength."

As the *Durham Syllabus* says, "It must be the aim of all Christians to hasten the time when education in England shall be inspired by the central purpose of a Christian faith." It is only as "believers in God" in Peter's sense that teachers can hope to interpret their syllabus in this light.

When we come to consider our methods, this must be at the back of our minds. Children cannot be taught the great beliefs of the Christian Church as direct theology, nor can they assimilate it all at once; they need to be taught concretely, by doing and making and serving, and they must be presented with the parts that eventually make up the whole. They will not all learn at the same rate, nor will they all respond in the same way; it becomes a necessary if onerous duty of the teacher to develop their faith in accordance with these factors. Full comprehension cannot be expected at fifteen years of age, but we can at least aim at making the cardinal truths vital and personal to our adolescents to such a degree that the Apostles' Creed is their vade-mecum and the Christian faith their certain Way.

This is what our Agreed Syllabus in the long run really means for us; this is the root of the matter. This is the challenge that we as teachers of Religious Knowledge really have to face; this is the doctrine we have to teach.

PART II
METHODS

PRELIMINARY COMMENT

"Men [and children] believe more from seeing than from hearing; the way is long by precepts, short and effective by examples."—SENECA.

WE may not agree with Seneca that the way is either short or effective by examples, but we certainly shall that teaching by practical methods is likely to bring about far better results than by mere preaching and talking. It is our business as teachers to use any and all methods that will make our lessons attractive and forceful, and in Religious Knowledge it is our duty to make the Bible vividly real and the Christian life an adventure full of challenge and vigour and colour.

It is to this end that these methods are offered. Some are suited to all types and ages; others merely for the brighter A streams of the Secondary Modern Schools; others, again, only for the Junior and even backward Senior streams. It is hoped, too, that not a few of these methods—especially those challenging the brightest children—may be found useful in the Grammar and Technical Schools. Some methods are extremely adaptable to a particular scheme, and will fit the current syllabuses of the General Certificate of Education in Religious Knowledge. Much will depend upon the time you are allotted, and also upon the existence or otherwise of a reasonably good Religious Knowledge library.

Many of these suggestions are already familiar in connection with other subjects; some will be recognised in a new guise; others may be quite new and even unusual. However much they may appeal— or appal—you will realise that they are not necessarily meant for you. But don't be afraid to try them—and give them a *fair* trial. That is, try them with your aim clearly in mind and feeling that the method chosen is the one that will successfully embody that aim. ALL these methods have stood the test of classroom practice; they are not flights of fancy born of hopeful theory. So if you fail it isn't necessarily because of the method; find out what went astray and how; put it right next time. Select a few that come easily to you and make them your own. Try out others as and when they can be fitted in; it is foolish to try twenty methods in twenty successive lessons. Where possible, keep actual records; collect class results; assess the relative value of the various lessons.

Let me add a practical note. No lesson on the time-table will succeed if you have to hunt round anxiously for books, pens, paper and the like at short notice. The atmosphere of the lesson is immediately ruined, and the gentle, subtle influence of the Religious Knowledge lesson is shattered even more easily by the least disruption of smooth working. So have your apparatus ready—paper, pencils, pens, plasticine, Bibles, notebooks—and see that the pencils are sharpened! Have it distributed quietly, collected quietly. Quietness as a form of respect for one another is a Christian attribute. Judge your time; a scrambled finish to a lesson ruins it. Weigh the pros and cons; assess likely and possible modifications to future work in the light of present experience.

Above all, remember that in my endeavour to keep to the bones of methodology, what now follows may appear extremely secular. This is quite intentional. I leave the spiritualising of your aim—to *you*.

CHAPTER VI

THE STORY

The teacher's inheritance; stages of development; types of story; content of
stories examined; lesson planning; telling the story; forms of story-telling;
detailed analysis and specimen notes.

THE Story, whether told in History, English, Religious Knowledge
or any other subject, does two things—it shapes standards and
ideals, and it interprets and illuminates facts. Because "the spoken
word is the remembered word" and tales heard during childhood
remain lasting possessions, much of the shaping of character is done
by this medium of education. It strengthens emotional power and
intensifies interest in both the subject-matter and the background of
the story itself.

Some of this may be due to the fact that the telling of stories is
an age-long practice that harks back to the days when the primitive
narrator, minstrel and troubadour were important people indeed.
They sustained noble traditions, roused inherent desires, awakened
dormant impulses to emulate; they intensified the thirst for adventure and achievement; they stirred in the young a great yearning to
be brave and virtuous and chivalrous.

It is in the steps of these that the teacher humbly walks. How
can he ever hope to measure up to their stature? He has so many
things to do, whereas these made story-telling their art and their
life-work. Be that as it may, our task is to educate the young by
using this method in order to inform and to inspire. By its means
we are able to put before them ideas beyond their immediate grasp;
we may give them knowledge of lands and peoples and customs and
manners that they would otherwise never receive. We must know
our audience if we are to succeed; we must know which stories to
tell, when to tell them and why. Not least must we learn how.

It may be as well if at this juncture we glance very briefly at the
developing interests of children, reminding ourselves that there is
no hard-and-fast line between any of them. First, we have what
might be called the Rhythmic stage of the very young child. This

is exemplified in stories involving vivid repetition, real adventures happening to animals and small children. Then we move to the Make-believe stage of the growing child. Wonder tales, Why, How, Once-upon-a-time and Long-long-ago stories attract this age. Whilst still in the Junior stage, children pass on to the age of Hero-worship. The instincts of aggression and curiosity are strong, as are the impulses of children to re-live in their own lives the events and experiences of peoples of the past. Primary Schools have here "their finest hour," a glorious opportunity to crystallise these strong urges into emulations, at least ideally, of great men and women of the Bible and history. There is always a demand for action, bravery and adventure. Stories of great writers, musicians, pioneers and law-givers are hero-tales of untold worth. Truth of spirit gives way to truth of fact at a later stage, as moving to the Romantic age of the Secondary School child we find that the more aggressive instincts are sublimating into some semblance of moral sentiments as the adolescent begins to crave for romance and chivalry—more often than not, of course, without knowing why. Stories of heroism stir strangely; the battles of virtue and vice are so very real. Here, your stories will have to be more selective and even less frequent; they must have a wider range, and they must be for the most part factual.

We begin to see some of the challenge and not a little of the difficulty in acquiring this art. For an art it certainly is. Some folks have a natural gift of narrative, like the tellers of tales long ago. They are able to hold the rapt attention of their listeners, their very speech molten by the fires of their own imaginations. These are to be envied. Most of us have to be content with the bare ability of putting a few ideas into some kind of ordered sequence, and only by sheer hard practice do we improve.

But even the natural story-teller benefits from a study of what is and what is not related to his art; and he improves by practice.

Let us, then, before studying further factors that will help us in the art of telling stories, look at some of the aspects of the story itself and how to prepare it for the telling.

If Bible stories are examined closely—indeed, this is true for all stories—it is seen that they fall into three main types. There is the straightforward plot, usually dealing with a single character or incident, e.g. Call of Samuel, the Lost Coin. Then there is the snowball type, where the main incident or character-study is expanded by a series of events, some of them toppling over one another in rapid succession as the whole action moves faster and faster in breath-taking and exciting accumulation to its conclusion, e.g. the Story of Joseph, the Fiery Furnace, Feeding the Five Thousand, the Conversion of Saul. Thirdly, we have the many-stranded type in which two or more plots and sub-plots, or several characters, stand out for contrast and comparison, and so heighten the excitement of the main plot or narrative, e.g. the Prodigal Son, with the two sons and the loving father; the Good Samaritan, with the three passers-by, the victim and the innkeeper; Moses and Aaron; the Two Builders.

Further discussion of these would be merely academic. They are analysed to help you to decide the type of plot to be unfolded, and to suggest lines of concentration to limit the bounds of the story. It is so easy to let an exciting sub-incident swamp the whole unless you are quite clear that it is only a sub-incident.

Let us go a step further with close study of the story. We are now concerned with content rather than skeleton plot, and must consider the historical background, detail and significance. We will examine these together.

Background should be prepared by reference to your books and special commentaries; get necessary detail quite clear in your own mind, and make sure it is relevant and necessary. You must also be reasonably sure of historical foundation. Is the story true, is it myth, legend, allegory? Can it be dated? Can it be related to any other subject—to Geography, to Science? The Agreed Syllabuses are most helpful, especially the 1949 revised *Cambridgeshire Syllabus*; and so is the *Teachers' Commentary*. All facts should be interesting and useful; mere frills are boring and irrelevant enough to cloak the real development of the plot. They should be accurate, of course; children have a pernicious memory for glossed-over remarks made in uncertainty of fact. Get information about setting, historical, geographical, cultural, clothes, customs, manners, occupations, tools, distances (Sabbath Day's journey), money (two-pence, widow's mite). These are the stuff of interest.

Then there is the significance of the story. What does it mean as it stands? What does it mean for us today? Is it merely a story of God in the past, of Jesus in the cornfields, of the persecution of the early Christians? Or is it something that has a message and meaning for us at this moment? Is it a question of right and wrong? If so, remember that standards have changed somewhat in 4,000 years. Is it a trait of someone's character? If so, is that trait as important to anyone today? What of the actual rites and ceremonies, laws and sacrifices? What of the implied direct speech with God in those days—and now? These are questions to turn over in your mind as you prepare your work. As you answer them to your own satisfaction in relation to each story, you may decide that it might be a better plan to break away from the straightforward narrative and approach the plot from an entirely different and new angle. Indeed, this is one of the best devices in story-telling, though one that defeats its own purpose if indulged in to the exclusion of other methods. Thus, why not tell the story of the Good Samaritan as the inn-keeper might tell it to a customer (the gaps can always be filled in by "hearsay"); or Miriam might tell the early story of Moses. Why shouldn't a rabbi tell of the visit of Jesus to the Temple at the age of twelve—and might he not recognise Him when He turned out the money-changers some twenty years later?

We have now examined in a very broad way the type of plot and the importance of preparing the content. We have therefore to devise a workable plan on which to base our actual lesson. The one eventually put before you is, of course, not infallible; but it has the virtue of sequence in a not-too-obvious framework, and has been used successfully by some hundreds of students—now teachers.

When trying to decide which parts of your scheme best lend themselves to story-telling, you will probably notice that they vary considerably in both quality and quantity of information. They seem to fall naturally into three types. Some are full of detail, much of it unnecessary to your immediate aim; others are scanty and woefully lacking in detail or specific information; and a few of both types will be so familiar to the children that you wonder whether your dealing with them yet again will be of any value at all.

This triple variation must now be dealt with, as we proceed to our framework. Before continuing, however, I must acknowledge my debt to the writers of a small book meant for Sunday-school teachers, but equally useful to teachers in day school—*Methods of Teaching*, Gill and Pullen (N.S.S.U.). Quite by chance I found that they had made an approach to story-lesson preparation much like my own, even to the division of story types we have now reached. Their precise and logical handling of each of these induced me to modify my own to incorporate theirs.

Let us get back to our lesson plan. First, state your A I M. At the risk of reiteration, let me remind you that this must be clear, as the whole development of the story depends on *what* you want to teach. Keep it specific, and keep it simple. Don't lose the clearness of "Jesus, the Good Shepherd" in the blurr of "Inculcating an understanding of the Shepherdlike care of Jesus for His children." Unless the aim is clear whilst the story is being prepared, all kinds of extraneous matter that you had intended to leave out will creep in, muddle the outline and cloak the truth you wanted to tell.

Having settled the aim, study the story more closely and settle on the point at which it appears to make its effect felt. This is the C L I M A X. It may or may not be exciting, but it is the sequel to the events preceding it. It is the working-out of the aim, which shows how important it is to have both quite clear. Now relate these two factors to the story. There is an aim and a climax. W H A T H A P P E N S I N B E T W E E N? How best to deal with the story in an effort to pass on to the children its full meaning?

It is here that we remind ourselves of the three types noted already. Is the story one with too much detail or not enough, or is it too familiar? Let us put them side by side, and with the points already dealt with, develop a workable framework by comparison and contrast (see p. 58).

From these you now have the nucleus of a lesson plan. You already had your aim and climax, and in the ways indicated now have the series of incidents or steps in the story working out the one in leading to the other.

Our next guide is no less a person than the King of Hearts, who said, "Begin at the beginning and go on till you come to the end. Then stop." The one weakness of this otherwise good advice is that the story-teller cannot fully accept the dictum—he must know where he is going, and should not start unless he does. But here are two excellent points—a good start and a sound ending. Until you are able to use the framework mechanically from sheer practice, and even when you can, it is better to prepare both beginning and ending as verbatim sentences. These will give a definiteness and crispness that will shape the good lesson.

Let us now note the Lesson Plan we have evolved:

ANALYSIS OF STORIES

Too Much Material	Too Little Material	Too Familiar Material
i. Note your AIM	i. Note your AIM	i. Note your AIM
ii. Note your CLIMAX	ii. Note your CLIMAX	ii. Note your CLIMAX
iii. Choose your form of narration	iii. Choose your form of narration	iii. Choose your form of narration
iv. List the incidents	iv. List the incidents	iv. List the incidents
v. Cut out the superfluous happenings	v. Amplify with further happenings	v. (a) Note those "sure to be known" by the children. (b) Prepare new relevant material
vi. Check sequence for continuity of the story	vi. Check sequence for clarity	vi. Check sequence for relative importance of facts
E.g. Incidents in the lives of Elijah, Isaiah, Ezra; story of Joseph; events in life of Jesus and of Paul.	E.g. The Lost Coin; Cleansing the Temple; the Captive Maid.	E.g. Christmas stories; Call of Samuel; stories of Moses; of Paul; many of the Parables and Miracles.
NOTE: Take care that the pruning does not leave a mere skeleton plot, or the result will be very dull.	NOTE: Take care that the new detail does not smother your aim. Weave in other characters. Introduce dialogue; have plenty of action.	NOTE: Children are usually more tired of the teller than of the story; tell it from a NEW angle. Base No. iv on your choice of narrator. Pass over v (a) quickly; dwell more on v (b).

1. Statement of A I M (simply, clearly).
2. The Story
    (i) *Opening Sentence—verbatim*. Make it arresting. Raise a problem, ask a question. Vary pitch and tone of voice. Sometimes make a general introduction; often plunge right into the story.
    (ii) *Steps of Development*—your list of incidents in sequence, plus background detail where necessary.
    (iii) *Climax*—try to make this the highest point in the tide of rising interest.
    (iv) *Closing Sentence—verbatim*. Make it sum up the story. Leave the children with a quiet statement, a problem, a question. If there is a "moral," leave it at that; don't ram it down their throats or ruin it by "explaining."
3. Class Activity and Expression. (Guidance on this later on in the chapter.)

Here are four different opening sentences for the same story to give you some idea of variety. They were provided by students.

    (i) "The Scouts are here! Run, tell Moses—tell Moses that the Scouts are here! Hurry!"
    (ii) "This morning we are going to talk about spies. What does a spy do? (Accept various replies.) Yes, he goes secretly into an enemy country to find out as much as he can about the enemy and the country. . . ."
    (iii) "Have you heard? Oshea and the others are back." "Back? Where have they been?" "Why—didn't you know . . .?"
    (iv) "Grapes—or Giants . . .?" (Note the value of pitch and tone—and pause.)

And here are four different closing sentences for another story.

    (i) "Borstal? Never again! I've learnt my lesson—and Dad's trumps!"
    (ii) "Yes, John had been the black sheep of the family. The only one who ever understood him was his mother. He was like the Prodigal Son who came home to his father. God is

our Father—and someone has said that God is a Father with a mother's heart."

(iii) "I was a long time getting used to having my young brother about again. Father said everything would work out for the best. He was right, of course; he always was."

(iv) "This my son was dead, and is alive again; he was lost, and is found."

(The simplicity of the Bible phrasing of this idea makes an excellent ending to the story told either in the straightforward manner or from the point of view of the father.)

Here is a pair of sentences to open and close the story of Christ's entry into Jerusalem.

"When General Allenby captured the City of Jerusalem in 1917, he approached the gates and was preparing to enter the city at the head of his victorious army. Suddenly he jumped off his horse and, instead of riding through the streets as a general might be expected to do, he walked. He had remembered something. I wonder what it was."

"And so, on a bright and glorious day, when Jesus is acclaimed King and Leader, there appears in the distance the glimpse of a thundercloud—the chief priests are angry because He heals the sick and gives sight to the blind and is the Hero of the people; we wonder—'What new mischief will the jealous priests and scribes plan—against Jesus?'"

Before leaving the question of preparing opening and closing sentences, I am reminded of a student who once objected that it was possible to get the closing sentence first and then to find an introduction that would eventually lead to it. This recalled the very sound words of Percival Wilde, who says somewhere, "Begin at the End and go Back till you come to the Beginning. Then start." This reversal of the King of Hearts' advice is both wise and salutary. And without pressing the moral it does emphasise the need to see the story as a whole, as a finished work of art, before attempting to present it to the class.

At the end of this chapter are notes of a specimen lesson embracing the points so far discussed.

Meanwhile, there are further considerations. Generally speaking, our stories fall into two broad types—narrative (i.e. description of scenes and incidents); and biography (i.e. description of the lives and work of the people). These may be further subdivided to introduce varieties of approach. The new angles thus presented provide more opportunities for teacher and class to share, and to some extent obviate the real danger of the teacher's adherence to the same method in successive lessons. Variety of approach helps him to get out of his rut.

The story, whether narrative or biography, may be oral or written. It may be told direct by the teacher or looked up by the children. It may be the work of a single child for the benefit of the whole class, working on references given him by the teacher in Bible and Commentary and text-book. Or a group of children may work on a subject and produce a composite account for the rest of the class or for a different class; it is often a good idea for children to visit one another with work of special interest; a fourth-year A class can produce pleasant stories and illustrations for a first-year class of any stream.

Where a story is well known, revision for the teacher and the joy of repetition for the children may be experienced as a complete class effort where the children build up the story as they go along. They will keep one another on the right lines, and drop severely on to those taking liberties with plot and background. They should be given the pattern of the story framework already discussed. Needless to say, there is incidental training in oral and written English here; so is there an indirect learning about lands and peoples and customs and manners. This is all to the good. Why not use Biblical material for English and Geography lessons?

Besides being oral or written, the story may also be imaginary or true. Further, it may be Biblical or non-Biblical, and may be given in either first or third person. The present tense, too, has a compelling forcefulness about it in story-telling.

The Agreed Syllabus and modified school or class syllabus provide ample material. All that is needed is the careful selection of such parts as best lend themselves to this method of teaching. All the familiar incidents of the Old Testament—Moses, Joseph, Joshua, David, the prophets and so on, and in the New Testament the stories of Jesus, the Parables, the events of the early Christian

Church—lend themselves obviously and easily. The biographical material is equally recognisable.

You will now see that variation of actual story-telling is almost endless; the following are examples:

Oral account by the children of a non-biblical biography such as St. Francis of Assisi, Schweitzer, Elizabeth Fry.

Written account by a child of an imaginary Biblical story such as Benjamin's account to his father of finding the cup in his sack; or what the boy with the loaves and fishes told his mother; or Matthew's call as seen by his assistant; or the Armour-bearer's story of Saul.

Oral account by a child of a true Biblical autobiography, such as that of Hannah, Zacchæus, Peter.

Where biography is concerned, there will be a temptation to drag in dates, schooling and superfluous information. These are usually dull and uninteresting unless brightened with action, so are better left out. Prophets, kings, disciples, great saints, pioneers, men and women of the Bible and early Church, reformers, historical characters—all these provide an ample selection. Many of them are given in the Agreed Syllabuses, and there are plenty of books on these lives for content and information. Tell these biographies in such a way as to show that God is a very real Person and uses such people —humble and insignificant as they were for His work then—even today. Further than "God may one day need you for some special job," don't press the moral. If your teaching is really up to date, you will use biographies of present-day missionaries who are doing every bit as great work as Augustine and Francis. Even as I type this, I call to mind a small newspaper paragraph in which a local church said farewell to a member about to leave for medical missionary work in Angola. What a good opportunity for a Religious Knowledge teacher!

The selection of types may be simplified if it is remembered that children like men and women of daring—Gideon, Michael, Niemöller; of legendary bravery—Samson, the Israelite Robin Hood, Nurse Cavell, Captain Oates; of adventure—Joseph, Judas Maccabæus, Grenfell, Mme Curie. They like, too, tales of romance— Ruth, John Williams; of simplicity—Jairus' daughter, Raikes; of drama—Peter, Jephtha's daughter, Cranmer; of pioneering—Amos the Shepherd, Shaftesbury, Barnardo, Elizabeth Fry. The history of the Christian faith through nineteen hundred years will provide counterparts of all Biblical stories. Selection of these will occasionally be coloured by the locality (e.g. see *Durham Syllabus*), where memory and tradition of certain brave lives will be strong—or ought to be.

Above all, remember that children are more interested in what folk do than what they say or think, so be sure the stories of these people are vehicles for action. Children love old favourites re-told in modern idiom, but they do not care for abstractions. Goodness, mercy, evil, justice, as such, are colourless and meaningless. These ideas and ideals need to be personified; leave the question of impression to the process of growth and development. Similarly, do not dwell overmuch on the sadistic features of a story. When children's eyes begin to sparkle villainously and voices begin to murmur gruesomely, it is tempting to wallow with them in the gore of martyrs and revel in the shrieks of the tortured. Don't. Where your characters speak—and they should—give them voices and dialects that fit, and vary the tempo of speech. In this way, children are helped to distinguish the peasant from the nobleman, the soldier, the widow, the fisherman. They quickly recognise the fat, greasy shopkeeper and the thin querulous stranger.

By the way, even the best of story-tellers occasionally loses the interest of one or two of his listeners. If you must correct a child, don't do so as I once heard a student—"And the fat, long-bearded rabbi looked at the tall innkeeper and said, 'Sit up, John, there's a good boy!'" The class laughed and so did I; the student looked bewildered. It ruined the story—and class control. Better to have fixed John with an eye, continuing the story the while, or even to have strolled to him and gently touched him, still telling the story. Sometimes it is effective to break off your story and *ask* John—"What do you think he said, John?" It brings John to heel and keeps the story flowing. That should be sufficient, for if your story is good, class opinion will settle John's hash. Which reminds me, don't omit humour from your stories. Without overdoing it, you can make scenes and incidents quite funny and give legitimate outlets for laughter—the pot-bellied dignitary, the waddling donkey, the obsequious publican. And the pompous rabbi tripped by running children and left enveloped in his robes is as comical as any top-hatted Englishman skidding on the traditional—if ephemeral—banana skin! Beware, however, in these as in any lessons, that you do not build up a reputation for being funny; it's disastrous. Make these aspects incidental and part of the natural flow of the story.

Background and setting should be clearly woven in as you proceed. Don't stop, for instance, to explain how Peter could see a vision on a housetop without sliding off. Call it a flat-roofed house and get on with the story. Quite often you will have to provide visual aids of various kinds, especially pictures, snaps and maps. It is fatal to pass these round the class during the story. Arrange them for the class to see after the lesson, in an orderly fashion; they serve as a reminder of parts of the story just heard, and add to the pleasure derived. A map, large and simple enough to be seen from the back of the class (go and see, *before* the lesson), or a large picture, or a large model, may be used for illustrative purposes throughout the lesson, but only if they *do* serve that purpose. Otherwise they are gratuitous distractions.

Sometimes it is a good plan for the children to try out some aspect of the forthcoming story first. Thus, the healing of the blind man might be begun something like this: "Close your eyes. Keep them shut. Now open your desk. Take out your Bible. . . . Now your ruler. . . . Now touch your neighbour . . . his hand . . . his jacket . . ." and so on. Bring a child to the front; let others pass by him whilst he pretends to be blind, marching, slouching, skipping . . . let him say what he "sees"—soldiers, beggars, children. It is in this simple way that children learn what it means to "see with your hands, or with your ears," or—and you will devise these—"to see with your nose." As the story continues, some of the children will quietly react, closing their eyes as they identify themselves with the blind man. They may even "shout for joy" at receiving their sight. It is detail they love; this is seen again and again in their intense delight in information about the homes of other people, their food, clothes, rooms, schools, teachers, modes of travel, what they learned, their books and their play.

It is obvious that the story chosen should have the necessary ingredients of appeal for any particular class, and that you are using language that suits each, too. Use your face and eyes, vary your speed and mood, adapt your inflexions; and when you are aware of

PLATE I

Creative expression—poster-colour paintings of Jacob's Dream.
A and B stream boys.

PLATE II

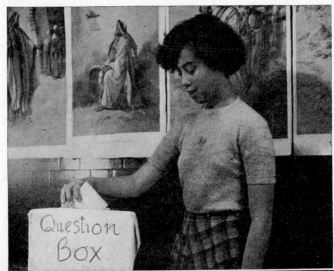

Above: The Question Box.
Below: Lettering for memory work.

PLATE III

Above: Shipwreck of Paul ; three-tone painting by an A stream girl.
Below: Various forms of written expression.

PLATE IV

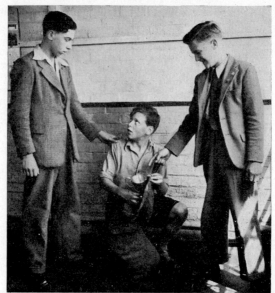

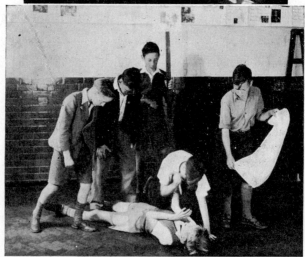

Above: Spontaneous mime; Benjamin finds the cup.

Below: Scene from original group-script; a story in the Apocrypha.

an audience without being lost in the telling, you will know how you are faring. The story is the greatest bond of affection, and the surest means of education there is, if the teacher has mastered the art. You don't need to be a genius; you need only recall that genius is 90 per cent. perspiration.

By now you will probably feel that once more here is a counsel of perfection. Perhaps it is. But story-telling is an art, and an art to be practised. And the suggestions made are the things to be practised. As time goes by and more and more children enter your world and walk side by side with the peoples therein, as they learn to tell heroes and heroines from villains and cowards, as they learn to live and re-live these lives, weep with them, laugh with them, rejoice with them, fight with them, they will eventually see the greatest Hero of them all—and bring Him into their own. That is the ultimate purpose.

CLASS ACTIVITY AND EXPRESSION

Finally, what outlets for the class are planned? Mere listening is not often regarded as a form of activity. It is, of course, if it has been conscious listening; it is a form of mental activity. If the children have been re-living with the teller the scenes of the story, they have had their outlet for the time being. Many a well-told story of just the right length can be left well alone. The class will have listened, enjoyed and lived the experience of it, and go away contented yet hoping for more, browsing and even brooding over the good story for some time to come. Many other stories, however, seem to be incomplete without some kind of manual or practical expression. This can be done in many ways; here are some suggestions from which to draw when dealing with the last part of our lesson-notes preparation:

(a) Re-telling a scene from another point of view, e.g. one of the shepherds in the nativity stories.

(b) Spontaneous or written dialogue, e.g. between two onlookers at Daniel in the lions' den.

(c) Simple play-writing, e.g. David and Jonathan.

(d) A letter, e.g. John Mark to his mother.

(e) Dramatisation, e.g. Prodigal Son—in tableaux or with spontaneous speech.

(f) Poems, e.g. crucifixion; blindness.

(g) Short question test.

(h) Note-making. The best type of notes are those made by question and answer; for some children, write the notes with blanks for them to fill in.

(i) Lettering, e.g. part of a text or a special prayer.

(j) Memory work, e.g. learning two or three verses bearing on the story or lesson.

(k) Poor man's Bible, e.g. scenes from Joseph; Jesus in the countryside.

(l) Models, e.g. tents, houses, temple.

(m) Drawings, e.g. Paul in jail; finding the scroll of the Law.

(n) Hymns and prayers, e.g. illustrative as found in the hymn-book or original ones.

(o) Questions I want answered.

There are countless forms of activity for all lessons, and these will lead to further forms of expression through discussion, research and constructiveness. Forms of activity leading to practical service are dealt with in a later chapter.

Quite a few children take their work home and get their parents —willingly or not—to help them. We cannot measure the influence or effect of this; we can only hope that it happens very often and takes into the home the attitude and atmosphere we try to engender in the classroom. Whatever you do, try to arrange that all lessons are rounded off with some kind of activity, and remember—if you are likely to need clay, paper, pencils, chalks—have them ready.

SPECIMEN NOTES

These will seem extremely full, and are made so quite deliberately to show the trend of thought and weaving in of imaginative background throughout the telling of the story.

THE STORY OF ZACCHÆUS
(Luke xix.)

Consideration of Aim

The secret of happiness; what wealth cannot buy; the joy of friendship; how Jesus understands the outcast.

Poor Man's Bible: by a C stream boy.

General Background

Jesus is passing through Jericho; the crowds are following Him mainly because He has cured the blind Bartimæus.

Zacchæus—a publican = tax-gatherer; a Jew working for Rome; a parasite.

Everything between him and Jesus:

　(*a*) wealth (from unjust extortion and the method of "farming-out" tax-collecting);

　(*b*) high position (Chief of Customs—over such men as Matthew had once been);

　(*c*) hardness of heart (from unpopularity and hatred as a Jewish traitor);

　(*d*) indifference (real or assumed—"he couldn't care less!").

But—*he was lonely*—had no friends; no one cared to be seen with "publicans and sinners"—household words. (N.B.—"A friend is one who knows all about you and still loves you.")

　—*he felt despised*—he was physically small; felt a sense of inferiority. This may have shown itself in his tendency to bully alternating with the desire to be quite alone. "Little in stature" = big in behaviour sometimes. (I think Zacchæus kept himself to himself.)

Detail

Sycomore tree = fig mulberry. Short trunk, many branches; easy to climb, even for a small man.

Note the ironic connection between this sycophant (parasite) and the tree he climbed; sycophant means "fig-revealer"—one who shakes a man as though he were a fig-tree until money falls from his pockets!

Why did Zacchæus climb the tree? True, he was short, but why sacrifice his dignity to do such a thing when probably boys and young folk were doing the same on the outskirts of the crowd gathered round Jesus. Was it just curiosity, or a desire to see the Man who sat with publicans and sinners? Was it the outcome of the bitter loneliness and disillusionment his reputation had brought him? Was it the urge of a secret craving for sympathy and friendship?

Too late, anyway. Seen by Jesus who reads the longing in his eyes; Jesus sees through the veneer and looks at the real

Zacchæus, who responds to the Master's smile. Here was One who could believe in him in spite of everything else.

Jesus invites Zacchæus to be His Host

From this moment Zacchæus is envied as well as hated; many of the crowd would have liked to entertain Jesus, for was He not the famous Rabbi—and as some whispered, the New Messiah? Hence the murmur (v. 7) that Zacchæus could not fail to hear and understand.

Note—"he stood"—could mean, he got up from a kneeling position before Jesus. More likely = he stood still, or he stopped in his tracks. They were angry with him and his new Friend. He would show them. By his declarations he put himself "in the right," and by so doing "excused" Jesus, too.

Note—the flow of declarations, with Jesus making no comment:

(*a*) Half his goods to the poor.

(*b*) From the other half, repayment fourfold. (Look up the Law references here—Lev. vi. 5; Num. v. 7; Ex. xxii. 1, 4, 7; 2 Sam. xii. 6.) Law demanded from a self-confessed thief, twofold plus "one-fifth part," i.e. 20 per cent. This indicates tremendous sincerity on Zacchæus' part, for the fourfold restitution was exacted only from the condemned criminal; as yet there were no charges against Zacchæus by the people or Jesus. Zacchæus puts himself in the worst light he can imagine. By now he is certainly kneeling, pleading; as he looks *up* at Jesus, pouring out his words, he experiences something he never felt before.

Zacchæus has Something that Money cannot Buy

Jesus now reinstates Zacchæus as a worthy "son of Abraham"; being a Jew Himself, Jesus realises what this means to Zacchæus—and to the people watching.

Zacchæus had been one of the most unlikely men to win, BUT "the Son of Man came to seek and to save that which was lost."

Here is your detail. Now try to decide how the story is to be told. Shall it be straightforward narrative; told by a disciple, say Matthew; narrated by one of Zacchæus' servants; as seen by one of the crowd; by one of the victims of Zacchæus' extortionate powers . . .?

When this has been decided, make sure that you know what the climax is, and where it comes. Then work out your headings leading up to the climax, and plan your opening and closing sentences verbatim.

This may give you some such scheme of notes as this:

THE STORY OF ZACCHÆUS
(*narrative*)

1. *Statement of AIM*

   How Zacchæus found the Secret of Happiness.

2. *The Story*

   (i) *Opening Sentence:* "Zacchæus had everything; and yet he had nothing. But when he indeed had nothing, he had everything! How did this come about?"

   (ii) *Steps of Development*

   (*a*) Zacchæus the chief tax-collector.
   — wealth and position ⎤
   — loneliness   ⎥ illustrate
   — hardness of heart   ⎥ from notes.
   — indifference   ⎦

   (*b*) Zacchæus hears of approach of Jesus, the "friend of publicans and sinners."

   (*c*) Zacchæus tries to see Jesus.
   — why?
   — his first attempts fail.
   — he succeeds.

   (*d*) Seen by Jesus.
   — hope and joy.
   — realisation of friendship offered.
   — invitation.
   — reaction of crowd.

   (iii) ⎧ C   Rising   (*e*) Zacchæus makes amends.
         ⎪ L   — defends new friend.
         ⎪ I   — defends self.
         ⎨ M   Higher   (*f*) Jesus' reply.
         ⎪ A   (*g*) At the home of Zacchæus.
         ⎩ X   — Jesus stays the night.
                              —Zacchæus a NEW man.

(iv) *Closing Sentence.* "Zacchæus never saw his Friend on
earth again, for two weeks later He was crucified. But
there is a little legend I like to recall of a very aged man,
small in stature, who tended the ground at the foot of a
very old fig-tree near Jericho. 'Old man, why do you
take so much care of that old tree?' 'Because'—and the
old man's eyes grow young and bright again—'from the
boughs of that tree I first saw my Lord.' Zacchæus had
found the Secret of Happiness."

3. *Class Activity and Expression*
   Select from:
     (i) Dramatise the scene.
    (ii) Re-tell from the point of view of "one of the poor."
   (iii) Dialogue between Zacchæus and Matthew.
   (iv) Drawing—Zacchæus in the tree.
    (v) Theme for Morning Assembly—True Happiness.
   (vi) Find other stories in the Bible about the "lost."
  (vii) Write "The Son of Man came . . . lost" in your note-
books.
 (viii) Print the same text in MSS. lettering for display.
   (ix) Write in ONE sentence what you think was Zacchæus'
secret.
    (x) Can you find a modern example—or write a short story
about a similar incident that might happen today.

It is always a good plan to READ THE BIBLE ACCOUNT as it stands, to
the class, especially if you decide that the mental experience of a
story well-told is sufficient class activity.

A Dialogue

ZACCHÆUS Good morning, Matthew.
MATTHEW Good morning, Zacchæus.
ZACCH. Do you remember when you worked for me?
MATT. Yes, I do. But I'm glad I left my job to follow Jesus.
ZACCH. I met Jesus yesterday.
MATT. You did? Where did you meet Him?
ZACCH. In the market-square at Jericho.
MATT. What did He say to you?
ZACCH. He said, "I want to come and stay in your house. Go
and get a room ready."

MATT.   That is just the sort of thing He would say. And did you?

ZACCH.   Oh yes.

MATT.   But however did you happen to see Him? You are so small and there must have been lots of people.

ZACCH.   I climbed a fig-tree.

MATT.   What! You—climbed a fig-tree! I can't imagine it. (*Pause.*) What did the people say when He came up to you and spoke to you?

ZACCH.   They did not like it at all.

MATT.   What did you do then?

ZACCH.   I ignored them at first. Then they began saying things about Jesus and me, so I stopped and spoke to them.

MATT.   That was the best thing to do.

ZACCH.   Well, I didn't want Jesus to take the blame, so I said, "I am a rich man, but I will give you back four times as much as I have taken from you."

MATT.   But you should only give them their money back and one-fifth. You're not a criminal!

ZACCH.   Well, I wanted to show them I meant what I was doing.

MATT.   I see. *I* found it was hard to make people see I had changed. Will you give up your high position?

ZACCH.   I do not know. I have not made up my mind about my business. There will be a lot to clear up. By the way, Matthew, where do you work now?

MATT.   Why, I told you! I am a follower of Jesus.

ZACCH.   I think that is what I shall do.

MATT.   If you want to, you will have to give up your high position.

ZACCH.   If I have to, I shall.

MATT.   If you do, the people will like you better, Zacchæus.

ZACCH.   I hope so, because I have not got many friends.

MATT.   You will have when you join Jesus, and you will have many enemies, too. Well, I must be going. Jesus is on His way to Jerusalem, and I shall have to be with Him. Good-bye, Zacchæus, and good luck.

ZACCH.   Good-bye, Matthew. I'd like to come now, but I have a lot of clearing-up to do. Perhaps I shall see you later on. Good-bye, Matthew. Good-bye.

This is the work of two twelve-year-old boys, following a lesson on Zacchæus given by a student-in-training. Nothing has been altered except spelling and punctuation where really necessary.

Scraperboard: "The Magi." By a boy aged thirteen.

CHAPTER VII

DRAMATISATION

Tableau; miming; plays, original and published; dramatic reading; puppetry; shadow plays; radio scripts; TV scripts; open-air drama; recordings.

DRAMATIC approach to a subject is, or should be except perhaps for the story, the most popular and most enjoyable method as far as the children themselves are concerned. Even in the higher Senior classes where the story is often regarded, quite wrongly of course, as childish, pre-adolescents will take a great interest and pleasure in their dramatic work.

There is a fundamental impulse to self-expression that finds an outlet in acting. Perhaps this is why the Nativity and Miracle Plays of the Middle Ages had such a vogue as a means of teaching religion. They dealt vividly with the dramatic truths of the Bible, and gave their watchers a sense of reality not easily forgotten. Happy those folk who witnessed performances by the Craft Guilds of the day, from the streets and windows, as the two-storied carts moved their lumbering way through village and town. Delighted the crowd who saw the Tale of the Flood with Noah's scolding wife to make them laugh; thoughtful those who watched the profounder story of Abraham and Isaac. And today in Oberammergau there survives the great spectacle of religious drama in the Passion Play of 1634.

How much greater the reality for the players themselves; the soaking-in of character, the understanding of cause and effect, the give and take of movement, the team-work of the players and scene shifters, the development of insight into the dynamic of the plot and purpose of the play. Acting a play is a creative and co-operative business for individual and group, and, obviously, the better it is done, the better the results all round. This does not mean that all children get the same value from dramatic activity, nor does it mean that all children should act plays, anyway. Indeed, to attempt a play with the dullest of our children may be to invite disaster; but there are some forms of activity that these children will find more suited to their limited capacities, and consequently more satisfying psychologically; these forms give them confidence in achievement and unlock doors to a freedom they might otherwise never experience.

In the following aspects of Drama you may discover what your particular group or class find most stimulating and you most educational, always bearing in mind that the approach is the lesser means to the greater end of religious training.

(a) Tableaux

Do you remember the lantern-slide? Lantern lectures have fallen into disrepute in these days of television and talkies. But here is the start to our approach to Drama. Just as the slide was the forerunner of silent films and talkies, so the static form of drama—tableau—may develop into the silent mime and talkie play.

Tableau drama is particularly good for the representation of simple Bible stories, parables, miracles and so on, and especially so for younger and backward children. Having heard the story of Joseph, for instance, they can set about arranging "lantern slides" of outstanding scenes to reproduce the narrative. Discussion of the plot and characters and scenes involves knowledge and understanding of the situations and facts of the story.

Much should be left to the ingenuity of the children, who will improvise scenery and costume. Don't worry if a boy uses the waste-paper basket and an inkpot to represent the sack and Benjamin's cup; merely make sure that the inkpot is empty. Look at the improvisation through the eyes of the children, and don't necessarily accept the idea that so-called C children have no imagination. When you have seen them use a T-square for Goliath's sword, a vase for the widow's cruse, a roll of wallpaper for the River Jordan, a blackboard map-rack for the elder brother's hay-rake, a chair for boulders in the Good Samaritan story, a wall map for the bed of the paralysed man, and the fire-bucket for a well—you may begin to realise that there is no end to imagination! But look out for your personal possessions, or your scarf and coat may do excellent service for a variety of Eastern costumes.

The idea of the method is, of course, that the children shall represent in picture form a still-life page of the story they are showing. One of the faults some children tend towards in this type of work, and indeed in all dramatic work, is that of dropping out of the picture. Having struck a pose, a child may relax without quite knowing it; his eyes wander, his limbs move, his whole pose wobbles. The reason is generally that the scene is being held for too long, and his interest is sagging as the physical strain tells on him. Class opinion settles the deliberate fidget. Competition amongst groups for the best portrayal is also effective. Children often need specific guidance and instruction in the necessity for being still, but usually the mere suggestion of "how still can you be?" works like a charm.

The best tableaux often result from life representations of the pin-man drawings already done by the children in earlier expression-work. When they have told the story in a dozen or so pictures in the form of a strip cartoon or Poor Man's Bible, they have something before them to portray; they will make their own alterations where and when necessary in the actual dramatising.

When the children have produced a number of tableaux, it is good fun and excellent teaching for groups of them to come out and set static scenes, whilst the rest of the class Guess What and Guess Who. This is a game that may well be held out as a kind of reward for good work. Occasionally, a keen group will do a scene from an incident not already dramatised or met by the class; guessing this gives real joy to all the children, actors and class alike. Indeed, this is an opportunity to set before the class a whole new incident for the first time.

(b) Mime

It is quite easy to pass from the tableau into the mime form. Your tableau characters, at first still, now move—still without speaking—into the successive scenes. As they do so they will discover that many of the former static scenes can be eliminated. For example, the tableau scenes necessary to the Good Samaritan number as many as eleven:

    (i) Farewell.
    (ii) On the road.
    (iii) The robbers.
    (iv) Attack.
    (v) Man left wounded.
    (vi) Priest sees.

     (vii) Levite sees.
   (viii) Good Samaritan saves.
     (ix) Innkeeper receives.
      (x) Good Samaritan leaves.
     (xi) Man recovers.

With the introduction of movement, so passing into mime, these may telescope into about four scenes:

      (i) Farewell.
     (ii) Attack on the road.
   (iii) Passers by; rescued by Good Samaritan.
   (iv) At the inn.

Here, again, let the children improvise and mime scenes for guessing. If you care to teach some of the easier conventional signs for miming to be found in any good book on the subject, by all means do; but the children make themselves very clear to one another—and that is all that really matters.

Once movement has been introduced, the tendency for children to drop out of the picture is stronger than ever. Be sure that every child has plenty to do. If the preparatory work in discussion has been well done, he will have begun to feel his part and will react to the rest of the cast. His emotions are stirred more than they were in the tableaux, owing to the new experience of movement. He can show a sequence of emotions, too, instead of one at a time. Thus, surprise can move into mimed repulsion, anger, sympathy.

For example, in the scene depicting the discovery of the cup in Benjamin's pack, the tableaux have portrayed only surprise, or only horror, or only anxiety, whereas the mime shows all these emotions as well as the gradual passing from the one to the other. These changes cannot always be left to the actor; his reactions need to be discussed. Let him put himself in Benjamin's position. Is he sure he hasn't got the cup? Is he annoyed that his word is doubted? Does he mind the men searching? Let them. They do so. There it is! How does he feel? What did he expect? Why? What has happened? Can he explain it? Does he fear the discovery? Why? Will anyone else suffer? Who? Do thoughts of his father affect his expression? How? . . . and so on.

Children will answer these questions, and add quite a deal more if encouraged. This indicates the need for *free* discussion in the right atmosphere. Various preliminary practices at facial changes and bodily gestures to be woven into the scene may be tried. Class voting will decide who shall play whom. This may seem unnecessary, but if the child has examples and something to think about in his portrayal to enable him to sustain his part, he adds a dynamic something to the whole that makes the mime real. It is this emotional playing that is important, for it helps him to absorb the significance of the story and, in particular, the part he is playing himself.

The chief temptation to the teacher is to allow familiarity with the method to breed carelessness of attack. This is seen in the casual, "That's the story; now let us mime it." The resulting shallow performance and dull atmosphere are to be expected. Each separate incident *must* be discussed, each character examined closely, each scene built up so that every aspect of its significance is covered; and all this is to be done in a spirit of reverent discovery that will enhance both preparation and final production. This does not mean that an occasional unknown mime should not be done. As in the tableaux, it makes an interesting diversion from the usual lesson.

Sometimes the mime may be done as the narrator reads the account from the Bible. The children then bring to life the reading, reacting in tempo and action to the quality of the reading. Several attempts may be made for constructive criticism; this will reveal many subtleties of the content of the passage not at first noticed.

A Narrated Mime is a good exercise for Morning Assembly, e.g. Acts xii. 3–17.

(c) Plays

With the play, the silent film of the mime passes into the talkies. Children love all forms of dramatic activity, but none more than what they call "proper acting," i.e. where they can not only move but can also speak. Never be shocked or too obviously amused at their gaucheness and vividness of dialogue. The boy who feeds the swine and thoughtfully says, "I'm going home to me Dad; he'll understand," has the right attitude; you would ruin it by demanding either Biblical or correct modern English.

Children are always ready to act spontaneously, especially in the

Junior School and the lower classes of the Secondary School. As they get older they lack natural spontaneity, losing it in a welter of self-consciousness; they prefer co-operative group preparation of the script, or a published play.

Original plays are always fun, and should be encouraged. The English lesson should be used for the mechanics of construction. Here, again, it needs teacher and blackboard, with class discussion of scenes and characters. Groups of children miming may be encouraged to speak, and the dialogue will gain impetus as the familiar mimed scenes develop.

Quite often there will be small sketches, such as the one given in the chapter on the "Story" of a meeting between Zacchæus and Matthew. Involving only two or three characters, these playlets give ample scope for repetition, so that the message of the theme or plot sinks in. Some of these make pleasing additions to the Morning Service.

The best subjects for original plays are those with dramatic plot— the Bible is so full of them, and the Agreed Syllabus makes selection extremely easy. But the possibilities of plays with softer characterisation—such as the story of Ruth, or David and Jonathan's friendship —should not be overlooked. With bright children it may be possible to weave plots around characters like Isaiah, Ezra, Onesimus, from background reading. Groups might work on separate scenes, and a co-ordinating committee would collate these, writing-in the connecting dialogue and editing the play generally, before further work is done on it. Such work needs insight and originality, and there is great reward in a successful result.

Excellent material is also to be found in the lives and stories of missionaries, reformers and pioneers.

Where a story is dramatised in this way, it is obvious that the number of scenes will be fewer than or entirely different from what was needed in the mime, for dialogue carries the plot much further than mere picture and action. Thus, our Good Samaritan play now becomes three scenes, each richer and fuller than the four of the mime and the eleven of the tableau:

    (i)   Traveller sets out.
    (ii) On the road.
    (iii) Next morning at the inn (a throw-back scene).

In spontaneous acting, children speaking their own idiom should be allowed to do so. When a play is written, however, it is often noticed by the children themselves that the dialogue needs considerable attention for a variety of reasons. They will suggest the alterations and improvements. If not, make these yourself for the group to discuss rather than as definite corrections done out of hand. Strangely enough, where the English improves there is a corresponding loss of vividness and directness. Biblical language creeps in, and there is a spattering of thee's and thou's. When actual Bible language is deliberately used, it is amazing how infectious is the lilt of its rhythmic prose and how well-spoken it often is—almost as if the children realised for the first time that such words need the best diction and articulation that they can command. Nativity plays reveal this more than any other type of play.

Needless to say, a considerable amount of background knowledge is indirectly obtained in the search for guidance on costume, customs, geographical and historical factors, apart from a useful familiarity with the Bible in the search for references and cross-references. There is encouragement, too, to the collection of pictures relevant to the work. Where the children decide to give a fuller showing of the play, work on scenery and posters (correlated with the Art lesson) make a pleasantly useful outlet for emotional interest. For classroom production, no scenery is needed. Pauses and announcements of the successive scenes are enough. Occasionally, a verse of a hymn, spoken chorally or individually, may be given in the intervals. A suitable gramophone record makes a change.

One of the dangers here is that these means become ends in themselves, and may smother the real purpose of the play. Guard against it. The desire to occupy as many of the class as possible is natural, but do not forget that they can often best be occupied as an audience. Players in such an intimate atmosphere as the classroom usually provide the more vital performance.

This brings us to the question of technique. How far shall we insist upon stage-craft? It is a mistake to do too much in the Religious Knowledge lesson. It is very possible to deal with some simpler forms of necessary technique in the English lesson, in such a way that the children see the need for and benefit of it; the right way to enter, to exit, to move, to sit, kneel, cross and so on. These things are out of place in the Religious Knowledge lesson, where an

PLATE V

Above, left: Puppetry—making a clay head.　B stream.
Above, right: Working the puppets.　D stream.
Below: Making the clothes.　B stream.

PLATE VI

Above: Scene from Tolstoy's *Michael*—by Yardley Wood S.M. Girls. (*Photo by Birmingham Post & Mail.*)

Below: Scene from original Nativity Play—by Highwood Primary School. (*Photo by West Herts & Watford Observer.*)

insistence upon them may create undue fuss and hinder normal portrayal to the undoing of much good work on the religious side.

What should be aimed at is care of speech and broad positioning; avoidance of congestion and talking away from the audience. The more thorough the approach to the play, the less likely is there to be any need for major interruptions arising from weak characterisation and stage-craft. Plan entrances and exits to open-out scenes and to focus the chief players. Use of high chairs, steps and platforms, all help in this. But while aiming at a good stage performance, prescribe nothing that will deprive actors and audience of a portrayal that is creative and absorbing. The hall-mark of classroom plays is sincerity, not technique. This is important, too, when children are learning their lines—as ultimately they will, whether you had intended that they should or not.

Before we leave spontaneous and original plays, a word of warning seems necessary. Not all Bible incidents, however vivid, are suitable for dramatisation. I once saw a D class act the story of Cain and Abel. Even allowing it a place in the scheme at all (a doubtful thought), I am quite sure such an incident should not be portrayed in the classroom by children of any age or ability. Again, Jesus Cleansing the Temple should not be acted, nor should the story of Ananias and Sapphira. These are all incidents—and there are others —that are either ethically wrong or that create doubt and confusion in the minds of children, and anything that undermines a simple faith should be avoided.

Now let us turn to the question of published plays. There is an increasing number of these now available of much better quality than were extant some years ago. Unfortunately, there are still many that suffer from both false sentiment and poor dramatic construction. These are usually the plays written "for" children, which generally means written "down" to children; the children are usually the first to realise it. If ever you are in doubt, better leave such a play unattempted. Get guidance from the right quarters, if you are in real difficulty. The Institute of Christian Education and the Religious Drama Society, with its quarterly *Christian Drama*, provide up-to-date information on these matters.

There are, of course, notable exceptions. Plays on religious themes by Hugh Ross Williamson, L. du Garde Peach, Freda Collins, and others recommended by the Religious Drama Society, are good.

Then, there are such plays as *The Man Born to be King*, *The Boy with the Cart*, *The Stars Bow Down*, *Murder in the Cathedral*, *Go Down Moses*, *Tobias and the Angel*, *Brother Wolf*, *Pilgrim's Progress*. Scenes from these complete plays may be concentrated upon most effectively as well as economically. You will find that all of them provide for sincerity of thought and speech, which should be your criteria of judgment. There is nothing merely pious or sentimental in any of them; all have a dramatic quality that is unmistakable. If you find that any play you have chosen—however good it is—seems to need a lot of explaining and rehearsal, it is probably too difficult for your group, and therefore unsuitable.

Some teachers think that no published plays should ever be done in the classroom, but if *good* published plays are done only occasionally, they at least serve as standards—of content, plot construction and quality—without which our children would make but little progress in the writing of their own. Besides, children like doing a printed play that gives a sense of completeness and rightness. So get your copies of printed plays (sets may be hired from Drama Libraries, which saves the expense of buying them), and use them.

Finally, how well we get to know our children in this kind of activity—and how well they get to know us. We discover in them traits we never suspected, both good and bad—originality and excitability, courtesy and officiousness; the shy become vocal and the reticent boisterous. And they find us patient or provoking, co-operative or bossy, encouraging or carping. Acting a play is more than a classroom exercise, especially in the Religious Knowledge lesson. It is a getting-to-know-one-another in a friendly, reverent, Christian venture that never palls if done in the right atmosphere, in the right spirit, for the right purpose.

(d) Dramatic Reading

(i) By the Teacher

In our anxiety to impart knowledge we may concentrate overmuch upon mere content in our lessons. We forget too often the inner urges of the spirit and fail to satisfy them. A good lesson may yet lack emotional education; and in Religious Knowledge a lesson may be devoid of spiritual experience. We must not forget that there are times when children gain most from merely listening, provided the experience shared between teacher and class is one of deep intensity.

This can obtain only when the contribution of the teacher is at a high level of achievement, and in the case of Dramatic Reading when the work is prayerfully—even powerfully—prepared. In any case, he must be a first-rate reader with a love for and a sense of the dramatic value of words and phrases in themselves, as well as vehicles of narration. He must be willing to study and to practise reading aloud, aiming at a rendering that is a work of art.

The exercise of this ability must not abrogate all other forms of teaching, but must be regarded as a means of generating, as it were, an experience at once vital and inspiring. There will be no follow-up beyond a quiet thinking pause in which the children would appear to come back to earth! Perhaps this sounds exacting; but the best literature deserves the best expression, and the best comes only of long and hard practice.

It is not difficult to find passages suitable; there are so many too beautiful and too difficult for children to render—yet how often we allow them to try. They would be sadly marred, too, if broken into snippets with "exposition." Even if selections are made, see that they follow in unbroken sequence. Choose from the Psalms and Prophets and Apocrypha; sometimes use a passage from Shakespeare or Shaw; and don't forget the poets like Milton, Donne and Thompson.

Some care should be exercised in choosing the best Biblical version. Much will depend upon the thought behind your dramatic reading. If your plan is to present to your class an experience rich in sound and dramatic power, without the necessity of their knowing the meaning of every phrase and word, to soak them in beauty, if you will, then the Authorised Version with its sonority of rhythmic language is obviously the choice. If, however, a piece depends to a large extent upon its meaning and clarity and forcefulness, then a suitable rendering may be found in one of the modern translations. Thus, Amos vi. 1–6 would ring as a challenge in the Authorised Version, but one of Paul's Epistles would present difficulty in anything but a modern rendering.

Where the reading is dramatic in the sense that there are several characters taking part in the incident narrated, variation of the voice will be necessary to portray these different people. The choice of such passages should be of few characters, for if overdone this effort at dramatic production may drift perilously near a music-hall act. Many of the incidents of the last days of Paul, found in Acts xxii to xxvi, are admirable for this interpretation.

It is absolutely essential in a lesson of this kind that there should be none of the gratuitous interruptions that so often spoil lessons. No one can appreciate a poem with a constant stream of visitors bent on various collections and note carryings. If there is no other way of getting complete security for at least this lesson, fix a notice on the door—"Please do NOT interrupt *this* lesson"—and lock the door as well. This is meant in all seriousness; a single interruption during a creative lesson is fatal—and you are creating a spiritual atmosphere so tenuous that the least noise may shatter it.

There isn't enough Dramatic Reading by the teacher; let us hope for great things in the future.

(ii) By the Children

In this form of dramatic activity, a passage of Scripture involving direct speech of several characters is chosen. Each character is then cast and, as the reading proceeds, says his lines naturally and vividly as and when they occur. The connecting-links of the narrative are read by a Narrator.

As in all other forms of Drama, thorough preparation is essential to the successful rendering of the passage to be given as a Dramatic Reading. The teacher must read and re-read the verses, saturate himself in their atmosphere, and try to grasp fully the amount of characterisation and the extent of dramatic power within the passage.

The voice parts of the several characters naturally have a colour and texture related to each, but the part of the Narrator is too often sacrificed to a coldly casual rendering in the belief that it is merely a connecting-link. But, as in radio plays, the Narrator's part gives scope for dramatic effort and exposition, and tone changes, inflexion and pitch should be exploited to the full. You will see the need for discussion of all spoken parts and of the various ways in which lines can be expressed. There is always the temptation to try to superimpose an adult conception—your own—on that of the child player. But children cannot possibly feel the emotions of the adult— of, say, Pilate or Peter in the Crucifixion narrative—and should not be forced to try to portray what they do not feel. Better the sincere inexperienced attempt of the boy than the artificial copying of the teacher's idea of what it should be. The feeling then comes from the heart, and this is always the important aspect of any characterisation.

It is a good plan to allow groups to study and present their own versions of passages relevant to the syllabus to which the teacher is working. In the life of Saul, for instance, there are several scenes that can be covered vividly by successive groups each dealing with their own chapters.

When a group succeeds very well with a passage, it should be given the opportunity of presenting the reading at the Morning Service; similarly, when the class reading for the week is announced, the passage should be considered as a possibility for Dramatic Reading. Both in the classroom and in the hall the children need stand only in positions that make conversation natural, with the Narrator standing slightly to one side as being the impersonal link. If his lines are a vivid contribution, it is a good plan to put him between the other characters, but never to the fore. Having discussed and prepared their lines, the children should not need to be reminded that their reading is more like acting than ordinary reading, that it should be in character and vitally alive. Their voices must cover the dramatic effect of gesture and facial expression and movement, and this is extremely difficult.

Crowd parts need a certain amount of drill to ensure uniformity, e.g. angels in Nativity scenes, or for planned chaos, e.g. cries of "Barabbas" and "Crucify Him," in Easter scenes. This implies the breaking-down of the whole into episodes that can be rehearsed separately, and then bringing together the parts to produce a balanced whole. What is said about Choral Speaking belongs here, for there will be several passages suitable for Dramatic Reading or Choral Speech that give unusual opportunities for training groups; it is not easy to draw a hard-and-fast line between the two dramatic types.

Here are some useful examples for Dramatic Reading:

> *Nativity Stories:* Narrator, Mary, Angels, Shepherds, Wise Men, Herod, Heavenly Host.
> *Easter Story:* Narrator, Jesus, High Priest, Pilate, Peter, Serving-girl, Crowd.

Elijah Stories: 1 Kings xviii. 17–39. Narrator, Elijah, Ahab, People, Prophets of Baal.

Fiery Furnace: Dan. iii. Narrator, Herald, Chaldeans, Fearless Three, Nebuchadnezzar, Counsellors.

(e) Puppetry

How far one can link Puppetry with the Religious Knowledge lesson may depend to some extent on the amount of correlation there is with the Art and Craft scheme. When the children already possess or make puppets in their craft lessons, it is usually very easy to produce puppets for their drama elsewhere; any one puppet in his time plays many parts.

The sketches for the puppet productions may be prepared in the English lesson, or begun in the Religious Knowledge period and finished at home. Children *will* do this with encouragement, and often get considerable help from various members of the family. Hand-glove puppets need no special dressing, but full-size puppets may be clothed in the Needlework lesson. Be careful not to use the Religious Knowledge lesson too often for such mechanics; it should not be a handicraft lesson unless you are very sure of the spiritual significance of what is going on. On the other hand, we do well to remember that the Master Himself was a carpenter.

Puppet plays should be simple and vivid in dialogue, with not too many characters. C and even D children—for whom Puppetry is most suitable—develop an astonishing spontaneity with three or four puppet Biblical characters. Brighter children will write their plays, but the backward ones are happier unfettered by scripts laboriously written and often unreadable when provided. They find nothing irreverent in making a puppet to represent God; He is usually shown by a benevolent head, made with express care. But it is not unusual for them to suggest that in the play He is heard off-stage and not portrayed at all. Accept such a suggestion without comment; it is a sign of reverence.

The subject-matter for these plays is obvious, but choose scenes with few characters. Manipulation of crowds is difficult and confusing; nor is there room behind the stage for more than a small number of children handling the puppets.

The story of Adam and Eve (noted in performance and reproduced here), Abraham and Isaac, Samuel and Eli, David and Saul (selected scenes), Daniel, Ruth and Naomi, most of the Parables, some of the Miracles, Nativity Scenes, Paul's conversion, Paul in prison, Onesimus, Peter's Vision . . . these make good puppet plays.

It is always sufficient to let the visual force of these scenes work upon the players and audience. Pointing morals and preaching ruin the atmosphere and destroy the simple acceptance of spiritual values given by children to children. Let them speak for themselves, however crude the result, especially the backward ones; where these are concerned, it is a miracle in itself to get them to talk at all. For those who have a bent that way rather than taking oral parts, there is great joy in designing backcloths and properties; and children will go to a lot of trouble to make sure that their crib, Eastern house and stall are authentic.

The Garden of Eden

(As played by Puppets devised by children in the lowest class of a Secondary Modern School.)

One day, Eve was walking in the Garden of Eden, and she saw a snake coming towards her. At first the snake flattered her:

SNAKE   Ah, what lovely round fruit over there. Why don't you eat one; you will soon get fed-up with these.

EVE   God told me to leave them alone (*pointing at them*). Besides, these are just as good as those.

SNAKE   What! These are as good as them—these scraggy, mouldy things? Go on, pick one. Nice, isn't it?

EVE   I really oughtn't, you know.

SNAKE   Go on. Save a bit for Adam.

                        (*Enter Adam.*)

EVE   Hello, Adam. Have a bit?

ADAM   No.

EVE   Have a bit, because the Snake said so, so it must be all right to eat.

ADAM   All right. (*He eats.*)

("*Then Adam and Eve knew they were naked and hid themselves. Later, they heard God walking in the Garden.*")

EVE   Go away!

GOD   So you have eaten of the fruit, have you?

EVE   The Serpent told me to.
                  (*So God told the Serpent off!*)
GOD   Adam, have you eaten a fruit of that tree?
ADAM   No, I ain't. (!!!)
GOD   You have.
ADAM   All right, you win. (!!!) Eve told me to.
                  (*And they were sent out of the Garden.*)

You may perhaps shudder at the crudity of some of this; it is quite untouched. It is interesting to note that although it was gently suggested that Adam might say, "No, I haven't," and later, "Yes, you are right," instead of the vernacular expressions, the original crudities persisted in successive productions of the play.

(f) Shadow Plays

Using the puppet stage, you can devise means of lighting figures and cut-outs to produce silhouettes and shadows of your characters, resulting in a fascinating effect. This is hardly the best place to go into mechanical details of these productions, and the best method of helping is to recommend *Shadow Play*, by Whanslaw, published by Gardner.

The method is amply and clearly described, and as far as utilising it as a method of dramatic production is concerned, you will see how to fit dialogue with movement of shadows as for puppets. Again it is the script that really matters.

(g) Radio Scripts

It is a very short step, if a difficult one, from Dramatic Reading to Radio Scripts. The essence of both dramatic exercises is identical, in that the dramatic force and content of a narrative or play must be put over by means of the voice alone. The absence of stage gesture and movement puts a premium on vocal interpretation. But few, if any, teachers expect to be supplied with such scripts for use in the classroom. As in the case of published plays, the home-made product is educationally and emotionally the better value. Children are familiar with radio representations of events; the medium is also familiar. That is why they find so little difficulty in regarding the possibility of portraying David and Goliath by radio. They are equally ready to suggest and provide commentaries, in the style of radio commentators, in the camps of Philistines and Israelites.

They will arrange close-ups of hero and villain, interview Saul, and thence lead up to realistic descriptions of the ensuing battle, with all its suspense of surprise, challenge and final victory of the right. Boys will rig up silver-papered microphones and provide announcers, trumpeters and heralds with zeal and facility; the girls may portray weeping Philistine women and exulting Israelites.

Script writing may best be done in the English lesson. It may involve an imagined re-telling of a Bible incident, or at the other extreme it may mean the spending of hours in search work to get the background right. Upper classes of bright children will, of course, find this form of dramatic activity more to their liking and ability than will children of poorer mentality; but there is no reason why all children should not, at some time at least, attempt the method.

Radio playlets should be based on a variety of material. Bible stories always appeal, e.g. Joseph, Moses, Call of Gideon, Call of Samuel, the Parables, Miracles, scenes from both Old and New Testaments, and incidents from the Apocrypha. E.g.:

STORY OF GIDEON

Scene 1. The Call—God or Baal?
      2. The First Blow—Destroying the Shrine.
      3. The Army—Choosing the Three Hundred.
      4. Victory—The Battle.

SAUL—A CHOSEN VESSEL

Scene 1. The Call—The Damascus Road.
      2. Paul the Preacher. ⎱ Scenes from the Missionary
      3. Paul the Preacher. ⎰   Journeys.
      4. Paul the Prisoner.
      5. Paul the Dauntless.

(Each scene is obviously a play in itself and the complete play might easily be an edited version of selected scenes done by various children.)

Such topics as the Story of the Bible, Missionary Work, Great Lives, Martyrs of the Faith, Reformers, etc., give scope for wider reading and search. Interludes to illustrate the significance of familiar texts are interesting to prepare, e.g. "to comfort the fatherless . . ." by a story of Dr. Barnardo; "to preach to the afflicted . . ." with Kagawa, Elizabeth Fry; "Go ye out into all the world . . ." with John Williams, Grenfell, Schweitzer. These scripts should be adapted for Morning Service on occasion, on the lines of the Interludes given in the Morning Service for Schools by the B.B.C.

The re-writing of prophetic utterances in modern speech for broadcasting is an extremely difficult exercise. It involves an understanding of the words of the prophet in their seventeenth-century idiom—quite a difficult feat. It then means a shaking-off, as it were, of the Elizabethan lilt by now familiar, and a reverting to one's own tongue. But it can be done. Here is such an example, the re-writing of Isaiah's Prophecy by a boy of fourteen:

> "From Jesse there will come a great nation;
> the Lord will be with him always and be ready
> to prompt him if he does not do the right thing.
> The world will be a wonderful place to live in;
> there will be no dangers
> and everyone will live as one family.
> At that time there will be a descendant of Jesse
> whom everyone will look up to.
> You will praise the Lord, too,
> for you will have found out what He has done for you.
> All the bad in the countries will stop,
> and there will be peace.
> Do not fear anything
> for God will always save you.
> You will be allowed to go to heaven,
> a place of perfect peace and happiness."

There is not perhaps high literary merit in this; that is not the point. To have produced such a crystal-clear statement is to have understood; who can measure the spiritual effect it must have had on the boy who produced it and on the class who heard it?

The pretended broadcasting of a prophetic utterance as it stands in the Bible context is most effective. A good reader can become a first-rate declaimer, whilst the words of Isaiah, Amos and Haggai in this guise become charged with a new understanding and power.

Elsewhere are suggested interviews with Bible characters on the lines of Radio Newsreel and In Town Tonight. These may appear to be extremely secular ideas, but approached in the right way will bring to children a new conception of both faith and the Christian way of life as they try to put into words what they believe to have been the thoughts of the Early Christians, the experience of John Mark, or of those who challenged the viewpoints held by Sadducees, Pharisees and Zealots. So, too, martyrs, missionaries and pioneers may come to the microphone to assert their loyalty to Christ; and what all these say is in essence what the script-writers themselves feel.

Other incidents that lend themselves particularly well to this mode of presentation are: The Story of Amos, Courtiers in the Train of Sheba, Two of Gideon's Three Hundred, David and Jonathan, Birth of Moses, Wedding at Cana, John the Baptist, Paul at Ephesus (including reports from the Chief Silversmith and the Governor of the City), Eutychus (after recovering from his fall).

(h) TV Scripts

Most children will have seen sufficient television plays, interviews, documentaries and the like, to be able to attempt similar scripts themselves. We should draw their special attention to such scripts as those for "Jesus of Nazareth," "Sunday Special," "Meeting Point," and encourage them to prepare challenging material for classroom use. It might be possible to film really good work and submit it for consideration, criticism and eventual televising.

(i) Open-air Drama

It is often a good plan to go outside—literally—with some forms of dramatic work. There is something refreshing about open-air performances; most of the work discussed here lends itself to simple staging in a garden or some natural hollow near the school—or even the playground. A whole project could be built on an open-air Eastern market.

(j) Recordings

Children enjoy hearing their own dramatic endeavours on tape-recorders. They should hear first-rate recordings, too. On pp. 139 and 210 references are made to valuable gramophone recordings and to these may be added Laurence Olivier's "Living Bible" series (H.M.V.)—an inspiration and example of great artistry.

CHAPTER VIII

QUESTIONS

Types of question, by teacher and by child; written and oral exercises.

"And it came to pass, that after three days they found Him in the Temple, sitting in the midst of the doctors, both hearing them, and asking them questions."

IT was a perfectly natural thing for Jesus to be doing, for children of his age—indeed of any age—love nothing better than to be able to ask questions, especially if there is any likelihood of their being answered.

Jesus was a Teacher—the greatest of all teachers; He taught with questions. He went on asking questions all His life; we might do better to ask more than we do. And yet how often in discussing a lesson a student has said, "You know, I can't get them to ask questions. I invite them—and they're just dumb!" With their reputation of being notorious questioners, usually at the wrong time, children have a distressing habit of shutting up just when you want them to help. It is largely a matter of atmosphere. Much depends on the lesson, its nature, the teacher and his nature. If the period of Religious Knowledge has developed the right atmosphere of naturalness, freedom of thought and speech, curiosity, then children will respond and react to ready listeners.

Let us look at this aspect of education as a teaching method, under the headings "By the Teacher" and "By the Children." In dealing with both written and oral approaches, we shall probably agree that the most important type will be the last—oral questions by the children.

By the Teacher

(A) Written

The type of question-work implied is obviously that in which the teacher provides on a given subject a number of questions of varying length, with or without references, which the children answer in their special note-books.

(i) Short questions requiring short answers. This type may be:

(*a*) A recapitulation of previous lessons, perhaps as a revision test, aiming at briefly noted factual knowledge. "Twenty short questions" should be as usual in a Religious Knowledge lesson as in History or Geography.

(*b*) A passage for study, with questions set on its content. This aims at comprehension of language and purport, and is an exercise that may equally well be done in an English lesson. The early Bible stories lend themselves very well to this kind of work; so do biographies of Christian men and women. Many of these questions should be done at the children's own speed and in their own time.

(ii) Questions requiring longer answers. The essay comes in this section; we should try to make the exercise different from the normal run of compositions, by providing opportunities for interesting and unusual pieces of work that result from a little imaginative play on the topic.[1]

(*a*) A useful first exercise is to set the re-writing of selected parables or miracles, e.g. Good Samaritan, Water into Wine, Prodigal Son, Crossing the Red Sea, in twentieth-century language.

A good follow-up is to have these read aloud and compared, and then to hear the same passage as rendered by Moffatt, Knox and Phillips, as well as in the Bible in Basic English.

This work will inevitably introduce new ideas suggested by new words, sequence of phrases, interpretation and so on; and these in turn make opportunities for simple examples of Biblical Criticism as indicated by the modern versions.

A literary comparison is not out of place—the best class effort, the best modern example, the Basic English form, and a re-reading of the original Authorised Version with its now clarified meaning and appealing beauty of language.

(*b*) In a similar approach, turn to selected verses of the prophets. Don't forget the lesser prophets who, besides Isaiah, had much to say that is relevant to the present day. Let the class read and choose the passage appealing to them most, and then turn it into a Radio Talk. You must give them a time-limit—say five or ten minutes. The class will go so far as to rig up a micro-

[1] Based on suggestions in *Religious Education in the Senior School*, R. L. Arundale (Nelson), q.v. I owe much to author and book.

phone and deliver their orations. Delivery is of prime importance—inflexion, pause, vehemence, tempo should be noted. Who knows but what "Comfort ye, comfort ye . . . ." and "What doth the Lord require of thee . . . ?" may reach a child's heart for the first time, perhaps without his being aware of it but accepting it for all time.

(c) Now send out your reporters amongst the people of Judah, Jerusalem, Nineveh, Babylon. Let them interview Potiphar, his wife, Judas Maccabæus, Caiaphas, the Innkeeper.

Get your written accounts of interviews during the Trial of Jesus co-ordinated, and see the greatest drama of history through new eyes.

Make a Radio Symposium of news flashes something on the lines of Radio Newsreel. Watch your chronology in this.

Extend this type of work into an attempt to produce a news-sheet, even a newspaper, such as "Vigil Romanus," "A.D. XXIX," "Stella Roma," "A.D. L." These will involve reports of all kinds—interviews, letters to the editor, diary of events, past news, forthcoming attractions, advertisements and so on.

In any case, note that written questions requiring contemporary background and views are invaluable exercises for the discovering of details and facts relating to the Bible, its people and times.

John Mark's Diary, Barnabas's letters home, the opposing viewpoints of Pharisees and Sadducees regarding the Resurrection, the knowledge of taxes, feasts and their origin, conditions of life for the Roman soldier, the Sanhedrin—these are typical examples of written work that give considerable pleasure in being off the beaten track.

(d) Summaries. Let the class take stories, simple ones at first, then those with sub-plots, and let them reduce these stories to chapter headings. This is good practice for story-telling, as it ensures that they know the story content before or at least by the time the work is finished. These chapter headings can then be illustrated on the lines of popular strip cartoons or Poor Man's Bible. They have added value if sent to lower forms and displayed on the walls; both creators and recipients derive much pleasure from this.

Teachers interested in filmstrips could encourage certain of the more talented children to illustrate their stories with potential film scenes.

(e) The type of work we have been discussing leads to some of a more difficult nature, covered in the chapter on "Search and Discovery." But in between there are written exercises which we might regard as assignments, topics, lecturettes; also dealt with more fully in Chapter X.

Book reviews of Bible stories may be tackled; it is often a good way to get these books read by possible shirkers.

Reports on suggested books for the School Library, wireless and other plays, letters to the *TV Times* and *Radio Times,* make pleasant exercises and involve patience in finding the necessary information.

For the slower children it might be a good plan to provide pictures of first-rate quality (including the Old Masters) for straightforward descriptive work or comment. These children might need guiding questions to help them in the best line of thought and expression.

(f) Rather more difficult in style is the written work involving critical powers. Thus, you may provide some children with three accounts of the same miracle and ask such questions as: Why did Matthew add this? Why did Mark omit that? Where did Luke get this? And thereby introduce the Synoptic Problem.

Or Gen. i and ii might be compared in style, content and sequence, your questions guiding the children in setting-out their answers and drawing their own conclusions.

Yet another exercise testing critical ability is an adaptation of the "three-sentence composition." In this, the children are set to tell in three sentences the story before them. This is a very difficult exercise, as you will see for yourself if you try to tell *Cinderella* in three sentences. It implies precision, clarity of comprehension and powers of condensation.

(g) It often happens that a film with a Biblical setting comes to the local cinema, e.g. *Barabbas, Exodus, David and Bathsheba,* or *King of Kings.* Many children will go to see such films; the stories should be studied closely with Bible and commentaries, so as to get the plots, background, costumes, manners, etc., really right. The children then see the film with more critical eyes; armed with accurate facts, they can note the liberties taken with the story and characters. Verbal and even written comments should be expected—and obtained.

(*h*) Use the filmstrip for written work. Show a maximum of five frames of a quarry filmstrip (see Filmstrips in Chapter XVIII). Allow the class sufficiently long for information to be observed, then let them answer previously prepared questions on the content or import of the frames studied.

It is desirable that children have their own special Scripture notebooks for this and allied work. These might be covered according to their owners' tastes in Scriptural designs, and be the personal property of the children. This encourages the wish to make the books pleasurable in appearance and content by the inclusion of pictures, texts, drawings, photographs and other visual material.

If there is a School Magazine, see that there is at least one article of scriptural interest—the best review, the most interesting interview, guessing the hero and so on. Reproductions of Poor Man's Bible strips are likely to give pleasure; competitions introducing Biblical and non-Biblical characters, texts and events are bound to have many entrants.

(B) Oral

Teachers learn early in their training the value of principle behind their practice. In their Mathematics, English and Social Studies lessons they strive valiantly to harness the two together, but all too often in the Religious Knowledge lesson, for some reason or another, principles are non-existent and practice is merely a series of dull precepts and exercises. We must bring educational theory into the classroom at all times for all lessons. Hence the value of oral questioning by the teacher; if he knows what he wants and why he is asking the questions, he is all the more likely to ask sensible, searching and motivated questions that will lead the lesson pleasantly to a required end and stimulate further interest in the work being done.

The broad objects of questioning are the testing of factual knowledge, the preparation of known experiences for acceptance of the new and unknown, the clarification of comprehension, the development of critical powers. Questioning may be a spur to the children and a check on the teacher who is over-anxious to tell.

Let us look at some of the types of questions possible, remembering that they overlap rather than remain in water-tight compartments.

(i) Recapitulatory questions are probably best used, either at the beginning or at the end; for the one they will link the threads of the previous lesson, for the other they will sum up the points of the lesson just given.

Obviously they should be vital and searching, not merely soporific: they should stimulate and interest and test the memory. Revise past work with a few pointed questions on the things you deem it necessary that the class should know. Add further questions to start their minds working on lines leading to your new work. From time to time you will discover that you have left out an important point yourself, or there is something they have not quite grasped. Teachers are so prone to use questions merely to find out "What they have remembered" when more often it might be better if they asked in order to discover "How much have I taught?" or "How successful have I been with my teaching?" In any case, unless you ask questions the various failings may be missed altogether, and might cause difficulties at a later date.

(ii) Questions serve excellently to introduce a new line of thought. You are going to study some of the healing stories of Jesus. Why not begin like this: "Who's ever been in hospital?" There will be a riot of answers covering all sorts of ailments and relations, and when these have subsided you can proceed to nurses and doctors, anæsthetics, operations, running the hospital, subscriptions; being careful not to go too far before you guide the class to a consideration of gratitude for healing—and to the greatest Healer of all.

Be careful of this kind of introduction. One of the most startling beginnings to a lesson I ever heard was that to a lesson on the Wise and Foolish Virgins. It was—"Which boys are in the Scouts?" The aim was Being Prepared! As the student said wistfully, afterwards, "You have to do something now and then—to make them think!"

(iii) Making them think is the work of yet another kind of question—the poser. Put your children in Jesus' position when He was asked if taxes should be paid to Rome; in the position of the poor woman who lost one of her precious coins; in the shoes of the runaway Moses told to go back to Egypt; in the seat of Judas at the Last Supper; as Elijah challenging the priests of Baal. . . . And then? What would *you* do?

From part of the class there will be a volley of suggestions for some of the situations; some of the answers will be foolish and thoughtless, quickly scorned to silence by the rest of the class; some children will be more hesitant, weighing the pros and cons before coming to a decision. Note the various replies—discuss, criticise, amend, approve. Look for the grain of sense in the most unlikely answer; compare the eventual decision with the actual narrative where your approach allows of it.

As a variant of the method, it is often a good plan to start a story and then leave off at a critical point, e.g. Jephtha's daughter, up to her unwitting welcome to her horrified father. . . . What would you do? What do you think happened? Why? Then complete the story, and continue discussion as far as is valuable.

Another type of poser is that in which a story or incident is related or acted without mention of the name of the central character—then, Guess Who?

These lessons can be pleasant experiences as well as very educational if well prepared.

(iv) Background questions must be considered.

Very often one needs to bring to an incident knowledge already familiar to the children but for the time being somewhat unconnected and piecemeal. Skilful questioning will bring this to the fore, and collate it into general background—the countryside, types of people, what they ate, what they wore, their houses, customs, feasts. . . . We have already noted children's delight in detail, and if this is well taught at an early age it will develop into a fuller appreciation of later studies; the building up of correct mental images in preparation for and support of new knowledge is a vital part of the process of learning to which the good teacher must at all times have regard.

(v) Often you will be using visual aids of some sort or another. It is important here to remember that when looking at something of this kind, children do not necessarily see what you see, even in the simplest of pictures. In the language of psychology, they perceive whilst you apperceive. They see only lines and colours and shapes, and often fasten on some entirely irrelevant part of the aid that attracts their attention; you recognise what the aid stands for, and interpret its aspects in vivid movement and incident.

The difference is obviously due to your wider experience. How, then, to lessen the difference in order to make the aid useful to the child, the lesson and to the process of learning? First note the salient points of the aid in the light of what is to be taught; draw out the significance of these by questions regarding them—What is this? Why is it there? Who can this be? Why is he there? What is he doing? What is he wearing? In this way their observation is directed and their attention fastened on the relevant factors of the aid. The answers are then connected and built up into a new experience for the children—at third hand, maybe—but something that they can modify and develop as new aspects of the experience are presented to them from time to time.

Let us realise, for instance, how glibly and easily we refer to the hills of Palestine, and how casually we indicate contours in an effort to explain to our children the unusual build of the country. But contours to the child do not necessarily mean hills; they are seen for what they are—squiggly lines. This means that we have to make them real by a practical approach such as modelling; even if it means a Geography lesson it is important you should do it, otherwise you are wasting your time in your Religious Knowledge lesson. Reference to the immediate locality helps, especially where there is a marked hilly district.

Similarly, ruins of churches are to children merely heaps of stones and rubble; they do not see history as we may. Here we must fall back upon their reading, stories, pictures, models, filmstrips and the like, before we can hope that they will begin even vaguely to visualise in those ruins the majesty and history that have gone.

All this drawing-out of relations must be done by questioning. The linking of the then and the now is of tremendous importance, and demands much patient insight into the child mind and child memory. Cause and effect have to be made relevant to the work in hand; beware of digressing when you are handling a visual aid— red herrings abound in shoals unless you ask the correct questions and collate the best answers.

(vi) This selection probably by no means disposes of all the types of questions possible. But they all amount to these, as far as one can judge, so let us consider the *answers*.

First of all, don't always expect the right answer to a question. (If a boy is not attending, it is always a good thing to get him to repeat the answer if he can. A follow-up question is also valuable.)

Always give praise where it is due, especially to the child who has a penchant for giving wrong answers. Put to the shy and nervous child questions he is able to answer; this is psychologically sound, for it gives him a sense of worth-whileness and progress.

Wrong answers there will always be. But it is as well to remember that a Religious Knowledge lesson in particular is no place for a show of disgust and impatience; with a wrong answer, pause and search for the gleam of gold that may be there. Ask yourself why this particular answer should have been given. Is it so hopelessly wide of the mark because of sheer ignorance on the part of the children, or was the issue too vague in your own mind and the question therefore badly worded? In any case, it means trying again. Re-word the question; the result often surprises and rewards.

Sometimes an answer is unexpected. The first reaction is to pass it over, even to snub it. But there may be a very good reason for that answer, so again—pause and penetrate, and a great deal of truth may be found in it.

Perhaps, after all, the questions are of more importance than the answers, for the teacher as well as for the class.

By the Children

Now let us turn to children's questions.

So often the teacher regards it as his prerogative to ask all the questions, quite forgetting that most children resent it—unless they have been questioned into complete submission. (It is always a salutary experience to watch children playing Schools and to note the assertiveness and questioning attitude of the Teacher—especially if you happen to recognise the teacher!)

But if the atmosphere is right there will be questions—plenty of them. Questions are the surest signs of mental alertness; the children are genuinely interested and trying to find out, sorting-out their uncertainties and false impressions. The child who asks out of mere fickleness is frowned upon by the real seekers after truth.

Often you cannot give the answers. Be absolutely honest and utterly sincere. Don't try to bluff—it's unChristian anyway, and you won't succeed. The children will distrust you and future lessons are already doomed. Try to remember that the questions they ask are of more importance than the answers expected. If you are beaten by a question, it may be possible to give sufficient answer for the time being; promise to find out more, and keep your promise. It may be possible to use such a question as a means of introducing a future lesson; on occasion it can gently be referred back to the questioner with suitable references in Bible or text-book.

The golden rule, however, is certain—If you cannot answer a question, say so. *Then,* try to find the answer.

Generally speaking, there are three types of questions one gets from children, whether written or oral. These are: the background question, the problem question and the awkward question.

(i) The background question explains itself. More often than not it is easy to deal with right away. It covers a gap you may have left in a narrative, an uncertainty raised in the child's mind, an item of knowledge the child wants to know either out of mere curiosity or because it is relevant to work in hand. Usually, the best method of meeting such a question is to give a reference for the child to follow, or to provide the necessary chapter or text-book with the information.

(ii) The same casual question may easily prove a problem. It is more likely to happen when you are on controversial ground, as when dealing with the miracles, both Old and New Testament. Each of these presents some new thought and belief; individual doubts arise, and uncertainty is seen to stumble into the face of a bewildered child. Why is this? he says. How can that be? Why did God let it happen? And so on. Old Testament stories that seem to point the cruelty and fickleness of God tend to counter much of the New Testament conception of God the Father if badly presented in class. No one can anticipate all the likely questions, but be sure there will be many. Take care not to let personal conviction outride the realisation that children are not necessarily ready for adult explanations. One of the best guides to these problems is to remember that we do not believe in Christ because of His miracles; we believe in miracles because they were done by Christ.

Sometimes an older child will pose a problem when he refers to something at home or in his own life that does not fit in with the way of life being presented to him in his lesson. You must decide whether the moment of the question is the time for dealing with it, or whether to have a private chat about it with the child concerned. In these days of mass gambling, pools, racing, under-the-counter and the like, posed questions are often of the kind: Is it wrong?

But how can it be wrong if my parents do it, and if everybody does it? Isn't the Christian just a spoil-sport? These are problem questions, indeed.

Written work often contains a problem question, though not actually asked. It is sometimes the smallest of daring comments, and likely to be missed in the marking unless you are quite alert to its significance. If you spot it, don't overlook it; it needs dealing with, and answering as far as is in your power to do so.

(iii) The awkward question does not always come at us with the ferocity of thrust given by a soap-box orator in Hyde Park. It may be quietly interpolated in the smooth flow of a lesson, or insinuated rather than propounded in written exercises. As indicated above, school and home environment have much to do with this kind of question. It sometimes brings with it a challenge to clash with home beliefs and home activities—who is right, the teacher or the home? Here lie the seeds of alienation.

Mixed classes make for awkward questions, too. A teacher recalls the eleven-year-old who paused in the reading of a Bible story to ask, "What's circumcised, sir?" He must have hesitated, for one of the girls giggled and the rest of the class stirred in a new interest. "Well . . . ?" She replied, "Please, sir, my little brother was circumcised last week." It was of no use skipping the question, awkward though it was; the excited interest was strong, too. So, together, teacher and class moved from circumcision as a means of cleanliness to a form of rite followed by the Jews—and Jesus was a Jew. The question never recurred in any guise. The main consideration for the teacher faced with an awkward question is to remain calm and detached—at least outwardly. Much depends upon his immediate knowledge, of course, and much of his answer will depend upon the age of the questioner; such a question in the Fifth Form might be deliberate, though not if the class were really concerned with their Father's business.

These are general points for both oral and written types of question. Let us look at them separately and more closely.

(A) Written

Many children hold back from asking questions in class. They may be reserved and shy; they may be slower thinkers than the rest; they may be merely lazy. But there are those few whose questions probably mean more to them than the answers they are likely to get. It may be that they are a little afraid of being laughed at, especially if they have been the unfortunate butts of ill-advised jokes earlier in their lessons. Some of them are not so much afraid of their classmates as of the actual mentioning of doubts and questions concerning the Bible and God. Irreverence is something about which they have a genuine anxiety.

All these types of children need encouragement, and perhaps the best way of getting their questions is to enable them to be asked in writing. In any case, a written question is almost sure to be better-expressed and more carefully thought out than the spur-of-the-moment oral one.

This is where we must consider the written form of question, then:

(i) (a) The Question-box. This is not a new contrivance, though it may be for the teacher of Religious Knowledge. Questions are written—anonymously if preferred—on slips of paper and posted in the box provided. There is the added advantage of comparative secrecy. The box should be available at any time, not merely in the lesson.

Teachers often complain that the idea fades out. Perhaps it is because it is overdone in other subjects or neglected. Question-boxes often lapse into a state of dustiness and dilapidation that defies belief; small wonder their uselessness, unless to advertise moth-eaten religion. Find out why the interest goes, if you have reason. Stimulate it from time to time by reminders, and even by deputing two or three likely children to submit questions. Have a Question-box lesson—once a term is ample; then ask for a boxful.

Some of the trouble is entirely due to the teacher's lack of interest. Not only is the box allowed to disintegrate, but the questions themselves are never looked at, and even if they are they are rarely answered. As one teacher has remarked, "There isn't time to do that *and* get through the syllabus." A teacher with that attitude should begin by disposing of the Question-box. Questions put in the box must obviously be dealt with. Some will need only a few words, others need references; some offer openings for simple search work, topic and lecturette preparation.

Recommend children to discuss a question with their parents before submitting it; it is often interesting to observe the effect of parent guidance. Some anonymity is removed by recognition of a child's handwriting; but to indicate this at large might result in fewer questions, especially from the very shy children most needing help.

The Question-box has a long-term policy which we are liable to overlook; in answer to the teacher quoted above, it is of peculiar value to the syllabus. If a note is made of questions common to the class or occurring often, use them at an early date or modify future lessons to incorporate them; many aspects of the syllabus are covered or approached in a way that amounts to co-operative work with the children—which is all to the good.

(*b*) Some teachers prefer to use a Question-book rather than a box. They say it is more compact and less likely to be ignored. This may be so, but it is also more easily lost. It hasn't the advantage of secrecy that the box has, of course, as the questions are open to all to read; whether this is a valuable aspect of the method or not should be considered.

(ii) Yet another form of written question may be encouraged in the Religious Knowledge Note-book. A special Question Page (perhaps the last one in the book) may be set apart for you to look at when checking work. It might be called "Things I would like to Know" or some such title, and would reveal a great deal to the discerning teacher.

(iii) A very useful exercise, and one enjoyed by all children, is the preparation of questions for one another. It is a kind of quiz lesson in which examination papers are set and exchanged and marked by the examiner. A doubt or a special interest in the questioner's mind is often revealed in such papers.

There is a *Bible Queries* booklet published by H. E. Walter with a variety of interesting questions, and the *Bible Quiz Book* by Hedges (Pilgrim Press) is also useful.

But a selection of class questions makes a more personal and therefore more interesting Class Bible Quiz, especially if bound in the Craft lesson and given the status of a book in the School Library for other children to use.

(B) Oral

This is the most important kind of question. It has not been avoided in general discussion, of course, but we must look at it more closely.

Given the sympathetic understanding of the teacher children are always willing to ask questions; sharing a story, telling an experience, criticising a piece of work—all these will stimulate a natural flow of comments that can be guided into a co-ordinated discussion if the teacher so wishes. Always regard such questions from the point of view of the questioner, not your own. The teacher is expected to know all the answers—or where to find them. It is therefore unwise to be dogmatic or doctrinal; it is out of place with children, in any case, but if you attempt to be either their desire to question will be curbed and adult precepts will probably muddle them into the bargain.

Let us remember that "out of the mouths of babes . . ." often issue truths that may urge us to reconsider our own assurances. If we are going to encourage freedom of speech and questioning, and advise the open mind—we must also remember that ourselves. On the other hand, a child often says, "What do you think, sir?" Then is the time to indicate that we do not sit on the fence; we must come down unflinchingly on the side of Christianity. Our point of view may make or mar the rest of our teaching for that particular child or class.

If there are two points of view, it is generally wise to put them. Even so, it does not follow that the child is either satisfied or answered.[1]

It is by their questions that a teacher finds to what extent he is succeeding; further, it gives him an idea of the line and level of thought and interest obtaining in his class. A child's question may reveal a weakness in background teaching or an overlooking of a vital aspect of religion. It may be a delayed question of the type that smoulders in the mind of a child for days, even weeks, before bursting into the flame of speech.

The kind of question of the "Is it true?" variety is one that never ceases to occur; and children do mean that question. This problem is recognised by the compilers of Agreed Syllabuses, especially those of the *Cambridgeshire Syllabus* who give special attention to it in

[1] Not long ago I became involved with the evergreen problem of Gen. i and ii, and on the following morning was politely but firmly proffered by one of the boys a copy of a magazine containing an article on the Creation. He also requested permission to leave early to attend his Assembly. I let him. I don't agree with his brand of religion, but his point of view is as sacred to him as mine is to me; it is up to me to respect it.

their notes for teachers. Children usually mean—Is it true in a very literal sense? Did it actually happen? They have to be shown that it is possible for truths to be conveyed in more than one guise; that the inner truth is the one to be sought. Hence the truth of myth, legend, folklore, parable and fable. Biblical criticism poured indiscriminately into young ears may do more harm than good. It is not always easy to assess how much to give and how far to go; only experience and understanding can show when a child is satisfied.

At the same time, it is essential that the leavers should be armed with sound arguments and sane notions regarding much of the harmful and specious nonsense—and, indeed, blasphemy—that they hear at street corners and will hear in factories, public-houses, halls and clubs. The need for assurance and security that adolescents so often sadly miss in their homes is shown by their questions. These lads and girls clutch at their teachers' advice as at straws, and demand support and strength without realising what they ask. They are vaguely aware that religion and life are in some way linked, and just at the time that their conviction begins to exert a powerful integrating influence upon their developing character, they go from us.

Leaving school, they enter a world that has all the forces to smash human personality. They are plunged into the turmoil of factory and shop life; they are confused and bewildered; their sense of right and wrong becomes numbed; their belief in God and Jesus trembles and totters under the scorn and sneers of the new world; their ideals begin to fade in the murkiness of the fascinating cheap world around them. How easy it is to fall victim to the ever-present waves of agnosticism and cynicism. How quickly do they agree to the ideas that this and that "really don't matter" and that such and such "are only natural" and "who cares, anyway!" This kind of climate is subtly cancerous, eating away the insecure childlike faith they once had. Can we do anything about it? We can—a little, at least, especially in the last year at school, when questions of right and wrong, moral, ethical and Biblical problems come to the fore.

More than ever today we need to remind our boys and girls that God expects explanations—let us put it bluntly, as bluntly as Jesus Himself said it—"they shall give account in the day of judgment." This is not to preach fear; it is to utter a challenge for them to serve Him in such a way that growing-up is a dedication of heart and mind, their bodies "a living sacrifice" and "temples of God." Agnosticism and atheism they will meet, but they will be the better able to see what sterile and worthless attitudes to life these are.

This is a difficult task and makes tremendous demands on our own convictions. We are the better for having met these demands. Apart from the inner impulse to live well, they will have received from us the analytical attitude of mind that will enable them to attempt to distinguish the real from the false, and the Christian way of life from the many attractive ways offered to them in the new world.

We must return to our oral questionings. Many of these will appear to be of a more adult nature—about sin, pain, death, temptation, disease and spiritual matters. These do not all need adult answers. The older the child, of course, usually the more explanation he will need; he has probably asked the questions before and has up to this point been satisfied with the answers; as he gets older he feels the inadequacy of these and asks for more.

There is no doubt that one question leads to another, and this is all to the good. It is by discussing answers to such questions that the adolescent unwittingly reveals his doubts and resolves his fears; in this way he becomes aware of his weaknesses and builds his strength against a future need.

Children will always want to know Why and How. Why did God appear to let Isaac *nearly* be sacrificed? Why did Israel think Yahweh could only be worshipped on their own soil? (Notice how awkwardly expressed these questions are.) How did the Israelites *really* get across the Red Sea? How did the walls of Jericho *really* fall? Why were the Samaritans looked down on by the Jews? Why *should* people suffer? *Why* should my mother be confined to her bed for eleven years: she never done nothing! *How* do people know about God?

In all these questions and others often more startling, you should never be shocked. Certainly if you feel so, you must not show it. Don't resent being besieged or even attacked; don't be afraid to follow-up an argument. Only in this way can questions be expected and encouraged. And happy is he that receives them. Happier still is he who can answer them.

All their questions cannot be anticipated, nor can all the answers be prepared, but Selby Wright's *Asking Them Questions* and the

Institute of Christian Education booklet on the *Teaching of Miracles* are very helpful, though of course not infallible. Some questions have a currency of their own throughout many schools and over many years. It is these questions that are met and to some extent answered in these books. The series *Questions at Issue* (S.P.C.K.) is valuable, too.

Questions Children Ask

Here, without any attempt to group them, is a selection of questions asked by children at various times, and noted for consideration:

How old is the Church of All Nations?

What is the cause of the trouble between the Jews and the Arabs?

How long is the Dead Sea? Why is it Dead?

Do you think a parson should say, "I couldn't care less"?

How can the Bible be a best-seller if nobody reads it?

Have you read the Bible, sir? If it's a library, why should you begin at the first book? Can't you begin anywhere?

Where is Judea and the Mount of Olives?

If God made me, how did my mother and father make me?

Who is God? If He made us, who made Him? He can't have made Himself, can He?

Is there a Satan?

Is there a Hell?

Is there a life after death? If so, it can't be very exciting, can it?

Is being tempted doing wrong?

Why do we call God Yahweh in school?

Why do we have Scripture twice a week and games only once?

What's the Virgin Birth?

None of these is easily passed over; only the background questions are suitable for brief attention. Many of these questions are the stuff of fierce argument amongst men; how are we to answer our children?

CHAPTER IX

DISCUSSIONS, DEBATES AND BRAINS TRUSTS

Approach through story work; training the right attitude of mind; running the discussion; formal debates and topics; Court of Justice; suggestions for Brains Trusts.

IT is very difficult to separate some methods for closer examination, since they are all so interrelated; an attempt to do so will involve a certain amount of repetition, but we must consider how some of the most vital contributions to the understanding of the Christian faith may be gained from classroom discussion of problems.

We are endeavouring at all times to present to our children Christianity as a way of life. It is our duty also to give them the tools whereby they can develop their own attitudes towards the challenge of life, and to help them sort out their own difficulties. It is essential in Religious Knowledge, as indeed it is in any lesson, that they know how to think and how to apply their thought.

The child in the Junior School is usually very ready to ask questions and to discuss matters raised in his lessons. In this stage, the best approach is often through story work. Teachers may find it a good plan, for instance, to break abruptly at a point where the central character has to make a decision or respond in some sort of way to a situation, and ask—What would you do? Why? What did he do? Why? Why not? Was it the right thing to do?

This can be done very successfully with stories of Abraham and Isaac, Elisha at Dothan, Peter and John before the Council, Zacchæus, with incidents in the lives of missionaries and reformers, and the like. Changes in standards will be revealed in the discussion —what was right in Old Testament days may be far from right to-day. Why? A story like that of Onesimus illustrates this method:

Onesimus runs away from Philemon and joins the Christians in Rome.
Paul gets to know him and who he is. *What is Paul to do?*

Onesimus admits to Paul that he is not really happy. *Why? What has he gained? What has he lost?*

Onesimus and Paul talk it over. *What do they decide?*

Paul writes to Philemon. *Who will take the letter? Why? Will Onesimus do it? Why? Will Philemon receive him? Why?*

The questions indicated are not meant merely as questions to be answered, but as pointing lines of discussion. The possible answers must be argued out; Onesimus is but human, and had been a slave; it would not be easy for him to make up his mind so quickly; there would be a great deal of temptation to do many things other than return to his master. Further discussion on what may have happened to Onesimus is useful here; remind the children that Onesimus = worth. The story is an example of love in action; further discussion on what it exemplifies might therefore take place on the lines of "Give the Story a Title"—or—"What does the Story teach us?"

Similarly, in the story of the Talents, children of this age are very ready to suggest that the dividend required by God is rather like the interest on banked money, except that the owner of the talent has to trade it to make his own interest. This leads to a discussion of their own and others' talents, ranging from ability to play football to love of animals and, surprisingly enough, often including such traits of character as sympathy, being friends, honesty and "being funny at the right time."

Children should then be led to see why and how these talents may be traded to the advantage of other folk in school, at home, in church, in their various clubs and in the wider community embracing all these.

When the Secondary Stage is considered, we see Discussion as a method come into its own, for it is a method that gives boys and girls a sense of growing up, a feeling of maturity. The pre-adolescent is developing physically, mentally, emotionally. He is a whole person. He is anxious to find a meaning for life and how he fits into it. At times, he seems to be over-reticent, he seems to have lost his earlier exuberance, and has to be drawn, coaxed and challenged. But he is ready to question another's point of view, often vehemently; and this is often the very occasion when he gives of his best in a discussion.

At times, too, he finds great difficulty in putting into words his own point of view; not always will he accept another's as sincerely meant as his own. This is important to remember, and the compilers of the *West Riding Syllabus* do well to remind us of the need to pay special attention to the method of guiding the adolescent's attitudes of mind and thought. They say, in effect:

Training is necessary to help the adolescent:

> To think honestly and sincerely, but to treat with respect the opinions of those who differ from him and who are also sincere and honest.
>
> To preserve an open mind, not rejecting or rashly adopting because it is something new.
>
> To apply knowledge and experiences of the nature of God and the example of Jesus Christ.
>
> To make a personal decision—and to live up to it.

If something on these lines can be borne in mind, his training in the comparative quiet of the classroom will stand the adolescent in good stead when he is likely to flounder in the hubbub of the office, shop and factory, in fierce one-sided arguments, and in face of agnosticism, atheism and hypocrisy that he will meet every day of his post-school life.

Starting a discussion is not difficult in the right atmosphere. When a class sense one on the way, they often move their seats, loll and become extremely conversational. Let them. Discussion thrives on informality; it dies in a formal atmosphere. You can't argue sitting stiffly in a desk ten yards from an opponent who isn't even looking at you.

For teachers who find it difficult to devise discussions, the books *Begin Here!* (R.E.P.), *I Believe* (R.E.P.), *Teenage Religion* (S.C.M.) and the *Focus Wall Sheets* (S.C.M.) are invaluable as guides. Some might like to follow the provocative "To Start You Talking" idea of the B.B.C. Discussion Groups. Another method that might appeal to the class is "We Beg To Differ." Selection of topics, or, better still, questions submitted for argument by the class, needs to be vetted carefully; some looseness might be allowed, too, whereby members of the audience could put in an opinion here and there and so widen the discussion.

Occasionally you can read an article from a newspaper or magazine, part of a play or some other extract, inviting comments and questions. Such topics as: the Effect of Films on Crime, Juvenile Delinquency, Sunday Cinemas, Sex, Is there an After Life?, Has the Atlantic Charter Failed?, Racial Hatred and so on, soon start the ball rolling.

Now and again, try dividing the class into groups each under a reliable leader. This obviates the feeling that some of the class might be saying things merely to please the teacher, as well as that others of the class would talk if only you weren't there! In any case, a small group of six or seven can really hammer out points at close quarters, and religion becomes something that matters intensely to each one of them. Another advantage is that more of the class are at work at any one time by this method of grouping.

Give a time-limit and allow free discussion—within bounds. Respect for one another and the need for relative quietness soon emerge. Occasionally there will be an outburst; treat it with friendly humour—a raised eyebrow can do much. (If you cannot curb noise and argument that get out of hand in this way, you had better leave discussion work for a time and examine the general discipline and working atmosphere in the classroom!) Don't be afraid to let one or two groups go to other parts of the building where they will not interfere with other lessons, or into the playground or on to the playing-field.

Since a discussion is really what the Bureau of Current Affairs once called "organised conversation," it is most necessary to summarise opinions crystallised in the discussion. Such summaries should be given by the chairmen or leaders of the various groups, with the teacher acting as President or Chairman whose duty it will be to co-ordinate the various viewpoints. Further discussion should then be encouraged until there emerges some kind of general policy or even a specific decision that can be stated in positive terms to serve its spiritual and inspirational purpose. The teacher's task is to preserve balance and relevance of the main issues of the discussion; he is often called upon to elucidate badly expressed ideas or to formulate clearly and simply what the groups are to decide. It is because of this that he can seldom be merely a watcher. If he is fortunate enough to have an outstanding boy or girl capable of handling the discussion, he can by all means stand aside; he will need to be ready, all the same, for the various duties that only he can perform.

PLATE VII

Above: Looking it up.　The R.K. shelves.
Below: Search work and assignments—a senior class.

PLATE VIII

STELLA ROMA

ROME CCCIV

EMPEROR ORDERS CHRISTIANS TO BE PUT TO DEATH.

MANY THROWN TO LIONS

The great Emperor orders all Christians to be exterminated. Many have been captured and have been put to death by the sword, others thrown to lions, and many burned.

Some of our own soldiers forced little children to fight the lions that tore their own parents.

Other Christians had oil poured over them, and set alight, and made to run around the streets.

Most of our arenas were crowded with yelling mobs jeering the Christians who awaited death.

COLONIAL NEWS.

GAUL

BETRAYAL in BRITAIN

ALBAN CHANGES RELIGION

It is reported that a well-known Roman citizen Alban has changed his religion and become a Christian. Pressure has been brought to bear upon him to force him to give up these strange ideas. But he is obstinate and refused to do this. He has therefore been deprived of his Roman citizenship.

SEALING of CATACOMBS

MANY CHRISTIANS DIE

The Emperor has ordered all catacombs to be closed up as it is thought that the Christians are holding their meetings there. When ...

NEWS IN BRIEF

NOBLEMAN DEPRIVED OF RANK

A young girl of XIII was deprived of his rank yesterday. This man Terves was found guilty of following the Christians. When he was asked to stop this he refused. He told many friends of his new religion. A Roman soldier heard of it. Terves was burnt at the stake built by his wife and children. Any other persons found following this Christians will die in the same way.

NEW HOUSES READY.

It is expected that the houses built by Balter Ltd will be opened next ...

LETTERS TO THE EDITOR

Dear Sir,

I read in your paper reports concerning the persecution of Christians. I think that this mass slaughter is useless. Why not our Emperor leave them alone? Is he afraid the Christians will become powerful? I think their bravery is amazing. Hundreds have been thrown to the the lions, others burnt at the stake, and still they refuse to give up their religion. I am seriously considering being a Christian.

A Roman Citizen

Dear Sir,

I cannot agree that it is a good thing to rid our city of all the Christians. I am a ...

A.D. L

CORONATION of HEROD AGRIPPA

∽ IMPRESSIVE CEREMONY IN CHALCIS ∽

With the coronation of Agrippa II today, the government of the state of Chalcis passed from the hands of the Roman procurator, Tenstius Caesenus, to the servant king of the Herod lineage. (Chalcis is a small state situated in the gorge between Lebanon and Anti-Lebanon.)

The new king is the only son of his father, Agrippa I, whose name he bears. His new kingdom, which is a gift from the Emperor Claudius, is indicative of the ties which still exist between the Herod family and the Roman rulers.

Amid the joyous festivities which accompanate today's ceremony, it is doubtful whether many remember the tragic circumstances commented with the death of the young King's father six years ago.

The strange occurrence was related to us by an eye-witness who was present at the circus at Caesarea on that fateful day. He said: "The King entered with his Royal escort and when he arose to address the crowd the sun glittered on his robes of silver tissue. When he spoke all the bystanders began to shout that his voice was that of a god and not a man. He suddenly he collapsed with violent internal pains and was carried out. He died five days later in terrible agony."

His son was but seventeen at the time and too young to assume the responsibility of kingship, and so for the last six years the state has been ruled by a Roman administrator.

The news, I imagine, will be especially pleased at the 'coming of age' of their king, for it is generally assumed that although like his father, he has been educated at Rome, yet he is known to be kindly disposed towards the traditional religious beliefs of the Hebrews, and views the writings of their prophets with more than mere tolerance.

Foremost among the young king's costumes today was the sister Berenice. Arrayed in her glorious scarlet robes it was ... See why she is famous for her ... she has been to ...

CONTENTS

	PAGE
CORONATION OF HEROD AGRIPPA	I
DISGRACE TO THE CITY	I
NEWS FROM THE BRITISH FRONT	I
INTERVIEW WITH GAMALIEL	II
FAST SPLENDOUR	II
THE LIGHTHOUSE KEEPER SPEAKS	III
INTERVIEW WITH JOHN MARK	III
MYSTERY OF MISSING GRAIN SHIP SOLVED	III
MAMMOTH MUSIC FESTIVAL	IV

DISGRACE TO THE CITY

No effort has been made to clear away the ruins of the Library, which was accidentally burned down over a hundred years ago, at the time of our resistance to the Roman Julius Caesar.

These ruins lie so close to the docks that lawless elements among the sea-faring men visiting our port have taken to concealing themselves by night among the ruins, from which they spring out to rob harmless wayfarers.

A particularly distressing case was reported this morning. It appears that Draco, the aged Greek physician, was called last ... to attend a case ...

NEWS FROM THE BRITISH FRONT

We are proud to state that our Roman armies have gone from victory to victory in Britain. The four legions, XIth Valeria Victrix, IInd Augusta, XIVth Gemina and the legion of Spaniards the XXth, have covered themselves with glory.

The invasion of this important island was begun seven years ago under the able leadership of Aulus Plautus with forty-thousand men. Landings were made at Rutupiae, Dubris and Portus Lemanis, and the whole force proceeded to Durovernum, where Vespasian, commander of the IInd legion, especially distinguished himself.

After the River Tamesis had been crossed the important town of Camulodunum, capital of the Trinobantes, was captured. The IInd then proceeded to the far west to Isca Silurum, the XIVth to Deva, the XIIth to Viroconium and the IXth to the east to Lindum. The IInd are at present engaged against the Silures, whose leader Caratacus is proving a worthy opponent to the gallant Vespasian, while the Ordovices of the north-west are resisting the XIVth legion with great obstinacy.

However the south and east of Britain are flourishing under the beneficial and just rule of Rome, and the city of London, founded by Roman traders and Britons attracted by Roman culture, has shown remarkable development, being a town of no less than fifty-thousand inhabitants. Camulodunum, Glevum and Lindum have been granted the status of Roman colonies, an amazing indication of the foresight and wisdom of our gracious Emperor. A number of prominent British noblemen have begun to learn the Latin tongue, and to adopt the worship approved by the Roman State.

The infamous ... ruid religion, ...

Above: News-sheet—class production. A and B streams.

Below: Newspaper—student production.

What we have considered so far are provoked discussions, raised deliberately by "questions of the hour." But it is not necessary to do this all the time. More often than not, the subject of a discussion arises from a lesson. Study of an incident or chapter may get held up by the uncertainty of meaning in a phrase or even a whole verse. What does it mean? Opinions are invited and discussion as to its most accurate meaning, backed up by reference to a text-book or commentary, often may continue for quite a while. The teacher is liable to succumb to the temptation to give immediate explanations instead of guiding the critical powers of his class in discussing the impact of a verse or a character or an incident met in the course of lesson study. This is a great pity, as it deprives children of the opportunity of putting into words what they feel themselves about things and people. Thus, during the study of the Crucifixion story attention may focus temporarily on Pilate. For the teacher to state Pilate's position, his fear of Rome and the people—in short, to explain Pilate's action—and then to proceed with the lesson, is to deter any expression of opinion and to stunt critical ability. How much better to ask—Was Pilate a coward? The invariable response is that he was, but there is always someone ready to question that assertion and anxious to say why. So—What do *you* think, John?—and off we go.

Again, the question of being called to do some special work—the early Leaders of the Old Testament, Abraham, Moses, the Prophets, Jesus, Martyrs, Missionaries, Preachers—how naturally discussions can arise from any stories of any of these. The question of Vocation and "talking with God" arises here, too. It was in such a discussion that a boy once said, "If God speaks through your mind, it's really a *hunch,* isn't it?" What a world of wisdom in that remark—and how sad to have given no opportunity for him to say it.

Throughout the discussion of problems and topics, it should be remembered that wherever possible the argument should touch the actual life experience of the pupils; they are developing in social consciousness, and in assessing the pros and cons will want to see how these fit in with their own lives as members of the community. This is especially true of the essentials of the Christian faith. Premature formulation is dangerous and confusing, but adolescents must be led to appreciate some of the maxims that help them to an understanding of life.

This may be realised when studying the Parables of Jesus. There is often a tendency to tell, teach and dramatise the content of parables without any reference to the background and context. The moral aspect is certainly necessary, but it is essential to come down to earth and discuss the problems each illustrates, at least with adolescents. Only in this way can familiar parables be made to illuminate the personal and social problems met by children in their own lives, such as—what matters most, money or goodness? what are the foundations of character? the meaning of responsibility; am I my brother's keeper? and treasure in heaven.

A word of warning seems necessary. It is easy to be side-tracked into discussions when other work should be in progress. It is often wise to say, "I'll make a note of it, and we'll discuss it later." But don't forget to do so.

Besides the topics mentioned in this chapter, here are some that may prove interesting and worth tackling because they are both real and personal to every boy and girl:

Why are there so many "varieties" of religion?
Why should the Christian religion be the best?
Why is it all right to tell a "white" lie?
What's wrong with Penny Pools or Poker?
Is it wrong to think about sex?
Leisure—I can do as I like.
Sunday is a day of pleasure.
Are you T.T. if you drink port at a wedding?
Is nuclear warfare so wrong?
Why should there be pain?
Is Pride a sin?
What's the harm in a little gossip?
Is it stealing to take something not wanted by others, like scrap, etc.?
Is it wicked to have a bad temper?

Many of these questions are the inevitable and eternal problems of sex and gambling and war, greed and dishonesty and indifference; couched in simple sentences, they strike deep at the heart of the bewilderment felt by children who are beginning to think seriously for the first time in their lives.

It may be necessary to have handy all sorts of reference books; Agreed Syllabuses often give both suggestions and Bible references. Occasional quotations may be used to support or to confute arguments, if thought helpful to do so.

But, as a rule, outside help is not needed, once adolescents really get down to argument and personal experiences; as a last resort, it is always stimulating to have a discussion on "Why our Discussions flop!"

Debates

Much of what has been said applies to the running of a Debate. It is really a formal discussion. The theme is announced, proposers and seconders for and against are elected, and their view-points are put to the audience. Questions may be dealt with, and after a given time a vote is taken to see whether the motion is carried or quashed.

The rules of the debate are as important in the Religious Knowledge period as in the English lesson; indeed, a religious topic can easily be debated in the English lesson, and so be given more weight by that curious paradox of time-table and subject importance! Any good English text-book will give you the necessary details of running the debate beyond what has been mentioned already. Here are a few likely motions that experience has shown to have been effective:

That all Sunday-schools be abolished.
That cinemas on Sundays are a good thing.
That to a Christian, all forms of gambling are wrong.
That suffering is due to sin. (Use Job.)
That miracles do not happen today.
That Science and Religion create conflict in the Christian's beliefs.
That only the Christian attitude towards sex brings happiness.

In case you should think that the Debate is a barren method, look at these comments made by thirteen-year-olds, on Sunday films. Every opinion, however gauchely worded, is alive with challenge:

God made the world in six days and needed a rest; so everyone should rest from work and go to church to pray.
People get bored in church because of the smell. It smells nice in the pictures.

If everyone worked on Sunday they would not be able to go to the countryside and see the lovely flowers and the trees, and they would miss the prayers God has granted to people.

If nobody went to church there would be no collections; therefore the poor wouldn't get any money—and even the parsons would starve.

Cinemas could show missionary films and have a collection so that they could help the missions better. You don't get much money in church collections, because people only go to get married.

If cinemas opened on Sundays, fathers would be in the beershops, mothers would be in the pictures—and where would the children be?

A *Court of Justice* is an interesting type of debate, and considerable value results from an occasional introduction of such a court. Take, for instance, the setting-up of a court trying Peter and John; or Paul before Agrippa; or even Jesus before Pilate. With the Bible story for background and content, adolescents make extremely good judge and jury, counsels for prosecution and defence. There is scope, too, for interruptions from the body of the court. Such a court needs a great deal of preparation; but if it is a success it is a spiritual innovation for everybody, and one that makes the whole subject of the Christian faith real and personal and challenging. Here, again, it is possible to produce such a court as an interlude in a Morning Service, so that the whole school benefits from the work of a particular group.

Brains Trusts

Popularised by the B.B.C. and adopted by various town and village organisations, the Brains Trust approach to discussion of questions and problems in religion is a useful one.

The idea is to have a committee or team to whom questions of various types, requiring factual answers as well as personal opinions, may be put. It is often a discussion in miniature, with the chairman crystallising the views into some sort of general statement. If the team is a class one, the pupils will select their own. Questions should be submitted beforehand where possible; a final arbitrator, it is necessary for you yourself to know the answers. Such questions should be based on the term's or year's work, with others of general interest.

The Brains Trust of one class can be taken to another and subjected to a battery of questions—a provocative and often salutary experience for everybody concerned. In passing—it is sometimes noticed that one of the best members of the team may be a pupil who is a duffer at putting into writing what he thinks. This is often true for all forms of discussion work, and is excellent training for that type of pupil because it is an effective outlet.

From the questions put, one or two may be selected for open discussion and even debate in some future lesson.

On a very special occasion, say for the Leavers, it may be possible to stage a most official Brains Trust, formed from Local Dignitaries, Education Office Administrators, Parents, etc. Such a meeting must be carefully planned, and attention given to seating, audience and so on. The questions should be obtained beforehand, and selected for variety and interest. Each member of the team should be vetted, and questions suitable for each included. This will obviate the member who knows everything and monopolises the session; nothing kills a Brains Trust more quickly.

Here are some questions asked of a Brains Trust:

Is it wrong to tell a "white lie"?

Is Mohammedanism a good religion?

It is right to travel on a bus without paying if the conductor misses you?

Do you think the Elder Brother behaved properly? After all, the Prodigal Son had had his chance.

Did Jesus let Himself be crucified because He knew He would rise again?

Why is there so much trouble in some countries over the colour problem?

Examination of these will show a good deal of thought and even anxiety as to what is right and what is wrong about Life and Faith. The core of all questions seems to be: "What can I believe in this world of strange contradictions?" Answer that for any child, and you have given him a standard for the rest of his life.

CHAPTER X

LECTURETTES AND TOPICS

Sharing information; talking on things children find interesting; expression of opinions; practice in self-expression; link with Project Method.

Lecturettes

CHILDREN in both Senior and Junior stages find great delight in collecting information. In odd moments and in English lessons, it is easy to persuade boys and girls to talk to the class on some subject of special interest to themselves, amazing in variety and unusualness of subject-matter. Aeroplanes, Butterflies, Diesel Engines, Embroidery, Shells, Campanology—and of course, Birds' Eggs and Stamps . . . all these are subjects for short or long talks. Besides, given time, children will go to a tremendous amount of trouble to look up further details and to provide illustrations of all kinds.

In present-day teaching a great deal of stress is laid upon individual and group work—collecting, compiling, sharing. More of it is needed in the Religious Knowledge lesson. It is nonsense to say that the children are not interested; if they are not, quite seriously it is the teacher's own fault; there is something lacking in his teaching methods or approach.

Once get the class to discuss matters, and you will soon find ample scope for harnessing special interests and hobbies. Here is a boy who interrupts a lesson on Palestine to say he's got some photos, his father's been there. . . . Right—how about a short talk, with illustrations? Encouragement and materials—and away he goes to prepare the talk, probably for the most part at home.

On another occasion someone mentions that he has a phylactery at home, found by his brother; here again is subject-matter for a talk. Or a lad specialises in stamps of the Eastern Mediterranean, and has a set of a recent issue; he is happy to talk about these and their significance.

Another day the class is studying, say, Psalm xxiii. You suggest browsing through other psalms, noting any differences. They find examples of Ceremonial, Individual, Nature, Wisdom psalms—

someone will talk on each of these, difficult though it may seem. The ever-green story of the Good Samaritan serves a new purpose as a start for the Arab-Jew question.

Talks on Biblical background are always welcome, especially if books of reference are available. Customs, homes, occupations and the like all make interesting subjects for lecturettes. The local church sometimes attracts as a treasure-trove of subjects—rubbings, tombs, effigies, lecterns, rood screen, stalls, roof, vaulting, types of architecture, tombstones and epitaphs, bells. . . . One of the best talks given to one class was by a lad whose father was a local bell-ringer.

This type of work should follow fairly set rules. A kind of roster should be planned, covering a long period so that pupils know within a little when they will be needed at least during the term. Be prepared to help with books of reference.

No lecturette should be of longer duration than six minutes. It is wise to limit a speaker who might otherwise be garrulous, and it heightens interest to have to give all one's facts in a set time. Discipline of speech and time is good for everybody. Following the talk, there should be twelve to fifteen minutes of question and discussion, during which the speaker can develop his views and clarify points worth the extra time.

From topics originally given there may arise subjects for another occasion; these should be noted, together with the names of the children showing particular interest in them, for they are the children to deal with them at a later date.

Topics

The word is used rather loosely. What is implied here is an extension of the lecturette. Often, it is found that the time-limit is really insufficient for the amount of material and knowledge acquired by the speaker, or the subject itself is worthy of fuller treatment; tied down to six minutes, the speaker cannot do either himself or his subject justice.

Also, whereas the lecturette succeeds well with Juniors, the topic is best done by Seniors, who will add to their factual knowledge their opinions and comments. The adolescent working on a topic can spread himself. He knows he can talk for twenty minutes, and even forty if need be, if he can find enough interesting material and has the ability to put it across. There is little fear that any boy or girl will talk for forty minutes. The giving of the talk fills the speaker with both pride and fear, but in the preparing of it he not only accumulates information that gives him at least the courage of having something to say, but he also learns to set it out for exposition in a logical and interesting manner. Of course, no two pupils react in quite the same way. Fifteen-year-old girls often produce better work than boys of the same age, but boys usually have much wider interests. For all of them, both lecturette and topic give training in self-confidence and in the ability to speak clearly and to argue sensibly.

This is invaluable training; its worth cannot be estimated, but it must have a telling effect when the adolescent is called upon in later life to defend or explain an attitude that he may uphold.

No rules about the use of notes need be made. Most children prefer to read their talks; some learn their work by heart; a very small minority speak from headings. The rare few who attempt to extemporise often fail dismally; they are usually the very cocksure ones who have done little preparation and are really interested only in the fact that they are on their feet in front of the class. Their failure is salutary, as a rule, and there is no need for further comment, except for a wise suggestion that work should be prepared. Do not let this deter the one or two who are on their way to being excellent speakers and who may wish to try speaking without notes. Remember, too, that the talks should be judged on their religious value and significance. Criticism of speech, mannerisms and exposition are out of place in this lesson. On the other hand, there is no reason why a talk on a religious subject should not be given in an English lesson for practice in listening and class criticism, and for training in the art of speaking.

Topics, like lecturettes, should best arise naturally from the Religious Knowledge lessons. In this way, children can find for themselves more information about, say, the Samaritans, Missionaries, Lives of Prophets, other religions. Many topics arise from discussion and search work. I have known the problem of J and E arise from an assignment on Saul, in which the boy handling it found a tangle of narratives that he could not unravel. Incidentally, I record my complete failure to reproduce the same conditions and results with another class.

Personal problems, such as unanswered prayer and bewilderment about gambling, often crop up either outspokenly or not very subtly veiled. A subject like Playing the Game may not strike one immediately as of religious significance, but recalling that "Christianity is playing the game better than the rules," it is easy to see how valuable such a talk might be.

Seasonal festivals give subjects, too. Few children realise at first sight that all except one of their holiday periods are connected with religious festivals. When they are introduced to the idea, they are quite ready to find out more about them. Harvests (coal and wool, as well as crops) with their pagan rites and origins; Christmas—the various stories of Nicholas, Carols, leading easily to a project and eventually to a Carol Service; Easter, Whitsun, leading to Jewish Festivals—best dealt with by a Jewish member of the school if you have one.

In the fifth year it is often possible to encourage papers on more ethical and spiritual matters—Sin; Forgiveness; What I Believe; What I Don't Believe; Duty; Science and Religion; Miracles; Modern Religions; Sects in Our Town; Sex and Religion.

Topics arise from Project work. Suppose the Project is on Hospitals. Opportunity for subject talks is provided in such aspects as Antiseptics (Lister), Vaccination (Pasteur), Penicillin (Fleming), Anti-biotics, Cancer Research, the Work of the Monasteries, Florence Nightingale, Missionaries, Transport for Emergency Cases, the Iron Lung, Mass Radiography. In fact, any project will provide topics as part of the general method, for often the best way for an individual to pass on to others what he has done on his own is to let him give a talk about it before the final co-ordination of the work in hand.

Newspapers give much food for thought and talk. The Racial question is always to the fore somewhere in the world; so is Nuclear Power; the Cold War; United Nations Organisation and various Relief and Educational Organisations; Discovery of Ancient Manuscripts; New Translations of the Bible; Archæology.

What should be clear from all these examples is the vast scope of both subject-matter and ideas for topics, as well as for sources of information. Too often our Religious Knowledge lessons are confined to the classroom and to the set syllabus. We need to relate our work more and more to the outside world through the children. The adolescent especially needs opportunities of seeing how Christian training squares with the world, and, what is more important, he needs the chance of putting into words just what he feels about things. He can't always discuss, he can't always frame questions. His inarticulate uncertainties demand the crystallising derived from reading about the subject. Where the subject is mainly factual, he has the additional training in the use of reference books and the satisfaction of being able to impart information found.

This type of work appears to involve much preparation and many reference books—and even to provoke severe headaches. In actual fact, no. Most Agreed Syllabuses give expert advice, guidance and references for the majority of topics likely to occur; commentaries usually help with the remainder. Keep a sensible perspective. These talks are not to be given to a body of learned judges, they are for the classroom; and as such they will often skim only the surface of both detail and information.

What really matters is the personal approach of the speaker to his work and to his search for satisfaction.

You cannot measure the effect of one small assignment of this nature spiritually, emotionally, mentally; nor is it wise to attempt to do so.

"Base of a cup found in the Catacombs, Rome."
Drawing by a girl aged thirteen.

CHAPTER XI

SEARCH AND DISCOVERY

Self-teaching; assignments; using reference books, and the Bible; the Synoptic Problem.

WHATEVER else may be our aim in Religious Teaching, we must not forget the place of the Bible in our lessons. It is our duty to give children the Bible, literally to place it in their hands, and then to help them to use it joyfully and intelligently. Knowledge of the contents of the world's best-seller is very much needed today. Apart from the fact that it has been considered too old-fashioned to read the Bible, it is very likely that in schools we have tended to do too much for children in simplifying the Scriptures in an effort to make them more attractive. It is time we let children help themselves, provided we do so in accordance with educational theory and practice.

That is why the method of setting problems for searching-out is so useful. It confronts children with a challenge for one thing, and it gives them a feeling of zest in the searching as well; there is satisfaction in the finding and there is more likelihood of learning. That is also why the method is so suitable for children of all ages, developing as it does a sense of initiative and self-reliance. If carefully graded, some easier exercises may be given to duller and slower children, but the bright ones certainly do excel; this is probably due more to their ability to concentrate and persevere than to anything else. Fortunately, most Agreed Syllabuses give Bible references, and use of these simplifies considerably the teacher's work. Where there is need for extra-Biblical search, the use of further good reference books will be obvious; the setting-up of a Religious Knowledge Library becomes more imperative.

Bible search need not always be a special assignment or a written exercise, but whatever it is, the real success lies in the child's giving to the class what he has done or found as an individual; sharing is an important part of teaching method. Nor should mere written or oral answers be sufficient. More often than not, illustrations can be effectively produced—drawings, diagrams, models.

Some of the best kind of search can be done in tracing background to familiar stories. In the story of Joseph, for instance—What *was* the coat of many colours? How did his people live, travel, trade? What were the local customs and superstitions? Why are there two stories? How do they differ? (Use a Moffat to disentangle these.) What is this mysterious J and E now discovered? Can it be related to the Creation and Flood stories?

A great deal of useful self-teaching may be done by this method, but the teacher should take care that guidance is sufficient for immediate purposes to prevent the child from wandering haphazardly around the subject. It is an important point to instil into the children, too, that the Bible itself has undergone more research than any other book of its kind, and that today there is a more accurate interpretation of its contents because of this research. Just as Bible scholars discover, so it is possible for children to discover. In this way, they find that the Bible has much to give for the searching, and, above all, that within itself it reveals to the seeker the gradual change of conception of God in man's eternal search for Truth.

Not the least important aspect of this method is that it caters for the individual and his own rate of progress. It gives him a chance to do something within his own ability and leisure to reflect; it obviates his being rushed or overridden in a well-meant desire to get work accomplished. Very often a child is observed to be quite oblivious of what is going on around him; his concentration is on his work and purpose, and what may seem to be day-dreaming is reflection in action.

This kind of work is best done in an informal atmosphere. It isn't always easy with a big class, but children should be allowed elbow-room for open books and maps and references. Where necessary, desks and tables should be moved. If the library is available, so much the better. Very often it is found that topics require more follow-up than the school library can provide. Permission to visit the local library should not be withheld; rather, such an idea should be put forward. It is a pleasant experience to find children searching in the local library after school and in the evenings as well.

Parents often lend a willing hand in search work; signs of parent guidance are often evident in the results, but the important thing here is the interest of the parent in his child's work.

For some exercises, a card of the nature of a Questionnaire may be prepared. The questions give a definite line on what is to be looked for; the value of the card to the child is the providing of directions for thought and search; to the teacher it is something that may be used again. These questions differ from those mentioned in the chapter on "Questioning" in their aim. Here, you are deliberately helping a child to get familiar with his Bible. It entails more preliminary work for the teacher than do some other methods, but once a selection of Search Cards is made, it serves many purposes over a long period. What is more important, perhaps, it gives the teacher time to attend to individual needs.

It is difficult to lay down any order or recommendations for special classes or grades. But here are a few suggestions and examples of search work and assignments for self-teaching.

You will be the best judge as to whether or not these actual examples are of any use to you; they may need modifying to meet a particular class and scheme of work.

(i) *Getting to know their Bibles*

Let's have a race.

Who can find . . . Isaiah . . . Genesis . . . Micah? (A pause between each to give time to find.)

Encourage the use of the index, especially for the finding of short books like Nahum, Hosea, etc.

Suddenly give a New Testament book. (Enjoy with the class the "catching-out" of some and the brightness of those not caught.)

Again, indicate use and value of index.

But also indicate the value of general awareness of books of the Bible—Psalms, Kings, Acts, Revelation, and so on.

Children enjoy this form of Bible Mental Arithmetic keenly. Team competition helps.

(ii) *Map Work*

Draw a map of Palestine.

Put in the Jordan.

When Jesus was in Nazareth He heard of many places that He might have longed to visit.

Use these references and mark the places on the map.

List them; say why He might have wanted to see them.

Gen. xii. 1–9; Josh. i. 1–7; Josh. iv. 1–7; Josh. iv. 19–22;
Josh, xviii. 1; Josh. xxiv. 1 and 22–8; 1 Sam. xvi. 1–13 and
31; 2 Sam. v. 1–3; 1 Kings xvii. 1–10; 1 Kings xviii. 1, 2;
1 Kings xviii. 17–46; 1 Kings viii. 1–11; 1 Kings v;
1 Kings xxii. 62–6; 2 Kings xxv. 1–12; Ezra iii. 1–11;
Neh. ii. 1–18; Neh. iv. 6.

(iii) *Bible in Everyday Speech*

Here are some Bible phrases which have become part of our
language. They are called IDIOMS. Find their sources by using
Commentaries and reference books.
Say what each means.

Set out in three columns:

IDIOM	SOURCE	MEANING
(*a*) Widow's mite.	Mark xii. 42.	
(*b*) Corn in Egypt.	Gen. xlii. 1.	
(*c*) Apple of one's eye	Deut. xxxii. 10.	
(*d*) Bricks without straw.	Ex. v. 7.	
(*e*) Salt of the earth.	Matt. v. 13.	
(*f*) Feet of clay.	Dan. ii. 33.	
(*g*) Eleventh hour.	Matt. xx. 1.	
(*h*) Fly in the ointment.	Eccles. x. 1.	
(*i*) The love of money is the root of all evil.	1 Tim. vi. 10.	
(*j*) Root of the matter.	Job xix. 28.	

(Note: Bible references are given only where child cannot find
his own.)

Add to this list any you happen to find or know.

(iv) *Familiar Texts*

Look up the following references.
In each there is a phrase or sentence that should strike you as
familiar or at least worth your remembering.
Write these down under the headings:

SOURCE   TEXT

Underline the three you like best.

1 Tim. vi. 12; Matt. v. 16; Is. xxxv. 4; Ps. xxxi. 24; Hos. x. 12;
Rom. viii. 37; 1 Pet. i. 25; Ex. xx. 12; Job. xxviii. 28.

Add any others that appeal to you for any reason.

(v) *Reformers*

Who were: Elizabeth Fry; Robert Raikes; Cranmer; Bunyan; Isaac Watts; others the teacher likes to add?

Say what each is remembered for.

Try to get a photograph of each; write underneath a summary of their work; label each: "We thank (name) for . . ."

If you could be a great Reformer, what would you like to do?

(vi) *Friendship*

What does it mean to be a "good friend"?

Make up six Laws of Friendship.

Explain—"A Scout is a friend to all."

Write a Prayer of Thanksgiving for Friendship.

Prepare an Order of Service—Opening, Prayer, Reading, Hymn, Benediction—with Friendship as the Theme.

Consider:

Luke vi. 12–16; Mark x. 32–45; John xiii. 1–17; re-read the relevant verses of the story of David and Jonathan; 1 Cor. xiii—Love is the foundation; compare with Eccles. vi. 14–17.

Look up further Biblical references, using index of Commentary and Concordance, on Friendship.

Comment upon: "A friend is one who knows all about you—and still loves you!"

The *Self-teaching Guides* of H. L. Holland and *Stories on the Apostles' Creed* (both S.P.C.K.) are extremely useful. This type of exercise should not be set merely for the sake of introducing the method of self-teaching, but as an end in itself for making the Bible more real and familiar it never fails to interest the children.

Do not forget the Apocrypha. Children should know how to spell the word, what it means and how it came into being. Their own copies of the Bible may not contain it, but there are editions available quite suitable for class use and for the library. There are several ways of introducing it, apart from a lesson on the Story of the Bible; text references help, and it might even become familiar to the class as the source of Bridie's *Tobias and the Angel*.

Although this is an ideal method for the avowed introduction of the Bible, it is obviously linked with the search work necessary for the information required in Lecturettes and Topics. Biographies, Local Histories related to the Growth of the Church, Study of Comparative Religion and so on—all have valuable ground to be covered by this method. (See e.g. (v).)

The Synoptic Problem

It is not altogether clear why this is called a Problem—apart from the Problem scholars have found it in their deeper searchings—but there does come a time in the Religious Knowledge scheme when the class realises that the four gospels are by no means identical although they have a great deal in common. They see, too, that John is apart from the other three.

Here is an excellent opportunity for search work of a simple but effective kind, that makes the problem an interesting piece of study rather than an academic pigeon-holing of known facts. You will need lots of copies of old, dog-eared Testaments, Gospels and Bibles, for you are going to cut them up. Some folk dislike intensely the idea of cutting up the Bible; they see some kind of irreverence in Biblical salvage. Perhaps that is why they prefer to leave so many Bibles about in such shocking condition—coverless, ripped, quite unfit for general use, and silent preachers of the disregard held for the Book. It is not unusual to find dozens stacked away in old cupboards, and a good many more unwanted ones in the local Sunday-schools. Use these, if available; if there is no immediate need for them, get them put away where children cannot see them—this is a service rendered. If the children themselves feel unhappy about cutting them, don't press or ridicule them; respect their reticence for what is holy. But when they see the result of reshuffling the verses and remaking the stories, they will gradually accept the idea.

Now, how shall the Problem be approached? A secular approach is simple. Obtain four newspapers reporting the same event, say, a football match. Examine these in class, and it is seen that although each describes the same match, there is a difference in style, detail, vividness, length and so on. The essentials of the match, like the score, the outstanding players, etc., are noted as being faithfully recorded; but there is obviously a bias of content and description that can be put down to the writer and his public.

Now, proceeding to the accounts of the writers who took it upon themselves to record the Life and Work of Jesus. What will the class expect to find? Yes, the main characters, their movements, the chief incidents—these will surely be mentioned by all or the story fails in its purpose. But there are bound to be differences of style, detail, vividness, according to the nature and ability of the writers and to the public for whom they wrote.

A few examples of similar and different records of the more familiar Gospel stories now follow. Here are the records of Jesus—His Life, His Work, His Teaching, His Death, His Resurrection. We are seeing that already some of the accounts are varying. Can we find out where and how and why?

This exercise is one that can hardly be left to one or two individuals; it succeeds as a group exercise. A good method of displaying what is found is to use two large cards—about 2 ft. 6 in. by 4 ft. Use one for LIKES—i.e. the descriptions common to the writers, and one for UNLIKES—i.e. for passages differing. Then make four divisions for the search results, these serving as guides in the search. The verse analysis to use is in the *Christian Education Handbook,* ed. Hamilton, (R.E.P.) Intermediate Course, Second Year, on page 34. The sections are:

> (a) What Jesus said.
> (b) What Jesus did.
> (c) What people thought of Him.
> (d) How He came to die.

This gives you the lay-out, as under, for pasting in the verses.

SYNOPTIC GOSPELS [1]

LIKES	UNLIKES
Matthew. Mark. Luke. John.	*Matthew. Mark. Luke. John.*
(a)	
(b)	
(c)	
(d)	

Before long, parallel verses begin to appear in at least three of the Gospels; John stands apart as it were, and it may be better to leave

[1] Leave the title until discovered.

him out altogether for the time being, to simplify the work of the children. Excitement and interest grow apace as sudden thoughts become hopes and hopes become facts. Long before the charts are completed, the idea of Mark's short Gospel being the core of Matthew's and Luke's account is put forward. Could it have been written first and then used by the others? If so, where did their extra material come from?

Even some of this extra material is common to both Matthew and Luke, with some left over that is peculiar to the one or the other. This common supply couldn't have been available to Mark or he would certainly have used it. The teacher may choose this moment to give the name Q = Quelle, or Source.

What of the rest of Matthew and Luke—quotations and stories, evidence from personal sources unknown to each other and gathered in their respective journeyings after the Master had left them? Further study of Matthew's extra material shows it to be full of Old Testament quotations, put in rather obviously for his Jewish audiences. Luke's extra material is so often straightforward, detailed and even medical (Luke was a doctor), and seems to have been written for folk needing simplicity and freedom from doctrinal preaching—perhaps the Gentiles.

The Gospels—at least the three concerned in the closer study— have so much in common; they have the same view-point. Hence, *Synoptic* (syn = with; optic = point of view).

As for John, he is entirely different in style and approach. So often his descriptions fade into his own philosophies; he is interested in the words of Jesus rather than in His deeds.

To pursue further than this the discoveries made would be merely technical and academic. In fact, in your wisdom, you may not have gone so far. But a final check on dates would not be out of place:

Mark (via Peter), A.D. 65; Luke, A.D. c. 80; Matthew, A.D. c. 85; John, A.D. 100.

There is further assistance and variety of approach in *Let's Read the Gospels*, Doidge (M.Y. Dept.), and in the *Christian Education Handbook* (R.E.P.); all nine of this series are treasure-troves of inspiration and practical guidance.

A quotation from the Primary School Report is not inapplicable here: "Intellectual processes will seldom function to their full capacity unless there is an emotional incentive behind them." The method of discovery, search, research—call it what you will—vitalises the functioning of these processes, because it is the children who make the first move; their minds are therefore active and receptive. They are approaching the knowledge themselves, instead of having it brought to them; and in the zestful search for information and truth, their energies become creative and their emotions are satisfied in exploration and achievement.

Scraperboard. "They that go down to the sea in ships."
By a boy aged thirteen.

CHAPTER XII

MEMORY WORK AND CHORAL SPEAKING

The need for memory work—a dying art; the pros and cons considered; choral verse-speaking—approach to and value of.

IN a great many subjects the pendulum of learning-by-heart has for too long swung too far in the wrong direction.

In our endeavour to broaden education we seem to have lost the desire to deepen it, and one of the joys of rhythmic pleasure has in some schools completely disappeared—to the detriment of education generally and to the children's loss particularly.

Long days ago it was expected of all children that they should learn by heart long passages of Scripture, regardless of the fact that these extracts were for the most part quite unintelligible because of their adult outlook and experience, and because they were never (or rarely ever) studied beforehand. Despite the unsuitability of such passages, however, there was a certain amount of incidental pleasure gained from the mere chanting of them in much the same unmusical monotone as tables were droned.

It was in this way that we became aware of and friendly with many of the Psalms and prophecies and poetic fragments of the Bible. At various times in life, some smatterings of these have often come to mind, and the joy of reminiscence has mingled with the earlier joy of mastery that the learning of them had originally given. Much of it, like much of the verse we learnt then, has been forgotten.

In these days of enlightened psychology, we have no faculty of memory to train; but with the discarding of old psychology has gone a corresponding disregard of old methods—which is not necessarily good pedagogy.

Learning-by-heart no longer trains the memory, as memory cannot be trained, it was said, so learning-by-heart became old-fashioned and fell into disrepute. This led to more disastrous errors —leaving children to learn what they liked, if they liked, and ignoring the memorising part of education altogether. It has meant a generation of children who cannot quote any of the Command-ments, the Creed, the Beatitudes, even Ps. xxiii—nor, of course, do they know quotable lines of Shelley, Keats or Shakespeare.

It is always easy to generalise, and in doing so to be unfair to those teachers who saw to it that their children should not go out into the world without these things. Such enlightened and far-seeing folk have been so few and deserve our gratitude.

In pushing overboard learning-by-heart, we have forgotten that we have robbed our children of much of the pleasure derived from the joy of repetition and the joy of remembering—life forces in themselves. The child who loves nursery rhymes, fairy-tales and jingles, who loves to skip and hop and revel in pagan chant and haunting rhythm, who even found the dirge of tables fascinating—surely he may yet find pleasure in the lilting verse and glowing prose of literature and the Bible.

Educationists who say "no learning-by-heart—it's out of date" have no right to dismiss it out of hand. It is time the pendulum swung back—part of the way.

The compilers of the Agreed Syllabuses have realised this when they say that the children should "commit to memory" such and such passages. What is this but "learning-by-heart"? Let us call a good spade a spade, and have done.

It would be equally wrong to go to the other extreme and allow the pendulum to swing right back. Never for a moment would we wish that children should be made to learn by heart many of the longest Psalms, or even the whole of Is. xl, "to keep them busy!" Nor should children be making these their own in spite of not understanding them.

But they should learn shorter poems of worth and impelling verses and passages—many smaller extracts rather than two or three scriptural marathons! And they should know what these pieces mean, and feel an inner impulse to possess them by learning them; and be aware that there are many other treasures in the Bible library. Not least should they be able to know where and how to find these gems.

This looks formidable; any task does in cold print. But it isn't. Teachers often find that the mere study of a passage is sufficient for some children to grasp its essentials. Further examination helps to fix them, and one or two efforts at reproduction will make the passage known. Other selections need more attention. Sheer imitation, challenge and rivalry all help children to master the lines. Those slower ones who manage five verses are as worthy of commendation as those who gallop through eleven or twelve; retention is often better, too.

It is useful to suggest a maximum and a minimum for learning. Children do not always need a reason for their learning. They find it in the fact that they have learned some and would like to master the whole; they find it in the sense of pleasure at things remembered; they find it in superiority over their neighbour, an *ad hoc* result of healthy competition in the classroom. The worst of all reasons is—because the teacher says so. It should never be.

Much of the cause for failure in the art of learning-by-heart is often due to the teacher's fear of indiscipline and noise. When asked why he would not let his children learn a poem or Scripture passage, a class teacher replied, "But they make such a noise! One starts to buzz—they all buzz—and so it goes on, louder and louder, until I seem to have lost control altogether. Oh no, I'd rather play safe!" Even in these somewhat noisy days of free expression and activity methods, this is a genuine cry. Children do get noisy when learning by heart. They say it aloud to see how they are getting on, apart from a conscious or unconscious verbal war with their neighbours. It is difficult to lay down hard-and-fast rules; so much depends upon the teacher and upon the usual atmosphere in the classroom. If the children work quietly in Geography or Mathematics, through their interest in the subject and their acceptance of a code of behaviour, they should certainly do so in their Religious Knowledge lessons; and learning-by-heart of a Scripture passage *is* a Religious Knowledge lesson.

The approach is important. Merely to say, "Turn to Ps. xxiv. Learn it. And do it quietly!" is to ask for noise and trouble. You will get it, too. You will sigh, shout for quietness—and then give it up. A pity.

Let us try to meet the case with an example.

First, the desirability of the passage. The best of all reasons is that it arises from a lesson. Here we are with the stirring story of David and Saul, interwoven with the deathless love of David and Jonathan. Saul and Jonathan are slain on the field of battle. Their epitaph; all heroes have epitaphs and memorials of some kind.

Theirs is in the lost Book of Jasher—the "Song of the Bow." READ it—dramatically, effectively. If it does not live for you, it will not for the children. If you are a bad reader (don't be afraid to admit it; admit it and put it right), get a child who will do the poem justice. Give him fair warning and time for preparation and practice. As the reading proceeds, note how the class begin to chime on the recurring "How are the mighty fallen." Let them. If they remember nothing more, they will recall those lines to the end of their days, and it will have been worth it.

Now let them have their own copies. If it is written in prose, have the poem copied from the Revised Version so that they can see it really is a poem.

Let them see how the chorus line occurs in ever-diminishing pattern—after six lines, six, six, five, two—as if the speaker's voice grows weaker and weaker in the overpowering emotion that presses his last words to a sigh.

Show how the poem epitomises the story of Saul and Jonathan, how colourful and picturesque is the language, how the lines flow. Is not such a fragment from a lost book worth the preserving? How was it handed down in days long ago? Why was it almost lost? How much can they themselves recall? Let them try. They will stumble, but will enjoy the trying, taking heart at the familiar chorus lines; individually, in sections, groups, collectively, always dwelling strongly on the vivid lines.[1]

Ulterior motives for learning should be extremely rare, but the added incentive of a rendering of a passage in the Morning Service is well worth while. A class of dull children will accept the promise at surface level, and work keenly to attain the honour; brighter children will see their part in the service as something that crowns their creative efforts.

Some of the Parables lend themselves to easy learning by heart, if taken pleasantly and with some ingenuity. In the inevitable Good Samaritan, for example, you have a Narrator, Priest, Levite, Samaritan; each can say his own verses, with the rest of the class miming if you think it necessary to occupy them. It is amazing how quickly each actor picks up his own verses and prompts his neighbour, and

---

[1] Further interest comes from strange places. If the class look up George Eliot's *Mill on the Floss,* they will find two of the lines on the last page; and as I write, there is a film at the local cinema—*They Were Not Divided.*

eventually learns the whole parable. The class, listening and watching, learn it too.

Again, show the class by means of the blackboard how Matt. vii. 16–23 fit into a parallel pair of verses; it takes them much less time to learn the story of the men who built houses.

Then again, in Ps. cxxxvi, the discovered fact that the repetition of the line "For His mercy endureth forever" *halves* their time and energy will cause children to *double* their efforts; children are mercenary creatures at times!

Here is a method of learning that may appeal to you, especially for Juniors and backward Seniors.

Write the passage on the blackboard.

Read it. Let the class read it.

Now let them read it again, accenting as they do so, and underline with coloured chalk the accented words. These are usually the key-words of the sentence; e.g.:

> I will *lift* up mine *eyes* unto the *hills*
> From *whence* cometh my *help*; etc.

Rub out the unaccented words, to leave:

> *lift*   *eyes*   *hills*
> From *whence* cometh my *help*; etc.

Let the class read it through again, the key-words being sufficient to remind them of the line.

Now rub out the unaccented words of the second line.

This leaves:

> *lift*   *eyes*   *hills*
>   *whence*   *help*

and the rest of the passage.

Let them read it through again.

Continue this right through the passage, until only the key-words of each line are left on the board.

The class reads the passage once more, and you rub out the top series of words entirely. They do so again, and you erase the second line . . . and so on. Eventually they come to the point when they have said it through without any guide words on the board at all.

They will know the passage by now, possibly some of them before, simply because of the intensive repetition of the whole unit, with the added excitement of beating the board as a happy encouragement. This does not mean that the passage is fixed; revision will be necessary to establish it in their minds.

This treating of the passage as a unit is most important in the process of learning; a verse-at-a-time method is not usually a happy one, as it fails to give shape and pattern that help the children in memorising.

Favourite texts—or rather, texts that should be favourites—and passages they like best in some aspect of their Religious Knowledge lesson may be noted in their anthologies, commonplace-books, or special Religious Knowledge note-books. These should be well-written, and illustrated with pictures and drawings and posters. Manuscript printing always appeals, and illuminated capitals may introduce the children to the beauties of early manuscripts and translations. What they are copying out, they usually learn automatically. A boy who undertook to letter the Prayer of Ignatius Loyola made two attempts he would not accept as his best; he handed back the original with the words, "I shan't want this any more, sir. I know it by heart after two goes at it." This was unconscious learning indeed.

By an approach on these lines, you will be able to cut out a good deal of tiresome chanting and anxiety over noise. There may well be a time when the class itself boycotts a noisy learner. After all, it *is* a Religious Knowledge lesson, and we have already noted that respect for others through quietness leads to the Christian attribute of Courtesy.

One of the major weaknesses teachers show in their hesitant work on learning is their failure to revise. They find it boring to hear work often, but in any subject, surely, it is quite useless to set work for learning and then omit to refer to it for weeks and even months at a time. Of course children forget most of it if they never have a chance to say it aloud. Let them revise their Scripture learning by saying their pieces at the beginning or end of the lesson—and why not in the English lesson on occasion? There are always those moments between the changing of classes, after registers, and so on, that are ideal for little extra practices; some teachers use them for class-reading, others for mental arithmetic or spelling. Why not sometimes listen to a memorised passage of Scripture?

So far, we have considered what is meant to be a constructive plea for learning-by-heart. In the Primary School there should be extensive verbal learning, satisfying the love of repetition and joy of mastery that young children possess.

As we move into the Post-primary stage, we adopt more subtle and more adult modes, not forgetting to study the passages and to give wider scope for personal tastes, trying to create the urge to possess things of beauty as part of the sentiment for things of good report; nor must we forget that even the adolescent loves to display his knowledge and memory.

Up to now we have had in mind those individual passages and selections recommended by the teacher or chosen by the children for individual or group learning. The place in memory work of *Choral Speaking* must now be examined.

Choral Speaking is of course no new thing; it is, rather, an old method of learning brought into line with the new psychology in accordance with modern educational principles. It incorporates all that has been said of the joy of rhythm, repetition and mastery; it takes stock of the pleasure of things remembered individually and collectively; it makes much of the need to analyse and discuss all material selected until it is appreciated, apperceived and understood before being learnt.

This is not the place for discussion of Choral Speaking in general; it merely needs relating to the learning of Scripture passages. But we should note right away that there is every reason why the learning of selections of Bible Literature should be done in an English lesson, as part of the appreciation of the written word and where Choral Speaking is probably practised as part of the English course. Many Bible passages lend themselves well to this form of learning; indeed, many of them were originally written for that express purpose. The antiphonal and interpolated chorus work of the Psalms shows this, and the parallelism of much of the verse structure denotes a form admirably suited to Choral Speaking.

The passage chosen must be approached with understanding and appreciation. Without slavishly analysing every syllable and phrase, it is necessary to explain words and idioms, content and context. Questioning will bring these things to the fore more pleasantly than mere exposition; the whole process should be one of search and discovery. Unless the passage is clarified the class will regard it only as a vehicle of barren repetition; and they will speak it so—without colour, feeling or warmth.

Most teachers are familiar with the Appreciation Lesson in English in the studying of a poem; something of the kind is needed for the Scripture passage. Free discussion opens up lines of thought. What is the background of the piece? Who said it? Why? Was it ever spoken in the Temple? Why? How? Does it lend itself to shared speech? Is it antiphonal? Does it lend itself to verse and chorus, group and group? Verse and several groups? Where is there opportunity for change of colour, tone, pitch, tempo? Is the piece unique, or is it an example of several such passages? Has it a title? Can it be given one?

By the time they have delved into the meaning, structure and background, the children will have acquired most of the content. What is more important, they will have been thinking together, and are ready to discuss and practise a variety of modes of expression, to select the agreed best, to give this light and shade; then to practise it in its finalised form until it is a spoken work of art by means of which the choir is expressing itself in active thought despite the fact that each member is not verbally active throughout the passage. Given in assembly or to another class, it is presented as something learned well. If a gramophone record can be obtained, so much the better; there are several recordings, e.g. H.M.V. B8271, "Psalm xxiv" and "David's Lament" (unfortunately now only obtainable second-hand). Let the class listen, compare and contrast; there is no reason why it should not do better than the recording.

Once more it is necessary to underline the need for a clear aim in the Choral Speaking lesson. Choose many short passages rather than a few long ones; spread the choice through the whole Bible.

What should children learn? That is not an easy question to answer; no one anthology ever suits all schools or all children, and the best one is always the collection made by the class concerned. The Agreed Syllabus will suggest many passages, but it is generally accepted that during their school life our children ought to study for learning at least the following:

Selections from the Psalms; Song of Songs.

Job xxviii.

David's Lament.

Is. xi. 1–9; xxxv; xl.

Story of Jerusalem (to be found best in *Voice and Verse*, C.U.P., pp. 31–8).

Decalogue (in a simplified form—perhaps best done by the class).

Selected Prayers, e.g. Loyola's "Teach us, good Lord . . ."

The Apostles' Creed. (Don't forget this is non-denominational.)

Some of the Parables.

The Beatitudes.

Gal. ii, v, vi.

Eph. vi. 1–20.

Phil. ii. 5–11.

Eccles. i, vii, xliv.

There is no doubt that the Psalms have a special place in the Religious Knowledge scheme. To be aware of the feelings of praise, thanksgiving, hope, even sorrow, is part of the Christian's inheritance, and nowhere is it better found than in the Psalms. If religion is caught rather than taught, here indeed is infection.

Children find most pleasure in those that express praise and thanksgiving, but they may well be introduced to those of adoration —viii, xciii, xcvi; confidence—xxiii, lxxxiv, cxxi; petition—li, cxxx. The article on Psalms in the *Teachers' Commentary* is a comprehensive guide. If the children turn to Ezra iii. 11, 2 Chron. vii. 3, and Ex. xv. 20 ff., they will find references to antiphonal singing of both Psalms and folk-songs such as the gruesome Song of Lamech, Gen. iv. 23, 24, the Song of the Water-drawers, Num. xxi. 17, 18 (compare our shanties), the Song of Deborah, Judges v. 2–31 (a *tour de force* of dramatic utterance). This guide to the speaking of the Psalms is underlined by the directions given in Ps. cxxix. 1.

Following a detailed appreciation of background, content and structure, the approach to speaking the selected Psalms may be made in these appropriate ways:

(a) *As a whole,* one group taking the first line of each couplet, to be answered by another group with the second line.

E.g. Ps. cii, x, xi, xcviii, and the Magnificat.

In Ps. cxiv there is a series of four-lined stanzas.

(b) *For Psalms with refrains*—narrator and chorus.

E.g. Ps. xlii, civ, cvii, cxxiv, cxxix, cxxxvi, cl.

Here is Ps. cvii, a Song of Thanksgiving, in detail:

Lost travellers arrive safely (vv. 4–9).
Prisoners are released (vv. 10–16).
Sick men are healed (vv. 17–22).
Seamen reach their haven (vv. 23–32).

There is a refrain made up of a cry of distress and shout of praise, and the help of the Lord is expressed after each division. These thirty-two verses make choral work both interesting and straightforward.

Ps. cxxxvi can be approached very simply; vv. 1–18 in groups of three; vv. 19–25 in groups of two; the whole class joins in the refrain and v. 26.

(c) *Question and answer* (e.g. Ps. xv, xxiv).

Ps. xxiv has as its background the return of the Ark, after the defeat of the Jebusites by David. It is therefore a Psalm of Praise and Joy; and probably sung in processional form as the Ark was brought to the Hill of Zion.

Thus:

vv. 1–2	processional chorus.
3	1st group.
4–5	2nd group.
6	chorus.
7	1st group.
8a	voices from the city.
8b	chorus.
9	1st group.
10	as for v. 8.

Incidentally, "Selah" is usually taken to indicate the end of a stanza. It should not be spoken, any more than we should say "full-stop."

In Ps. xlvi, there is a change of person concerned in the groups of vv. 1–3, 4–6, 7, 8–9, 10, 11.

(d) *"Snowball learning."* The class numbers off for verses.

Each learns his own verse for successive class rendering.

All move up one and learn the new verse, and so on.

Strangely enough, although the method appears to create a "wrong order" of verse learning for some of the children, the true pattern evolves quite safely, probably due to the continuous class sequence of repetition.

The element of rivalry should be brought in here.

Children should be helped to see the Psalms as the literature of the worshippers who "went to church by staying outside." In the days of the worshippers, only the priest entered the sacred precincts and the people stayed in the forecourt. This will entail mention of the Holy of Holies, the Holy Place, Altar and so on. A model of the Temple is almost indispensable to make this quite clear, but pictures are better than nothing. It might be possible to visit a Jewish synagogue, or to invite a Jew to talk to the children on the Psalms and present-day Jewish worship. You may even be fortunate enough to get help from a Levi, or a Cohen (cohan = high priest), both of whom have the power to claim certain rights in the synagogue.

A final word of guidance. As in all other subjects, be very sure that the material chosen for choral speaking is within the range and age of the children. It is obvious that bright children can tackle work quite unsuited to those of much lower mentality, and that the fourth-year class can manage passages beyond a first-year class. In individual learning, a child will sometimes be found working on a text or passage that you may think unsuitable for all sorts of reasons. Beware of damping his ardour by careless criticism or condemnation, unnecessary questioning or over-anxiety. The child has a reason though he may not be able to put it into words; that he has chosen the piece should be reason enough. But by careful observation and wary guidance, it is possible to show him similar pieces of greater appeal and worth that otherwise he might never have discovered. After all, the Bible is a big book!

A verse-speaking choir may attempt more ambitious work. Having practised the art of speaking together intelligently and learning-by-heart systematically, the class may be ready at some point for something on a grander scale than mere class verse-speaking. Let them try scenes from such a play as *The Man Born to be King*. It will be a change from the Bible—possibly at this juncture a good thing; and the message will be the same—certainly a good thing.

The Easter scenes are especially effective, and can be rehearsed with more time than other scenes at other times of the year. A practical set-up is to have your choir at the back of the darkened hall, behind the audience. You need a central Cross cross-lit with two red spotlights to cast two shadows, one on either side of the real Cross. If on a dimmer, lighting may be varied in intensity to heighten the emotional effect.

A useful selection of scenes is:

Eleventh Play. Scenes 1, 2, i, iii, v, vii.

These in sequence, with appropriate music at the beginning and end, the Bach Chorale "O Sacred Head," after Scene 2, i, take about thirty-five minutes. A longer period might pall if not on a high standard; if well done, more than this length of time might become emotionally unbearable.

Something of this kind is a crown to achievement that children will seek, and the presentation to both school and adult audiences gives an experience that all who speak and listen will never forget.

And this, after all, is just what memory work implies—the experiencing of the Scriptures in such a way that there is joy in remembering what has been so well-learned in the past.

Not the least value of all this work is the presentation of the Scriptures vitally and attractively.

Encourage the Bible-reading habit; by doing so we may hope to bring back the Bible where it belongs—in the home. During the Festival of Britain, on a visit to Central Hall, Westminster, the Queen Mother said these words, "I can truly say that the King and I long to see the Bible back where it ought to be, as a guide and comfort in the homes and lives of our people. From our own experience, we know what the Bible can mean for personal life." It may be through the teachers of the present generation that the Bible returns home, brought back by the children to the parents.

Introduce them to the International Bible Reading Association, the Bible Reading Fellowship, the Scripture Union, or even devise readings as a Project in the Religious Knowledge Syllabus. In this way, when they have left school, they will again and again come across the very passages that gave them pleasure and strength as children; the words of the Bible cannot but give them hope and courage when as men and women they meet the problems of their new world, and when, perhaps for the first time, they realise that the Scriptures shall be "a lamp unto their feet" wherever they go.

CHAPTER XIII

VISITS AND SCHOOL JOURNEYS

Making them of value; planning, doing, assessing; training in what to look at and for; records; suggested visits.

WHO has not at some time in his career as a pupil or teacher been on a school journey? What a farce this can be, involving as it so often does time off from school to travel long distances to a famous spot, to meander round and round places of historical fame, to be given mental indigestion by garrulous, lisping guides, and to return footsore and weary with pages of meaningless notes and piles of official photographs and booklets that are eventually and often surreptitiously deposited in the waste-paper basket.

This kind of school journey is a shocking waste of time, money and energy. It is to be hoped that such visits are rarer than once they were.

There are probably all sorts of ulterior motives and lesser reasons for going on a school journey, but educationally it is obvious that the value lies in the fact that children are able to satisfy that inner impulse to discover by being on the very spot where such and such happened. It is first-hand experience of many things that could be merely vague and meaningless through exposition even with the help of pictures and models. To visit a modern edifice like Coventry Cathedral, to see the birthplace of a great reformer, to read the epitaph on the monument of a fine missionary, to handle precious documents, vestments, relics—these are the stuff of reality.

But that desire to find out must be a real one, arising naturally from a lesson, a challenge to find out more; if this is so, then there is point in the visit.

For any school visit to be a success there must be a definite scheme of planning from start to finish. If there is not, it is of the type already indicated and had better not be begun.

The scheme is best examined under three headings—Planning, Doing, Assessing. To make this practical, let us assume that a special visit is taking place, and obtain our guidance from that example.

PLATE IX

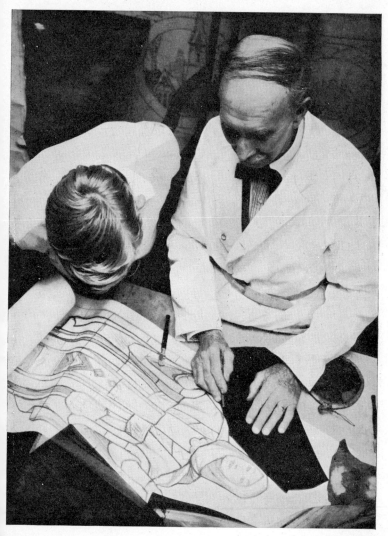

Going outside.   A boy watches a craftsman at work on a stained-glass
window for St. Aldhelm's Church, Edmonton.

PLATE X

Above: Project—a Bible Library in match-boxes.   B stream.
Below: Model—a Cinema.   B stream.

(a) Planning

Firstly, why are you going?

Has the idea arisen from a lesson, or is it someone's hope that such a journey might be worth while? Is it to a village church, a monastery, an abbey, a famous birthplace? Clearly, there must be some reason behind the visit, and from this discussion will arise so as to clarify and focus, as it were, the object of the visit. Children must know why they are going, and when they have arrived, what they are to look for. So you talk about the place, where it is, why it is being visited; in this way you stimulate interest and pleasure at the possibilities of the visit.

Secondly, what is to be found out?

There must be discussion of exactly what has to be sought for on arrival and how this can best be done. There must also be a clear indication of the tie-up of this visit with work already done in the Religious Knowledge course, or with some aspect to be covered later in the term. In other words, the aim should emerge as clear-cut as it can be made.

Thirdly, how are you going to set about it? What is your plan of action?

Suppose the visit to be to a village church. Be sure to obtain permission from a responsible person before presuming a welcome. Then get to work in the classroom. Divide the class into groups and individuals who will each be responsible for some particular part of the intended plan; take care that the sections of work do not seriously overlap, and that the over-all purpose of the visit is covered.

Discuss with the class the things they will find of interest: church records, stained-glass windows, brass rubbings, church plate, vestments, famous burials, quaint epitaphs, the font, choir stalls, carvings, architecture, tower and bells, historical background, church and village relationships "then and now," chats with the verger and vicar.

From these aspects and others that will arise will be judged the need for note-books, writing and drawing materials, odds and ends of things necessary to the various activities planned. It is important not to be casual and haphazard; much forethought is required. It is equally essential for you either to make a preliminary visit or to get as much information as possible before the actual class visit takes place. This is not so much to provide material as to give you a sense of awareness of what to expect.

By the time the groups have been fixed and the individuals know what they are to do, a keen sense of competition is already aroused. This is all to the good, easy to stimulate and maintain.

In their search for preliminary guidance in books of reference, children discover words like apse, nave, reredos and architectural names that baffle them. It is advisable to try to explain these before the visit, and then note them for further attention on arrival.

There is always the possibility that the implication of the visit may develop an historical bias, for history and religion are inseparably bound. The historical side cannot be eliminated altogether, even if this were deemed a good thing to do, but it is necessary to keep a clear idea before yourself as well as before the children that the journey and the visits are concerned with the religious aspect of the place, and that what they find will help them the better to understand the place of religion and the church in bygone days; it may help them to estimate the place of these in the present day, too. It should.

(b) Doing

Once arrived at the church, allow a little time for the strangeness and newness of the experience to give way to the sense that this is the object of their visit. After this preliminary interest has faded, it is time to see that the prepared plan is begun and guided into the right lines of action.

Group leaders are despatched with their groups to their respective duties. Be on the alert for emergency guidance and supervision; the best of children sometimes forget to behave and to work. If arrangements have been made previously for help at the church from a special guide, choose a convenient moment for his help. Not at the outset. Children need time to sort out first impressions, and after satisfying an initial interest in their own work, will find his talk of more value; their questions reveal that. Besides, the guide is there to clarify and amplify what the children are finding, not to deliver a lecture *in toto*.

Following out their prearranged work, the children are quickly finding their own sermons in these stones. It is a pleasurable experience to find each one bent on his particular job—the photographer taking snaps of church and workers, the artist sketching gargoyles, effigies, figures and scenes inside and outside, or copying an illuminated manuscript sufficiently well to guide him in the making of a better copy at home or in school; another is writing the prayer he has found on the main door or on some tomb; over there is a lad poring over an old church record, whilst two boys are energetically preparing a brass rubbing; the girls are listening to the vicar's explanation of the vestments, or admiring and sketching the plate used only on very special occasions.

Before long, two or three reporters are returning from the village where they have been interviewing local celebrities. They have been trying to assess the value and work of the church in the village today, and will no doubt have much to report.

Soon—usually much too soon—it is time to leave. Be sure to give a preliminary warning; children do not like to be dropped on at two minutes' notice, any more than adults do. They need at least a quarter of an hour to finish and clear up.

It is good training in Christian courtesy to ensure expression of thanks to vicar and guide, in reverence to leave the church quietly and all places tidy, in thoughtfulness to close all gates and doors and leave by the pathway despite the attraction of a short-cut over the graves. The opportunity for a prayer both before and at the end of the work should be considered, and there is always the practical sign of gratefulness in a group collection for the Church Fund Box. It is these things that underline the fact that the visit is one associated with religious training; in the long run, these are the things remembered when the details of architecture and history have been long forgotten.

(c) Assessing

This is often where the best of visits and journeys fail. The ends of those other visits came with the return to school—in fact, many of them with the boarding of the homeward bus or train. Let us get this visit correctly and sensibly finished.

The children have come back with dozens of rough notes, sketches and drawings. Now is the time to consolidate what they have done. Sorting out, accepting and rejecting is the next business. First, the other groups want to know what their co-workers have to offer. Lecturettes and talks will have to be prepared and given, diagrams and drawings need to be finished or re-drawn, photographs and descriptions must be examined. Critical listening is not an unimportant result of this. If one of the children makes an error of judgment or fact, someone is sure to be able to correct him—pleasantly but firmly. If another makes a sweeping conclusion regarding, say, the position of the church in the past or the present, general discussion will reduce it to a more likely statement.

Now follows the collation of the facts and illustrative materials obtained into a form for critical assessment. It is important to remember the relation of this work to the Religious Knowledge scheme. Eventually, out of the apparent conglomeration of details and notes, there emerges an approved selection of accounts and drawings and pictures that can be put together into some form of consolidated record. This is always exciting. It sets the seal, as it were, and gives thereby a sense of completeness and finish that is reflected in the children's pleasure and interest for a very long time. If there is a typewriting class, or a girl who is learning, some of the accounts may be typed to save laborious and often bad handwriting. A solid portfolio, indexed, containing the particular assignments of the children—with their names and suitably designed and headed—can be made in the Craft lesson. The permanent result thus produced may be exhibited, and should be given a place of honour in the Library for the benefit and general pleasure of other children in the school.

This co-ordination of work done is valuable, too, as the culmination of co-operative work. The class will have learned in this, if in no other way, that the best results come from harmonious working together, and that each individual contributes to the work of the whole.

Not the least value of this type of work, resulting from the visit, is being able to assess from it the position of the church in the lives of people today. Children are always interested in two aspects of this kind of experience—why such a grand old building of a past age was once so important and popular, and whether or not this same church means anything to the community today. Religion should mean something to folk nowadays, they argue. What is lacking that old churches are neglected and badly attended?

These matters make for intense argument and often heated discussion. Let them argue; let them plan another visit—perhaps on a

Sunday when they can attend a service in the little old church about which they now know so much. The rest may be left safely—to Providence.

You will say that all this involves a great deal of effort—is it worth it? It is. It is something worth the doing and worth doing well. As a Project it might usefully occupy the class for a whole term; as a visit for strengthening some part of the syllabus, it can be fitted in to cover, say, two periods per week for about three weeks; as a brief visit, it may well answer many of the immediate questions of the class and whet their appetites for something more. Much depends upon the amount of work planned and the amount of detail expected, but only the visit arranged with a plan of action can succeed in its purpose.

Other types of journey may be off the beaten track. Here is a missionary ship in dock, refitting prior to another voyage, e.g. the Society for the Propagation of the Gospel ship *Centurion*, or the *John Williams* of the London Missionary Society; a visit to either of these would be both exciting and educational. The possibility of visiting various societies and hostels will be dealt with in a later chapter from the point of view of Practical Service, but a few suggestions here will be useful.

Thus: Salvation Army Hostels in big cities, Children's Homes, such as the Waifs and Strays Homes, Dr. Barnardo's Homes, Schools for the Blind, Deaf and Dumb (a heart-searching visit this) and the offices of the British and Foreign Bible Society. From each of these is obtained a tremendous amount of information about the work attempted and done for the good of other folk, usually for the helping of the down-and-out or otherwise unfortunate children and people. Children are not likely to forget a visit to a Blind or Deaf school; and it might mean a big brother or a big sister adoption of some of the children at these places.

In all these visits, our business is to give the children first-hand or good second-hand experience that they might never otherwise obtain except vaguely and uninterestedly from some text-book or talk. In this way they learn what altruism is, what it can do and what they themselves owe to other members of the community around them.

CHAPTER XIV

LINKING THE OUTSIDE

Linking the class lesson with the outside world; visiting speakers; the class goes outside.

ONE of the charges levelled at present-day teaching of Religious Knowledge in schools is that it takes little if any account of its relation with the outside world; critics say it is too much bound by the four walls of the classroom. Yet it is quite a simple matter to relate the two, harnessing outside help in such a way that the children are made to realise that beyond the school walls there are folk who are working together for the strengthening of the Christian faith.

Probably the best way to link the outside with the classroom is to bring into the school representatives of these efforts for religion and Christian teaching. Just as in Social Studies we bring the postman and the dustman and the fireman to speak to the children about their work as serving the community, so in our Religious Knowledge lessons we can invite the vicar and the verger and the welfare worker to come and talk about their work—also for the community.

As far as the church representatives are concerned, few children, even if they attend church, really know who these folk are and what they do. One of their own number may be a server; he should be encouraged to explain his duties. It might be possible to get a local vicar and a Nonconformist minister to come at the same time, and discuss their particular work and where and why they differ.

When the need for a certain speaker is realised, be sure to get one with reasonable facility of speech and ease with children. Nothing bores or irritates a class more than spiritless inadequacy in a visitor; once they have got over the initial interest and welcome, children so obviously indicate their approval or otherwise of his ability. Get him to tell of *his* particular duties, inviting him to bring examples if advisable or possible; even a visitor is the more welcome if he has interesting visual aids. Special vestments are always an attraction. I have seen a Jewish worker hold a class fascinated with his display of scarves and phylacteries and books of worship, which, with his intoned prayers and readings in the original tongue, made a great impression on his hearers. A Roman Catholic friend might also visit you, and there is every reason why someone from the Church of England should come along and explain the Order of Service and Prayer Book to our children of the Protestant Faith. Whenever possible and practicable, such a talk should be followed up with a visit. In fact, an organised "tour of the churches" might be considered—not forgetting the Roman Catholic, Friends' Meeting House and Synagogue.

Very often, in the locality, there is a retired missionary—or one on furlough; he will be most willing to come. But if unable to secure a speaker on this great work, write to the Secretary, Edinburgh House, 2, Eaton Gate, London, S.W.1. You will be able to benefit from the tremendous work for young people that the Schools Committee is doing, and even send through them boys and girls to one of the Conferences organised for Secondary Schools on Foreign Missions and Missionary Work.

Visitors from overseas who are interested in education usually have much to say on Religious Education; they believe England to be a Christian country and are always anxious to find out why and how the Christian faith should have made the country what it is. Indian and African students will talk about the variety of sects and religions in their own countries, about the colour bar and racial prejudice. This may give a lead to discussions and talks on the great religions; or it may be the explanation of some of them; or it may be the culmination of a series of lecturettes on them. The Colonial Department, Institute of Education, University of London, will help in arranging for speakers.

In Somerset there is a school which has established a warm friendship with a Franciscan priory. Children visit the priory and the Brothers visit the children, and a mutual understanding is thereby engendered.

The Secretary of the Student Christian Movement might be invited to speak of the work of the Movement throughout the world, especially at schools where Junior branches have been started. It may not be generally known that residential and holiday conferences are arranged, whereby thousands of boys and girls are helped "to see the Christian faith, not merely as a subject of study at school, but as something which happens in the life of the whole man within the setting of the total human situation." Write to the Schools Secretary, S.C.M., Annandale, North End Road, London, N.W.11, for further information.

Doctors, Nurses, Hospital Chairmen, speakers from the R.S.P.C.C., R.S.P.C.A., the Y.M.C.A. and Y.W.C.A., Probation Officers—the list is inexhaustible. Make good use of these people when and where possible, especially to strengthen a particular part of your scheme. Such visits to the school must not be overdone, of course, especially if other departments are working on the same idea; frequency may destroy the value. In any case, these visits are adjuncts to rather than substitutes for religious training.

Sometimes it is good for the school to go outside. A local church may be presenting scenes from *The Man Born to be King* or a Miracle Play; a dramatic society, *Murder in the Cathedral*; a choir is performing an Oratorio; an organist is giving a recital of Church Music; there may even be a suitable film. It is usually possible to take a group of children, perhaps the whole school, to these performances; obviously, the children must be prepared with sufficient background and reason for the visit to be spiritually satisfying. At Christmas, many schools have their Carol Service in a nearby church, so that parents and friends and old scholars can join in the Christmas Story. At least once a year, and perhaps at the end of every term, it should be possible to hold a Leavers' Service attended by all children due to leave school and drawn from a wide area. This public avowal of their faith should do much to strengthen boys and girls as they realise they are not alone as they prepare to enter their strange new world.

One of the most valuable outside helps is a Bible Exhibition. It is possible to make models, collect genuine objects, manuscripts and so on, as the result of a project on the Story of the Bible. There used to be an excellent authentic Bible Exhibition provided for public showing by Mr. R. E. Ford, of Bedford. In this Exhibition were shown a complete collection "from Hebrew scroll to modern translation." Children were able to see for themselves massive scrolls such as Jesus read in the Temple, copies of early manuscripts, first translations, original Taverner's, Breeches, Treacle and other Bibles, every modern version extant, and so trace vividly the growth of the English Bible from its source to the present day. At the time of writing, the Exhibition is not available, but it is to be hoped that this is only a temporary hiatus. This reference may, however, give some reader the idea of preparing an exhibition in his own school, on the lines here indicated.

A useful link with schools and the outside world can be made through the British and Foreign Bible Society. In the first place, arrange a visit. At 146, Queen Victoria Street, London, E.C.4, quite near to Blackfriars Station, there is a wealth of information and a warm welcome is extended to visitors of all ages. In the Library are housed thousands of volumes—Bibles and related books, in half the languages of the world and in many dialects of those tongues. Interest is sustained in such things as Mary Jones' Bible, miniature testaments, beautifully written manuscripts and the unending variety of strange languages. Braille Bibles are a feature, too, whilst the packing rooms are veritable geography lessons shot through with the Message of the Bible. When next planning a trip to London "to the Science Museum," add a visit to the British and Foreign Bible Society; there is no fear that the children will find it dull.

There may be near, or at reasonable travelling distance, a stained-glass factory—or better still, as is the fortune of my school, the studio of an individual craftsman. A visit to either of these reveals to children the draughtsmanship, technique and accurate Biblical knowledge required by the designers of the many and varied memorial windows to be found in churches. Some idea of the care needed for repair of ancient and valuable stained-glass by modern craftsmen may also be gained. Children will by this means appreciate the better both colour and design as well as the particular historical and Biblical significance of such windows, and may be urged to attend more closely to these in their visits to churches long after they have left school.

It is by bringing the outside world into the classroom, or by taking the children into the world outside, that we link the two together; and it is by linking them together that we help our children to realise over and over again that they are only a small part of the great company working in strangely varied ways for the Kingdom on earth in this and other lands. If only because of this, our planning should never be careless or slipshod, our visits should never be haphazard, our follow-up should never be slapdash. Only the best is good enough, for it is done in the name of Religion; and regarding our children as Christians in the making, it is done for God.

CHAPTER XV

PRACTICAL SERVICE

The practice of Christianity; suggestions for school clubs and societies; good deeds; altruism.

SIR WILFRID GRENFELL once said, "Following Christ is doing something, anything, well," and an old West Country phrase has it, "Du gude if tha can, but du zummat."

The essence of Christianity is to do as the Master did—to do good. There is no doubt but that the present-day trend of doing so much for children may cloak the idea that they ought to do something for other folk. Service without payment is a rare thing these days; perhaps the school is one of the few places left in which to sustain it— by creating the right attitude and the right opportunities. In their lessons children should be guided to see that they have possessions and talents to be dedicated to the service of God, through serving and helping others—their hands, feet, eyes, voices, health, strength, happiness, sympathy, the power to think, draw, design and make; the hymn they sing so often, "Take my life and let it be consecrated, Lord, to Thee" should be made real to them; it can so easily be mere lip-service.

What shall we help them to do? There are the usual outlets for service through their Youth Clubs, Scouts, Guides and related groups, as well as in the Boys' Brigade, Girls' Life Brigade, St. John's Ambulance and so on. The daily good deed is sound enough, and yet so relatively few of our children belong to such groups, leaving a majority to whom the daily good deed is anathema.

These require specific guidance, and they have not far to look, as we can well show them.

Working Squads, Handymen and Repair Brigades—with shovel and barrow to tidy waste plots, to assist in school and other functions with hammer and saw, or merely to heave and move furniture. The gardeners can take over the allotment of some sick holder, or attend to almshouse gardens or a neglected green.

A branch of work appealing to cyclists is a Messenger Club.

From time to time there are opportunities to deliver church notices, envelopes for a good cause, urgent cancellations and important messages of all kinds.

A Helpers' Club with its own motto and badge—and could not all these clubs have some sort of distinguishing badge?—would appeal to some children, especially if it met after school and were open to requests of all kinds.

There are always demands for Hospital Visitors, not only for someone belonging to the school, but for other unfortunate folk. A class once adopted a stranger, a lad who had no relations near him; when he was better and left the district, the children immediately found someone else. Incidentally, very often in the play-ground or on a school journey, someone is unlucky enough to have an accident. Besides the teacher, reliable boys and girls can see the child home and explain carefully to an anxious parent, and help where they can. Someone can run the child's usual errands, do his paper delivery, nurse the baby, get in the coals; others can supply magazines and books. Baden Powell said, "Sympathy without relief is like mustard without beef," and here are chances to provide the beef of willing service. Nor is it necessarily the help of these workers that is the most important factor: it is rather that these may be the very means of bringing into otherwise barren lives the spirit of Christian service they have never known before.

In one school there was a lad suffering from the effects of in-fantile paralysis; he would never walk, he had his lessons in a wheel-chair. His mother was anxious, but she needn't have been. First one lad, then another, and another . . . until quite a group vied with each other for the opportunity of wheeling him to and from school, lessons and in the playground. It was always a joy for the headmaster to glance out of his window to see the boy in his chair with his bodyguard of drivers; and the laughter they used to share was indicative of the deep-seated sympathy felt by all of them. The strange thing was that it was the unlikely boys who helped most; but perhaps it ought not to have been strange!

From time to time there are reports of horrifying disasters in some part of the world—accidents, fires, floods, earthquakes. Funds are launched, collections made, sales and concerts held. It is not sug-gested that this can be done for every call that comes your way; but there are occasions when there is a special reason for your interest, as when children are immediately concerned, e.g. the Save the Children Fund.

February 22nd is Thinking Day for Scouts and Guides the world over, commemorating the joint birthdays of the Founders of the Scout and Guide Movements. On this day, the Guides give one penny each "to help to develop the world friendship of the movement." It might be possible to have such an annual School Thinking Day Fund, to provide some small financial aid to a chosen cause. The anniversary of the school's opening might be a good day, or the birthday of a local celebrity who is interested in the school.

Development of synthetic drugs has made it possible to cure many types of leprosy. It is possible for individuals or groups to "adopt" a leprous child and to pay for a cure through the British Leprosy Relief Association, 8 Portman Street, London, W.1, which will give further details, if your children show interest. The cost is £10 per year—not a heavy charge for so great a work, less than 2s. a term from each child in a class of forty. The Queen and five other members of the royal family all support children and adopt others when these are discharged as cured.

The adopting idea may spread to missionaries, and there are always excellent opportunities of doing so through the various Missionary Societies; if there is a missionary with local connections, so much the better. Have his photograph and letters displayed, together with pictures of his overseas home, the natives at work and at play, maps showing the locality and its relation to the rest of the world. One of the children might make a collecting-box modelled on the lines of a native hut or the mission station.

In this neighbourhood there is a Girls' School which takes a practical interest in a local orphanage. During the holidays in particular, the older girls look after the small children, wash, dress, take them out, and even help with the more menial and less exciting work in the Home. It is an interesting comment of the headmistress that the most successful helpers are often the girls of less than average ability. We can hardly guess the educational and psychological value to these girls of this opportunity to serve; spiritually theirs is a great increase in stature.

Rangers have been known to take blind girls to camp with them, making themselves responsible for their happiness. This is an excellent idea that surely need not be confined to Guides and Rangers. Is it not one that could be carried out by children generally, this looking after those who are blind and denied the normal pleasures of their more fortunate friends? There are Youth Clubs whose members take blind friends for tandem rides into the country; our boys and girls are potential members of Youth Clubs. In the chapter on "School Visits," a visit to a Blind School was suggested; perhaps the idea of adopting might arise from that; or the visit might arise from the adoption.

Flag-days are often a nuisance, even to the most generous givers. But some of them are worthy of special consideration for the exceptional work they help. Try to make sure that the children do know what that work is; we rather take it for granted that they know what happens to the money for, say, Remembrance Day poppies; it is doubtful if many children could say much about the Alexandra Rose Day, Daisy Day and similar good causes. The Christian basis of the work should be explained, and the need to *do* something about it emphasised.

In a tiny room at the British and Foreign Bible Society Headquarters is its famous Stamp Corner. There, children may see stacks of stamps sent from all over the world; there they are sorted and packed for export. Amongst these piles of stamps are many English stamps, collected by English children. This is something all the children of any school can do—collect sacks of stamps and forward them to the Society. With the money raised from the sale of these stamps the Society supports the work of five colporteurs—in Bolivia, Vietnam, Burma, Algiers and the Southern Sudan. Here is material for your Religious Knowledge lesson, too. I hope your beginning of such a lesson is more propitious than mine. I asked, "What— or who—is a colporteur?" There was dead silence; it was evident that the word meant nothing to these thirteen-year-old children. Then, "Did he write 'Deep Purple', sir?" I can't imagine Cole Porter delivering Bibles, but it did cheer up the lesson for us!

Towards Christmas the thoughts of many children, naturally enough, go to carols, cards, presents and parties. A Carol Choir might be organised to sing at prearranged points—hospitals, orphanages, homes of parents—bringing both pleasure and pennies for good causes. It should be easy to find children not likely to receive Christmas-cards and toys, and equally easy to get one or two more fortunate children to send these. Incidentally, after Christmas collect unwanted cards and send in bulk to the National Children's Home and Orphanage, Highbury Park, N.5, or to some other good cause. Silver paper and tin foil may also be collected for good causes, e.g. the fund for Guide Dogs for the Blind.

It may be possible to arrange a party once in a while for old folk, or for slum children. A Christmas Tree Service might be held at which decorations and toys and presents are affixed and removed to appropriate music. Children should make their own gifts for such an event, or use their talents in concert work for a similar occasion. Indeed, the making of presents and the using of talents for other people's happiness is something to be encouraged at any time. In a classroom stood a pile of good things brought by classmates for one of their friends then suffering from poliomyelitis. "We made them, sir," was proof enough of sincerity and happiness found through personal giving. This was in the lowest class of the first year, and only a day later in the lowest third-year class gifts were being sent to one of their number—a blue baby—then in hospital.

A Sick Fund for class members seriously ill would give an opportunity for practical sympathy; it should be run on committee lines and not dictated by the teacher.

By the time you have scanned through all these ideas and thought of riders to them, you will be feeling that they are quite impossible; this is because all of them are claiming immediate attention. It is impossible to undertake them all; they are meant only as suggestions that might meet your interests and those of your class.

What we are about is the development of a sense of altruism; service above and before self. There is little enough in the world today; perhaps we can do a great deal towards making it real and effective in the future.

CHAPTER XVI

PROJECTS AND CENTRES OF INTEREST

What a Project is; what it entails for the teacher; what it means for the
child; the Nativity Play as a Project; ultimate aims.

SOME words in education are used so glibly that we often tend to
overlook and even forget their exact pedagogical meaning.

Projects is such a word; and since this is a book of method, it
might be as well if we spent a few moments in reminding ourselves
of its significance before we apply this particular approach to
Religious Knowledge.

We know that children usually find their main interests in real
situations rather than in mere subjects. Their reaction to these is
"purposeful activity" prompted by their natural instincts and interests. A problem or a situation stirs their curiosity, and they want
to do something about it—to look, handle, throw, lift, make,
destroy. . . . When we teach children in the classroom we are prone
to divide experience artificially into subjects, using books and tools
to support our purely logical approach. But text-books can, and do,
become millstones, and children are not happy in their school work.
This is where teachers using the Project Method score, for "the
conception of projects . . . is at bottom a revolt against the tyranny
of the text-book, and a partial return to the broad and leisurely spirit
of inquiry" (*Modern Education,* Raymont). Some class teaching is
necessary, as is admitted by Raymont's "partial return", but the
accent of the project is on the "spirit of inquiry", into some real
purpose, with a plan for the job in hand and a result to assess.

Finding out is fun, given the reason, the stimulus and the tools.
In it are the beginnings of group work for both Primary and Post-
primary children. Juniors particularly do not differentiate between
subjects, whilst the adolescent needs opportunities for individual and
co-operative work "characterised by marked creativeness and adventurous independence." Social training, social service, and eventually
altruism—the springs of Christian conduct—are often best achieved
in this way, for the adolescent is in process of self-education.

The essence of the Project, then—and of the Centre of Interest which is but a Project in miniature—is that the purposeful activity of the children is guided by a knowledgeable teacher, from the inception of the idea to find out about something, to the culminating record of what has been found out in the process. A really successful Project always creates a desire to go on finding out—indeed, new ideas constantly arise as the original interest develops—and unless this attitude of mind is created the work has failed, for the finished schoolwork must never be regarded as the end of the adventure.

What is this purposeful activity? In brief—expeditions, explorations, discoveries, search, collection of materials and specimens and facts, model-making, aids, records, books, talks, lectures, discussions, dramatic presentations, exhibitions. . . . It is not strange that most of these should be chapter headings in this book, for in the Project is the co-ordination of all methods and approaches suiting all types of children from the brightest to the dullest, so long as they are planning and doing, and sharing.

Most teachers are familiar with some form of Project work, and not a few may feel it a waste of time, savouring of inefficient guidance, ineffective meanderings and useless collections of charts, drawings and note-books. That is a pity, for a Project efficiently carried out "according to plan" is immeasurably useful. Of course, it is only likely to be so when the accent is on planning and when the teacher becomes a super-leader.

The attitude of the teacher is absolutely essential to the success or otherwise of the work. He must see the skeleton of the Project—the purpose, the plan of action, the doing and the final assessment of what has been done. He must be willing to exchange text-books for voyages of discovery; he must be able to put up with noise and movement and chaotic classroom conditions. He must be available to discuss and guide and explain, as well as to appreciate the immediate and future needs of his children; he must know something of the psychology of the growing child, how to sublimate the energetic powers of the extrovert and how to nurture the child sensitive and lacking in confidence. He must be able to handle discussions well, for from these the chief educational values are obtained. Children under him will learn to think sanely, logically, quickly; they will learn to be tolerant of the other point of view, they will agree to accept and forgo, adapt and refuse, in a spirit of self-control and friendliness. It is the teacher who shows them the most difficult task of all—how to evaluate the information gained by a number of individuals, to assess the worth of the project as a whole, and finally, how to prepare the lay-out of the finished work as a permanent record.

Many of these experiences are sheer ethics, based upon the Christian principles of give and take that we often suggest might permeate the school curriculum.

Knowledge of the Project Method is probably based upon its use in History, English and Geography. Religious Knowledge has rarely, if at all, been included in such a Project. It hasn't been noticed as a possible link, and very often as a lesson has had to make way for the time-table changes necessitated for the Project. This is a great mistake; it suggests that the subject is of little account and ignores completely its power as an integrating force in the curriculum. It is difficult to see how a Project in History or English can be done really satisfactorily without some allusion to and research into the religious aspect and background; a Project so devised is certainly the poorer for the omission.

There is obviously room for Religious Knowledge in the average Project, but our task is to consider the subject as the basis of a Project in itself.

The possibility has been indicated already, in the chapter on "School Visits and Journeys," where a Project on the Church was introduced. The study of the Village Church makes an admirable section of a Project in Church History; there is an excellent article by Rev. Canon H. Herklots, on such a Project, in *Religion in Education,* Vol. 17, No. 1. An Oundle experiment is reported in Vol. 18, No. 2. Here are further suggestions:

Hospitals and Healing (see *Project on Healing,* Arundale, R.E.P.).
Good Causes (Barnardo's, Salvation Army, etc.).
Sunday-schools (references in your library will start you off).
Comparative Religion.
Freedom of Worship (from the Four Freedoms).
Festivals (Food, Timber, Coal, etc.).
Prayer (see *Prayer Project,* Ferguson, R.E.P., 6d.).
The Lord's Prayer.

The Creed.

History of Education (especially locally).

Nativity Play (or other religious festival play).

Tableaux and Pageants (missionary, Biblical, historical).

The Bible Library.

The Religious Knowledge Classroom.

A New School Hymn-book.

Prison Reform.

The Prayer Book.

Societies for Prevention of Cruelty to Children and Animals.

A Missionary Exhibition (British and Foreign Bible Society will help here).

The best Projects arise from the children's suggestions, but something on the above lines is interesting as a guide to what may be attempted. In working out the Project it will be necessary to weave in several of the other subjects, but the chosen theme will be where you intend it to be—at the centre. In this way, the children will see for themselves the influence of God and the Church in the shaping of lives and events through the ages.

Let us take an example from the above list, say the Nativity Play, and see how this may be done. The Project may easily arise from classwork before Christmas, and the idea of writing a play may even come from the English lesson. Careful reading of Bible stories and background will result, and the mechanics of the writing may safely be left to the English periods. Geography and History must be brought in for exactness of detail of customs and costumes; there will be research, collection of pictures, illustrations. The play now on the way, we consider production and all it involves. Costumes, scenery, properties, effects and all the paraphernalia of stage presentation. How will the other subjects help? Let us go to extremes and examine the extent to which each subject may be drawn in:

Mathematics	Measuring for stage, curtains, properties, calculation of costs and expenses; box-office arrangements; programmes; refreshments, seating.
English	Mechanics of writing the play; rehearsal, speech, verse-speaking choir; letters to parents, etc.

Art and Craft	Scenery, properties, backcloths; posters, tickets, programmes, stencilling, fabric printing.
Needlework	Costumes; alterations; curtains.
Domestic Science	Refreshments for audience and players; dyeing materials; laundry.
Science	Lighting; wiring; properties.
Music	Choir, carols, orchestra. Music of the period; interval music.
Handicraft	Heavy properties and staging; effects; crooks, crowns, swords, wings, etc.
Geography	Palestine at the time of Christ. Customs, country, travel, etc.
History	The period concerned; Romans and Jews; prophecy.

There will be general preparations, too, involving—producer, stage manager, property men, prompter, make-up, wardrobe mistress, effects, curtain controllers, stewards.

Casting is important; give opportunities to the shy and retiring. All members of the class should do something in the actual performance; they must feel as important to its success as the chief characters, proud of their craftsmanship and of their service as individuals to the group.

Probably the greatest value of this particular work is in the rehearsals—it is certainly the most enjoyable—when the children are really learning to listen, share, help and accept fair criticism; this is when the best training in team work, attention and unity of purpose is done, although the end crowns all.

Our job is to make the child a thoughtful, useful citizen, able eventually to educate himself by similar methods of enquiry, observation and discovery. This is more likely when the Project arises from his own interests rather than when imposed artificially by the teacher; indeed, the only time it really does succeed is when his inner impulses drive him to "learn through action." By this method he may well acquire new interests that he will carry into adult life; the joy of achievement and mastery may urge him to take wider opportunities as he feels the need for self-expression and service, and the right use of his leisure hours. More than ever in these rather selfish days do we need potential citizens who will do this.

Nor let us overlook the need for routine work, repetition, and revision in the course of the Project. There is always danger in Activity Methods, and this is one—that things are done haphazardly. Effective and efficient work often means drudgery, but if they see the end, children willingly persevere at the means. They will draw and re-draw, letter and re-letter, write and re-write, to get the perfect finish; and this desire is good if it is from inward urgings towards craftsmanship and perfection. It is only when ordered by the teacher that this aspect of the work becomes irksome and meaningless.

You will have realised the need for a library for this kind of work. Have handy references by you, and build up a collection of others where and when possible; use the local library—and borrow, remembering to take care of and return such books when no longer required.

A last warning—don't necessarily and habitually drag in all the subjects. If Music and Physical Training don't fit, leave them out.

There is no doubt that the Project does help children to develop their imagination; it gives them a sense of the purpose of life; it helps them to overcome difficulties and to learn to concentrate until the purpose is achieved; it exercises their sense of social and community liabilities as their personal resources develop. What a tremendous work may be done in the Religious Knowledge Project when these powers drive spiritually, for they are the very forces at work in Christianity—the putting of service before self.

CHAPTER XVII

SCHOOL WORSHIP

The Morning Service; preparation; hymns and tunes; prayers—the Lord's
Prayer; readings; music; notices; B.B.C. Service.

THE 1944 Act requires "collective worship on the part of all pupils
in attendance at the school."

This is covered by the School Assembly or Morning Service. It is
recognised that whatever class and individual instruction may be
given in Religious Knowledge lessons, there should be a form of
corporate worship expressing outwardly and publicly the beliefs
inculcated in our boys and girls. The essential aspect of our educational system is that it is Christian, and this religious element needs
vitalising and even publicising.

For too many children the Morning Service is the only form of
collective worship they know, for neither they nor their parents ever
go to church. It is as well, then, that we make this act of worship
spiritually valuable. We cannot afford to neglect or blast the tender
shoots of religion in our children by cold, dull, haphazard attempts
at worship.

One of the greatest enemies of the School Service is boredom.
Boredom arises from lack of appeal and satisfaction, and quickly
begets inattention. All aspects of our Service must therefore be
within the scope of the children, and as far as possible nothing
should happen that might create the feeling of sameness and monotony. In a word—the letter of the Act must not usurp the spirit of
the act. Only thus can we meet the challenge of the indifference
and paganism of the twentieth century.

A warning against the dangers of casualness was given by the
Scottish Commission as long ago as 1932, when it said:

"the common practice of assembling schools for morning prayers
is one which deserves careful attention. If this is purely a formal
occasion, consisting of a short hymn and hurried prayers followed
by items of school business, its influence may be positively harmful."

In other words, the Morning Service must never become a ceremony for beginning the day, as ordinary and innocuous an effort as clocking-in or opening the shop. It must indeed be, in the words of the 1944 Act:

"not merely an opening ceremony, but a preparation for the day, the influence of which will be felt throughout the day."

Hence the need for honest and painstaking and prayerful preparation on the part of the headmaster and teachers responsible for the Service. Children quickly see through falseness and insincerity, never more so than in the School Service, where we are catering for young, critical, sensitive minds. Can we afford to offer less than the best?

Accepting these principles, we turn to the practical aspects of the Service. It is obvious that the hall shortly to be used for Physical Training, Dancing, Singing—and in these days of overcrowding even as an extra classroom—for fifteen minutes or so must somehow be made a place in which the children there assembled may feel the very presence of God. It has to become a church, a holy place, despite the noise of traffic outside and the cramped conditions within.

We cannot control the traffic outside, but we can do something about the movement of the children into the hall. There should be quietness. The accompaniment of suitable music helps to create the reverent atmosphere aimed at, and the presence of flowers pleasantly adds to it.

Staff should not line themselves along the wall merely as policemen; the watchful eye destroys whatever illusion of reverence may have been provoked. The power of suggestion is strong, and the child whose eyes happen to wander to a teacher bent in reverent posture will respond much more quickly and thoughtfully than one who receives an angry frown or an ugly gesture. Besides which, for the staff to join in the Service as members of the school strengthens the sense of corporateness in the worship.

There are schools where "the service gives a teacher time to do some marking." Surely there should be ample time in a well-organised time-table for marking apart from this period which we ought to consider one of the most—if not *the* most—important of the day. Is not the teacher, too, the better for the day's preparation?

Quietness and reverence of entry and positioning, then; and likewise, for the exit, which can be brightened by a rhythmic accompaniment on the piano or gramophone.

The Service

What of the Service itself? It should bear the hall-marks of taste and discrimination. In the first place, we must avoid anything that smacks of haste and lack of preparation. There should be a reason for everything said and everything done, and a reason thought out a long time before the actual service.

Nothing ruins the atmosphere of worship more surely than scrappiness, undue rushing and slipshod handling. What should we think of a minister who stopped to discuss a tune with the organist, or who allowed a substitute to blunder hopelessly through the reading of the Scriptures? Then why in school? It does happen, alas; and when it does it blunts all sense of receptivity the children possess into something somewhat akin to disgust.

This means preparation a long way ahead. There should be a Calendar of Services for at least half a term in advance, put in a place where the children can see it. It should indicate the Themes and Topics for successive weeks, and the Daily Thought relevant to the Theme. Also it should show the passages to be read, the class responsible for the reader and the hymns. If a tune is to be changed or selected later, the new tune should be noted at least for the pianist —and not after the hymn has been announced! Check verses against new tunes, as they do not necessarily fit in actual rhythm or length; thus, a hymn of five four-lined verses cannot be sung to an eight-lined tune.

Here is an example of a Calendar week:

Theme for the Week: Happiness.

Date	Thought	Reading	Class	Hymn
June 25	Joy of Living	Ps. xcvi. 12–17	4A	223
„ 26	Joy of Beauty	Ps. xc. 1–9	2B	14
„ 27	Joy of Sight	Mark viii. 22–25	1D	11
„ 28	Joy of Music	1 Sam. xvi. 15–18, 22, 23	3C	10
„ 29	B.B.C. Morning Service.			

Each Service is a unity within a larger Unity of Thought. Themes should cover an extensive field of Christian Worship, and need never be so often repeated as to become dull by repetition. There are available nowadays many books of Themes and Services, and new ones are constantly appearing. Once the theme is chosen, the readings and hymns will centre in the subject, too. To select, match and fit— in other words, to prepare a consistent unity—is tiring and often sheer hard work. Only those who have had this duty to perform know just how tiring it can be. None of the books of Worship and School Services seems quite to fit, excellent though they are; there is always adapting, scrapping, editing—all worthy work, the results justifying the toil. Like so many anthologies, none entirely suits; the answer is prepare one's own. This might be a useful Fifth Form Project.

We have spoken rather glibly of selecting. What and how do you choose and weave into the Service? What do you consider in choosing hymn, prayer and reading? Why this hymn and not that? Why this prayer and not that collect? Why this for one department, that for another? Why this version and not that for the reading? Why this poem and not that parable? Countless questions. Let us try to find some practical guidance on these matters, and take each section in turn.

Hymns and Tunes

Most schools use particular hymn-books. Like good dictionaries, these are often either in short supply or are in poor condition. We ought not to expect our children to enjoy the singing part of Morning Service if they have to share one amongst four because of shortage or "because that page is lost, sir." If in no other way, this may be partly rectified by having class anthologies of specially selected hymns; included in such copies could be a number of hymns not in the hymn-book, of recognised quality and literary worth.

Quite often, the theme may be illustrated equally well by any one of four or five hymns. This allows for variety and avoids the over-use of the same hymn. But it is equally certain that another theme can be matched only by the very hymn you have already chosen. In early preparation this difficulty may be met by matching the only hymn and selecting another for the more general case.

Some hymns are much too long. Many people refuse to cut verses, but surely, if children enjoy a hymn because it is the right length with the cut when they would be bored with having to plough through extra verses without it, the cutting is worth while. Obviously, the omissions must not break the continuity of thought in the hymn; a good way of shortening a hymn is to read the first verse (or verses) effectively, and then continue singing the rest.

It is not beyond the powers of children to re-write a hymn, or to modernise it by revising the wording. Archaic words and phrases, e.g. "Thy unction grace bestoweth," "Thou Holy Paraclete," "and portion evermore," "a temple meet for Thee," must be explained. Inverted sentences, e.g. "be darkness at Thy coming, light," "pent be each warring breeze," "whose canopy, space" often cause confusion. Phrases relating to Biblical background can be made real by reference to customs and manners of the times. Thus, "gird up your loins," referring to the tying of a robe or cloak around the waist for ease of movement, may have a new meaning for children who have sung it for months without knowing what it meant. It is a good plan to go through hymns that have been known for some time, to find out if there are any parts, even words, that create misapprehension.

Tunes make for controversy. When someone says, "My favourite hymn is . . ." or "I like . . ." what he usually means is that he likes the tune. On rare occasions he may indicate that he means the words. But more often than not, hymns gain popularity through their setting; there is frequently an outcry when a familiar hymn is suddenly put to another tune. See to the setting of the hymns, then. Many hymns are faulty both in language and setting; some may be remedied in literary quality; many more may be improved by being sung to better tunes. In some hymn-books there are still legacies of the lugubrious writers who in past decades won over our fathers by the sickly viscosity of their melodies. It is time we broke away from these and followed the lead of Vaughan Williams and Parry, Shaw and Dearmer, and benefited from the virility and strength of their settings. True, some of these latter are already adopted and even familiar; that is all to the good.

We should beware of advocating modern tunes merely because they are new, and of discarding altogether the old ones. We are probably too fond of many of the tunes of our youth to recommend wholesale exclusion. But there should be discrimination. Let us wean our boys and girls from weak, treacly tunes, and rear them on those that are vital and crystal and clean. Very often the B.B.C.

uses a new tune that appeals even at the first hearing. Get it and teach it. The time for teaching is in the Music lesson, not during Religious Knowledge lessons or Morning Service; but a full rehearsal can be held at the Service before the tune is actually used for a hymn to be sung later in the term.

Folk-tunes and secular airs are sometimes used for hymns. Some people have yet to be completely converted to the general use of these, but probably admit liking the Londonderry Air for "O Son of Man." It is an interesting experiment, where a hymn is known by more than one setting, to put to the vote the tune preferred.

Descants add to the pleasure of hymn-singing, very often from the sheer sense of competition presented by the two parts. The musical beauty of such additions to a setting should be brought to the notice of the children. Variation may also be made, especially in long hymns, by having verses sung unaccompanied, by boys only, girls only, this class and that class, choir and school, solo and school, and so on. When a hymn has an historical significance in tune or content, this should be indicated clearly, e.g. Bunyan's "Pilgrim's Song," and many of Wesley's hymns. Those related to familiar Psalms can also be mentioned, e.g. Ps. xxiii and "The King of Love."

Although we look for a high standard of hymn-singing, it is possible to spoil the spontaneity of praise if we are over-pernickety about it. It is rare that a school of three hundred and fifty children sing out of tune; if they do, the reason is usually physical—lack of room, poor ventilation, wrong tempo, hasty breathing, slovenly stance; correct these and the standard is improved. Children should, in any case, be reminded that their singing is an act of praise and worship, and only the best in voice and song should be offered to God.

One of the problems of hymn-singing for many Secondary Schools is the increasing number of boys whose voices are changing. A good music teacher will give a basso profundo harmony to several well-known tunes that will give them tremendous pleasure in singing, and add harmoniously to the general effect. The psychological value of this provision for the encouragement of these lads is obvious. An occasional quiet whistling for these, too, especially for tunes of a martial character, like "Marching" for "Through the night . . ." proves well worth while. Verses of other hymns could also be given to a hummed background. We should aim at preventing these lads from feeling that they are out of it because they cannot sing any more. They should be helped to feel that they still belong to the Service—and the school, and must be brought in at all costs. It is all the more imperative when we realise that within a very short while they will be leaving; it would be wrong for them to do so feeling that they were already unwanted in things of the spirit.

A somewhat daring innovation, but one that may be tried, is the singing of some tunes as rounds or canons. "Glory to Thee" (Tallis) is such a tune. Some schools try jazz and "pop" tunes.

A final word of warning. We are conservative folk, and our churches still tend to keep to traditional hymns and tunes. We should beware of spending so much time on new hymns and tunes that we forget the old ones. That would be a great pity, for our children would be sadly disappointed on going to church to find that they didn't know the hymns; we shall have done more harm than good, for familiarity with the tunes makes for enjoyment, and if we don't enjoy a church service we are not likely to go again. Besides which, it is our duty to teach children the fine old hymns that have stood the test of time and usage, even if their full import is not always understood until our children have become men and women. It is not our business, perhaps, to fill the churches, but we certainly must not be guilty of helping to empty them.

Prayers

Much of what has been said about hymns and tunes applies to the prayers. Let us get rid of any that savour of false piety; let us be certain that the wording of those we use is within the mental grasp of the children, that they are pleasantly phrased and of high literary quality. Prayers should be free from archaisms and clumsy inversions; they should be the vehicles of simple, beautiful thoughts in simple beautiful language. These thoughts should be of the Father God, of adoration, thanks, forgiveness, courage; thoughts related to life, home, school, work and play; thoughts of friends and enemies, old scholars, new-comers; thoughts of others a little more distant—of the Queen, Parliament, judges, doctors, miners, factory workers, newsmen, writers, musicians; thoughts that bring a sense of reality to children because they are of people and things of their own environment and experience.

Children should be helped to see that prayers are not means of pleasing God, nor are they the pennies that work a kind of beneficent slot-machine; prayers are rather the acts of filling the mind with the thoughts of Him by which we can best live.

Prayers should not be long and wearisome or monotonously the same. At all times they should be spoken slowly and quietly and pleasantly, so that their meaning is registered by the listening child. Many should be of the sharing type in which the children have set sentences such as, "We thank Thee, O Lord," at given intervals. Phrases like "We beseech Thee to hear us" should be explained. "Let our cry come unto Thee" has been known to mystify a child into remarking that he isn't crying—and has he got to?

Where prayers and collects are used because of their applicability and acknowledged beauty of language and phrasing, great care should be taken to explain precisely their meaning and why they are used at all. "Prevent us, O Lord" and "Suffer us" occur in these and startle the thoughtful child. Other phrases occurring in formal prayers are: "catholic church," "apostolick," "remission of sins." Even the word "church" itself is not necessarily clear to all children, some of whom regard it as meaning the building down the road or at least their own particular church. These types of prayer obviously need pruning and free paraphrasing; none of them should be used so often as to become over-familiar and unattractive. An occasional adult prayer of the Church Universal should be used, however, to make it familiar if for no other reason; such a prayer is the General Thanksgiving, which all children should learn by heart.

Silence and reverence are essential. Children may be encouraged in both by the introduction of moments of silence and the use of silent prayer. The use of special prayers such as:

"God is among us; let us keep silence"

or,

"We have much to tell Thee; help us to speak;
Thou hast much to tell us; help us to listen"

followed by a pause, is most effective. All pauses should be brief; children fidget quickly.

A verse of a hymn is often a prayer in itself, e.g. "Breathe on me, breath of God . . . ," and can be used as a prayer.

Prayers for children for the most part need directness and robustness, but there is always room for a short interpolation of more delicate phraseology and spiritual thought that a sensitive child will seize upon gratefully; we should not overlook the individual in the mass.

There is no doubt that children need guidance in prayer—what it is and how to approach it. It involves a technique as do all arts, and prayer is certainly an art. Getting to *know about* God indirectly, through study of the Bible, nature, discussion and so on, is fine as far as it goes, but we have not put children in rapport with God Himself unless and until we have shown them that they have yet to get to *know* Him. Just as we never know our friends except by converse with them, so we can never know God except by direct approach and personal contact through conversation. When we do, we find we want nothing more than to worship Him and to serve Him, and prayer reveals to us how we can do that with His help and promises. This is what we have to teach our children; they should be helped to see that there are prayers of worship and praise, of thanks, of admitting wrongs and asking for forgiveness, of trust for care and deliverance, of pleading for others before asking for ourselves, and of saying nothing at all, but just waiting for the inspiration of God.

I am indebted to a late member of my staff for the following notes on her class lessons in Prayer; these notes are entered into the children's Religious Knowledge note-books, too, for their future use and reminding.

Prayer is

Talking to God.

Listening to God.

We can do this anywhere and at any time, but we all need special times for prayer.

We can use the prayers of other people or we can use our own prayers.

"Speak, Lord, for Thy servant heareth" (1 Sam. ii. 9.).

Talking to God.

Thanking Him.

For all the ordinary things He gives us every day.
For special things.

Ordinary things
>   Nature.
>   Homes and relations.
>   Food and water.

Special things
>   Health and strength.
>   Jesus and His love.
>   The Church (explained).

> "All good gifts around us
>   Are sent from Heaven above,
> Then thank the Lord, O thank the Lord,
>   For all His love."

> Thanks be to God for His unspeakable gift (explained).

How to get ready to pray
>   Say a verse of a hymn praising God because He is so wonderful and kind and loving.
>   Think about a lovely picture of Jesus or about something He did.
>   Then remember that our Father is just like Jesus.
>   Try to think of Him as very near.
>   Remember that the more we pray the *easier* it will become.

Telling God about the wrong things we have done
>   This is something like spring-cleaning.
>   We ask God to make us feel sorry.
>   We ask Him to forgive us.

My prayer (child to make up and enter his own)
>   Please forgive us this day
>   For all the wrong things we have done
>   And all the sins we have forgotten.

Praying for other people
>   1. Our parents.
>   2. Our friends.
>   3. Those who are ill, crippled or in any kind of trouble.
>   4. Those who work for us.
>   5. The Queen and statesmen.
>   6. Missionaries and people who live in other lands.
>   7. Doctors and nurses.

"Prayer is like a mat on which we bring other people to Jesus."

Praying for ourselves

That God will show us what He wants us to do, and help us to do it.

For anything we want, or help we need—but we must always remember to say, "if it is best for us."

God always answers even though He says "No."
(Explain, with examples.)

Listening to God

Leave a little time in which to be quite quiet.

God will show us what we have done wrong.

He will make us strong to do right.

He will tell us what He wants us to do for Him.

A Selection of Original Prayers

We thank Thee, O Lord, for all the wonderful things Thou hast given us, for our homes and friends, school, and play, and all things Thou hast made.

We thank Thee especially for sending Jesus to us, and for all Thy great love.

We pray for all people who live in far-off lands who have never heard the name of Jesus.

We remember all the missionaries, doctors and nurses who go to other lands to heal the sick and teach the people.

We pray this in the name of Jesus Christ our Lord. Amen.

A Prayer by Peter and John

Help us, good Lord, all the day,
And give us power to help others;
Keep near to our hearts, good Lord,
And help us all our lives,
Through Jesus Christ our Lord. Amen.

O God, please make us have courage to go out into the street where all those wild men are. God, please do not let us be scared, for Jesus Christ, our Lord.

O Lord, give us courage to do what you want, so we are not afraid to die, because we do Thy will.

O Lord, do what you will with us, for we trust in Thee.

O Lord, give me courage so that I may say the words Thou hast taught me, to fight without fear, and to make my enemies friends.

Please God make us brave enough to go out and face that crowd of people and talk to them in many ways so that they do not come on us as angry people.

Without further comment, let me add this quaintly real prayer of thanks.

> We have received beef, tongues, and tea,
> And certainly from none but Thee;
> Therefore with all our power of songs,
> Thanks for the beef, and tea, and tongues.

Needless to say, all prayers prepared by the children are considered for inclusion in the Morning Service; the children usually prefer that the Leader of the Service speaks the prayer, and all prayers are anonymous.

The Lord's Prayer

Whole books have been written on the Lord's Prayer both for schools and for churches. But special mention of it must be made in this chapter.

We know only too well how easily it becomes a mere meaningless mechanical repetition. Most dull children, and not a few of the brightest, have notorious variations in their personal versions of the prayer. "Harold be Thy name" is not entirely apocryphal. It is up to us to make sure that the Lord's Prayer is meaningful for all age ranges and types. Every child should be word perfect; it is not enough to accept that he is, we must see that he is.

Children must regard the Lord's Prayer as the family prayer and as a challenging prayer. Jesus said, "Our Father," not "My Father"; and to underline the ideal of brotherhood each line implies, each phrase needs to be illustrated with stories and readings both Biblical and secular. Lives of missionaries and great reformers are especially useful. Aggrey, Williams, Slessor, Xavier, Morrison . . . they speak for themselves, for others and for us. A very valuable book with

PLATE XI

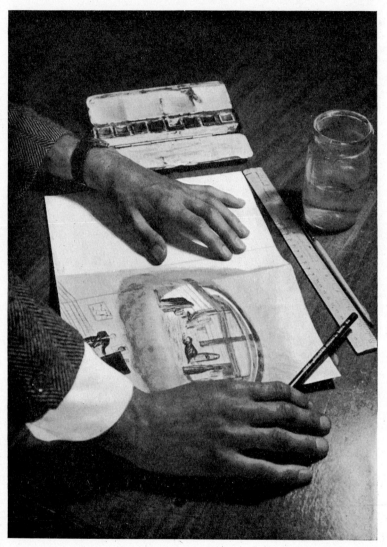

Expression work—Book Jacket. B stream.

PLATE XII

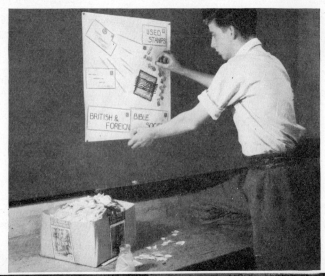

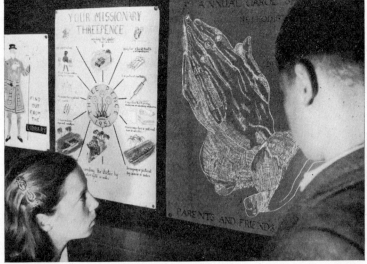

Examples of Posters for display in School and Church.   All streams.

this approach is Vera Walker's *Paternoster Tales* (S.P.C.K.), containing true stories of men and women whose lives illustrate the clauses of the Lord's Prayer.

Look up with the children the two versions in Matt. vi. 9–13 and Luke xi. 2–4. Note their differences (possibly due to the fact that Jesus gave the prayer on two separate occasions), and remind the children that the preference for Matthew's version dates from earliest times, when it was "the prayer of the faithful." We know that they said it three times a day, so wonderfully new it was to them—so new and so daring that it was only after sincere, prayerful thought that these early Christians even voiced it. It was far from routine then; how near to casual repetition it is now.

Understanding it better, children will say it better. They will need guidance on phrasing, e.g. "forgive . . . as . . . forgive . . ." without the pause before the "as"; help must be given in matters like tempo, gradation of expression, rise and fall of voice. There must be agreement if several teachers are training their own classes, and even full-scale practices to attain the required standard of speech, understanding, tempo and expression. There should be no departure from that standard at any time. Variation may be introduced sometimes by singing the Lord's Prayer to a monotone, a simple melody, or with a choir, a more elaborate setting; it should also be spoken inwardly as silent prayer, or voiced individually, in groups or in unison. These variations should be rare, but often enough to make the children aware of the need for perfection in speaking the Family Prayer.

Readings

It seems almost unnecessary to stress the importance of ensuring that the readings—Biblical or secular—should be within the powers of appreciation of our children, although of the highest quality we can select. Of course, in a full assembly there will be tremendous gulfs between mental, spiritual and even physical capacities, but some kind of yardstick must be considered when the readings are being chosen.

For the most part they should be dramatic, direct and simple, though not to the complete exclusion of less easily understood passages of spiritual depth. Stories, parables, Old and New Testament incidents for the greater part appeal to all children, whilst a leavening of Pauline precepts (in a modernised version for clarity) and prophetic writings both vary and strengthen the Service.

There is a welcome tendency to introduce secular readings more often, and most recent publications of Services for Schools in book and anthology form contain many secular readings as a matter of course. Excerpts from *Pilgrim's Progress*, poems of Studdert-Kennedy and Masefield, plays of Shaw and Shakespeare, all make vital contributions, especially when chosen to underline the Theme or Thought of the Service.

The reading is one part of Morning Service in which children really can share. Whilst it is possible for them to take prayers, they are not really happy, for the act of public prayer is a difficult one. Not that public reading is much easier, but it does lend itself to practice in a way that prayer does not. Practised the reading must be. Even poor readers can be coached in a short, simple reading, and so be given the opportunity of sharing. Prefects should take part, not merely as a duty, and members of the staff will take their turn if they so wish.

The opportunity to read in the School Service should be reserved as a real privilege, and not the least point to remember is the noting of good readers for future special occasions, like the Service on Parents' Day, Prize Day and so on.

In selecting the readings, you should give thought to its mode of rendering. It may lend itself to a variety of forms—direct narrative, dramatic reading with several voices, choral speaking in unison or in parts. If so, the most effective method should be used. Now and again it is possible to give a modified paraphrase of an incident, leaving the children to guess the names of the characters. Sometimes a short incident in the Bible story may be paralleled with one from the life of a missionary or Christian martyr. A poem written by a pupil makes for great interest and effect. Don't overlook the emotional value of having the whole school say in unison such pieces as Ps. xxiii or cxxi.

Another point to bear in mind with regard to the selection of readings is the use of various versions and translations. The Authorised Version should be used whenever the rhythmic beauty of the language is essential to the thought of the passage, provided it is also clear in meaning. Sometimes a selection is clearer in the Revised Version, whilst the use of versions by Moffat, Knox, Weymouth and Phillips make many rough places plain for the children. A reading of a familiar story from the Basic English version is effective, and the New American R.S.V. and the New English Bible are useful, too. Many teachers will welcome the Plain English translation of the New Testament, by Williams.

Scriptures familiar to us may be quite meaningless and dull to the children, for the very simple reason that they are often chosen from our own point of view. It is salutary on occasion to ask oneself: "Now, what does this word or that phrase mean to Bill Smith? Has he the faintest idea what it is all about?" The attempt to answer that will help you to decide the source of a reading, as well as to go to the trouble of clarifying the parts most likely to frustrate Bill Smith.

There is often an opportunity to introduce a humorous reading, if only to let the children see that there is room for humour in a Christian life; they see so many so-called Christians with expressions like the frontispiece to Lamentations, that it comes as a shock to realise that Christ Himself had a good laugh at the expense of some of His hearers. Isn't there something exquisitely funny about the struggle to haul a camel through a needle's eye? A whole service may be given to humour, and involve whimsical readings, Biblical and non-Biblical anecdotes, and even humorous music.

Music

We have already referred to music in school worship. There is no doubt that its use is essential to the smoothness and pleasantness of the Service.

Apart from attention to hymn-tunes, care should be given to the selection of voluntaries and incidental music. A rhythmic piece for entry to the hall should give place to a few bars of a rather more restful type to introduce the mood and atmosphere of worship. This is usually on the piano, but records of orchestral, organ and choral music should often be used; choir and solo items are always eagerly —and critically—welcomed by the children. What more moving moments in an Easter Service than the Bach Chorale "O Sacred Head . . . ," followed by the triumphant "I know that my Redeemer liveth!" It is even possible to include an original setting of a hymn or verse made by one of the children.

An individual performer as vocalist or pianist is reasonably possible, but music by an indifferent violinist is rather unwise. The school orchestra, if there is one, should at least occasionally accompany the singing or play a piece within its capacity.

Following the Benediction, the pianist should play quietly a few bars to sustain final meditation, then lead into a strongly rhythmic march for general exit. If there are notices, the quiet music will indicate the end of the Service, and after the notices the brighter music will imply the exit.

Notices

These are necessary evils more often than not, especially when the Morning Service is the only time the children can be brought together, except by cutting across the time-table. They should come at the beginning of the Service, though occasionally announcements at the end are effective. Reference to courtesy, manners, positive rules, matters that affect school tone and tradition are of great value, but this is not the time for acrimonious wiggings and sarcastic criticisms of behaviour; reading the riot act is a waste of time usually, but it is surprising on how many occasions one still finds this procedure almost part of the Morning Service!

Matters of discipline can so well be approached from the angles of outside opinion and school tradition; that certain things are "not done" for the reason that boys and girls are preparing to be citizens and at best Christian citizens seems to be the best attitude to take. It is a long-term policy, of course, but will more likely succeed as a form of training than hundreds of riot acts. There are, unfortunately, even in the best of schools, those occasions when a culprit has to be dealt with severely and publicly for some misdemeanour; but surely the end of the Morning Service is the wrong time to do so. It is much more effective to call a full assembly for that specific purpose.

B.B.C. Service for Schools

This is of very great value to all schools, and where possible the series should be taken throughout the term, especially as a Theme is usually worked out during that time. The Service makes a definite change from the normal School Service, and creates an atmosphere peculiarly its own. The dramatic nature of the weekly interludes is appreciated by all ages, and may set an example, too, for their own efforts in the writing of radio scripts.

The *Radio Times* gives details of the Service well in advance. The subject and thought should be put on the notice board or a blackboard in the hall, clearly enough to be seen. It is important to check hymns, verses and tunes, and to indicate on the blackboard any alterations and variations as compared with the school hymn-book. Try to provide the children—at least one between two—with the Special Prayers used in these Services; with these, the school joins in corporate prayer with children throughout the country. Now and again you will find used a hymn that is not in the school hymn-book. Make a note of it (for the particular Service it will have to be put on a blackboard for the children to read and sing); when two or three of these are noted, provide them for general school use. The B.B.C. are sure to use them again.

The school should be ready for the opening bars of the introductory music; this is always announced and should be noted on the board. There is absolutely no need for the leader to speak during the Service; he should listen with the children who will learn from the Service sequence just when to sit, stand, join in prayer and sing. At the end of the Service all should wait quietly until the final bars of the postlude have faded, and then file equally quietly to their classrooms.

One important point is too often overlooked in these Services—the reception. The set may be a poor one, but even more often is a good set badly tuned. The result is harsh and discordant; the children without knowing why become fidgety and disinterested. Reception must do justice to the fine work being done by the B.B.C. for the schools.

If the school hymn-book includes complete Services for Daily Use, these make happy variations from the usual Service, with sung chants and responses as well. The inclusion of these must be taken into account in that early preparation considered at the beginning of this chapter.

Where there is opportunity of having a Service at the end of school-time, there is equally wide scope for themes and types of Service as outlined above. Some schools make a practice of ending with an act of worship when it is difficult for all sorts of reasons to open the day with one.

Summing up

Most of the aspects of Morning Service have been covered from a very practical point of view. Much of what has been said may seem to be either unnecessary or advanced; if it has made you think that much, all to the good, for many of our School Services are still below the standard we ought to reach. The key is preparation, there is no doubt about that. Patience in this, in modifying, adapting, adopting new ideas without discarding the old ones that have proved good, always approaching school worship from the angle of the child—these attitudes of mind will serve us all in good stead, and help us to make a Morning Service that will be "not merely an opening ceremony" but will be assuredly a daily preparation "the influence of which will be felt throughout the day."

Scraperboard: "That peace which the world cannot give."
By a boy aged thirteen.

CHAPTER XVIII

AIDS AND ACTIVITIES

General principles; blackboard; pictures; friezes; murals; maps; posters; diagrams; episcopes; films and filmstrips; slides; models; charts; notebooks; news-board; flannelgraph; miscellaneous forms of expression; library; broadcasting; television.

"WE shall be missing the greatest chance we ever had of making Education a living thing unless we take the fullest advantage of the new medium of visual aids." The Parliamentary Secretary to the Ministry of Education makes this comment, and in so doing points the value of aids and activities in the classroom. Not that there is anything new in the medium; visual aids have been used as methods of teaching for many moons. What is of more concern is that these same aids should be allied to principles recognised as essential to educational progress, and their full value thereby obtained. As the Minister of Education has recommended, in Administrative Memorandum No. 367, "there should be a progressive development of the use of Visual Aids in Education."

The accent is on "progressive development," which can come only if the aids themselves are understood for what they are and are used intelligently and educationally.

In this chapter, then, we shall consider all the aids possible, regardless of whether they are adjuncts to or bases for our lessons.

Much has been said in recent years about aids—visual and otherwise—and we are all very much aware of the fact that teaching is extremely barren without them.

On the other hand, there is too often a tendency to use aids merely as ends in themselves, so that lessons pass into periods of craft and entertainment. This is probably most noticeable in the film and filmstrip lessons, mainly because of the pressure of the hire time-limit factor, which results in an enforced use of the material whether or not it is immediately applicable. Besides this, there is sometimes the case where one teacher makes use of films hired by another on the ground—"we might as well show it now we've got it." It is a poor sort of economy that discounts so casually the educational value of an aid.

This is obviously wrong; there should be a more rational and restrained use of all material and aids in general. Use them—but use them discriminately. Use them for what they were intended—as aids. Ask what the aids are meant to do; see them for what they are—second-hand, even third-hand experience of first-hand ideas. And when using them be sure that they really are suitable for the class you are teaching.

Then, as far as is possible, take care that the children see what you want them to see. The displaying of an aid does not necessarily mean that they grasp its significance. You want them to see it with understanding, so, knowing how the aid is going to help, point out, question, draw their attention, direct their interest, and thereby relate it to the subject-matter of the lesson. Only in this way is the aid of any use at all, and unless its purpose is defined it is a waste of time having it there. Remember, too, that an aid made by the children is often of far greater value than one specially provided for them; so don't begrudge the time taken to make it—*if* it is going to be an *aid* in the pedagogical sense of the word.

This means that there is always need of a supply of materials and tools. Be a hoarder, but see that this does not lead to a collection of mere junk to lumber the cupboards. Tins, boxes, string, coloured paper, pieces of cloth, glue, paste, plasticine, scissors, knives, folders for pictures, box files, old Bibles . . . keep these in a store cupboard, and keep the place tidy and clean at all times.

Many aids are also activities. Even a visual aid like a picture involves activity—mental activity—in the interpretation of it. But we shall not attempt a distinction other than to try to consider first the more obvious aids. Over 80 per cent. of these are for the eye; let us remember that the best visual aid in manners, bearing, belief and Christian attitude towards life is—the teacher.

(a) Blackboard

Sadly neglected in these days, and badly, too, is the blackboard. Chalk and talk teaching has been discarded, much of it rightly so, but the talk has come back without the chalk—and that is worse. Use your blackboard. Write on it the names of disciples and prophets and martyrs, dates and sects and countries. Draw rapid sketches of Palestine, the Fertile Crescent, the Eastern Mediterranean. Use plenty of colour—brown for hills, green for valleys, blue for rivers, yellow dots for towns. Illustrate with fishing-boats, pennants, tents. You don't have to be an artist; wholesome fun at your crude drawings may be a happy means of fixing facts, especially with the friendly challenge of "you do a better one."

Some teachers may find it helpful to draw their pictures on paper first; others put faint dots on the board before the lesson and join these as and when necessary. There are plenty of simple books available to the keen teacher, for guidance on blackboard drawing—*Black-Board Drawing* and *More Black-Board Drawing* by Higham, and *Black-Board Self-teaching for Teachers*, by Peake, both published N.S.S.U., are good, as is Whanslaw's *Drawing Bible Pictures* (R.E.P.).

Blackboard summaries of lessons used to be an essential part of a successful lesson, and were once expected in all College Lecture Notes. They were invaluable for revision and recapitulation of facts. Don't forget your blackboard!

(b) Pictures and Photographs

Get into the habit of collecting pictures; the class will gladly help, and organise a committee to handle and file them until applicable to a lesson. Most sources are obvious, but do not overlook church magazines, *Studio, Life*, the daily papers, *TV Times* and *Radio Times*.

The various firms advertising pictures for Religious Knowledge lessons will submit specimens, and the Institute of Christian Education have an excellent List of Pictures for the guidance of the teacher.

Choose all pictures as works of art; use nothing shoddy, sentimental or sickly in subject-matter or portrayal. See that the costumes depicted are genuine and that the background is accurate. Make sure that these and copies of the masters are discussed and understood. Explain the halo in classic pictures and the stylised approach of the painters. It is good to introduce as a complete contrast works of art by artists of other countries, e.g. those illustrating the *Life of Christ, Parables* and *Son of Man* by Chinese artists, published by the S.P.G. It is strange to Western eyes to see Jesus with Chinese features.

It is not enough to mount pictures and merely to fix them around the room. Arrange them pleasantly; small ones, with the Biblical context shown, should be mounted on large sheets of paper or framed in brown cardboard. Don't let them hang so long that they fade and curl and collect dust; a top flap will keep off quite a lot of dust. Change them often enough to prevent the familiarity that breeds indifference. File them away for future use under headings such as—Country, Parables, Old Testament Stories, Missionaries, Great Men and Women. . . . Some of the more connected pictures can be inserted in an album, suitably covered and designed, as a class or individual collection. This might be lent to the library for others to browse through.

Before disposing of worn and torn pictures, see if they contain characters or background that can be cut away and backed for model work or the flannelgraph.

Interesting and colourful pictures can be made by layering. The cut-away pieces are pasted over one another to produce a raised effect that may be enhanced by the addition of further cut-out animals and people.

Remember it is a Christian attribute to take care of and return promptly and neatly all loaned pictures and photographs; much indirect training in respect for the property of others, in taste and thought, may be given to the children by your own attitude towards borrowed and expensive materials.

One of the biggest temptations is to show an illustration merely because you have it. More often than not it bears no relation whatever to the scheme and is actually of little value, as the children have insufficient background to bring to bear upon it. If you must use it, it may be worth adjusting your syllabus enough to take it in or make a special lesson for it. Otherwise, file it and use it at a more suitable time.

(c) Friezes

When a number of pictures and photographs have accumulated it is often possible to arrange them into series or sequences along the wall of the room. They should be fixed in definite patterns— Parables, Stories of Jesus, Old Testament Heroes, Martyrs through the Ages, Great Hymn Writers, Churches in Other Lands and so on. The children should be encouraged to decorate the frieze framework, and Bible references should be looked up and inserted. For C and D classes verses of carols may be lettered and illustrated in series; many of these are suitable for miming exercises. A frieze prepared in an upper class could be loaned to another for a special series of lessons or as encouragement to efforts by that class to produce something similar. Interesting friezes can be made from the children's own drawings and maps. Some excellent guidance on India, China, Palestine, Africa and the South Seas is found in *Frieze Painting Books* (E.H.P.).

(d) Murals

This is an extension of the frieze idea; permanent murals should be possible. They should be designed and prepared carefully before actual application; they can then be fixed on the wall or, preferably, painted direct, especially if the room is the accepted Religious Knowledge room. Poster colours are most effective, and are easily removable if and when necessary to change the murals. The worst mural could not be uglier than the bare walls of some classrooms—which is a very good reason why painted murals should be tried! An interesting change is made by adapting the montage mural, in which parts of the mural are superimposed on the painting, e.g. a fishing-net from a piece of tennis-netting, cut-out leaves of trees, etc.

(e) Maps

Indispensable for good background teaching as maps are, it is amazing how neglected they are. Good maps of the Ancient World, of Paul's World, Palestine in the Time of Jesus are essential, not only detailed but also as outlines for classroom use, if teaching is to be effective.

Even the inevitable Missionary Journeys are useless without maps, and Palestine becomes much more understandable if geographical details are shown of places Jesus visited—the Jordan Valley, the Hill Country and showing how a man travelled from Jerusalem *down* to Jericho.

Obviously, coastlines of this area are so simple that even children can draw full-size maps for their own and the teacher's use. Class Bible Atlases, such as those of Philips, or the Westminster Bible Atlas are invaluable; indeed, no class should be without a copy for each child; and the library might well contain a full Westminster Atlas for reference.

There should be a good supply of blank maps of these same regions, so that children may keep their own; these should be slipped into a Commonplace-book or Record of Work done by the children; or they may be fastened together to make an individual Bible Atlas.

The main value of Map Work is to ensure familiarity with, and hence knowledge of, the location of places and events recorded in the Bible stories. If children want to complete or re-draw and colour their maps at home, encourage them to do so, and give them necessary materials to make their work smooth and interesting and their zeal joyful.

Some children may like to cover Paul's Journeys with stamps—Cyprus, Palestine, Greece, Italy; an exciting and new approach to maps may be made in this way.

(f) Posters

Use of bright colours in broad application is necessary to the value of good posters. They are silent teachers, and make cleaner impact by their simplicity and wholeness than by efforts showing finicky detail. One has only to study the effectiveness of ordinary commercial posters to see this.

Posters should illustrate Bible background either accurately or with controlled imagination. Bible subjects and themes related to religious teaching are always in evidence. Thus, we have such topics as: Christmas in Bethlehem; Christmas Today; Carol Service; The Holy Places of Jerusalem; Bible Exhibition; Oberammergau; China Today; Bible in Japan; Colporteurs; The World's Best-seller; Sunday-school and Church Anniversaries; Church Appeals; Ten Commandments; Bible Reading Groups; Nativity Play; Missionary Propaganda.

Children reveal amazing talents and individuality, but if they need guidance there are plenty of posters and artists (such as Fougasse) worth imitating.

Gummed paper of various colours may be substituted for poster-colour and paint. Simple ceramic posters can be produced by super-imposing objects and drawings to give a raised effect. Silhouettes give clarity and are startling in effect.

(g) Diagrams

The chief danger about diagrams is making them so full of detail that their essence is hidden. Keep all diagrams simple and to the point. Bear in mind that they are formalised representations, and are often not understood by children however simple they may appear to us. Unless pains are taken to be sure that everything in the diagram is grasped and related to the lesson, it may be as meaningless to them as a machine blue-print may be to us—even after it has been explained. For most children, diagrams remain sheets of paper with lots of lines and labels!

The best diagrams, obviously, are those made by the children themselves.

Useful opportunities, however, do occur for diagram work. The plan of the Temple is possible, as is the diagrammatic representation of the Story of the Bible in Skinner's *Concerning the Bible* (Sampson Low). If figures are introduced, they should be pin-men.

Other forms of diagram are suggested in: the Derivation of the Synoptics (after a lesson on the problem), illustrations of the Massoretic Text, the Books of the Bible, the Decalogue, Service, Growth of the Church (a good form is a diagrammatic tree). One of the best examples of work to be done by children with little or no guidance beyond the references is a representation of the Hebrew Universe, dealt with more fully under the heading of Models.

Many aspects of Missionary Work, especially statistics, lend themselves to diagrammatic form. Thus, Hospitals, Religions, Birth and Death Rates in various countries, Subscriptions and so on. These should be attractive and striking to the eye, colourful. They must be accurate, too; for instance, if percentages are used, the total of the parts must make up 100 per cent. They must be up to date. The children must keep to *one* idea for each diagram, make all printing very clear and leave the diagram to speak for itself. The use of blocks, circles, signs, pin-men, formalised figures, as in commercial advertising, is recommended.

Sources of information include *Whitaker's Almanack,* the *Christian Year-book,* leaflets from the British and Foreign Bible Society, Missionary Statistics.

Good opportunities of using diagrams arise when there is a local Missionary Week or Visit; have the children's work exhibited in churches, school, shop windows—where they can be seen.

(h) Episcopes

These and related projectors are extremely useful assets to teaching. Technically, they are machines in which an arrangement of mirrors is devised to allow any pictures to be thrown on to a screen in the same way as a specially prepared lantern-slide. The value is in vivifying the ordinary picture or photograph, and there is no doubt of the attraction of the projector for children. These types are cheaper, too, than the lantern-slide projectors.

There is a loss-of-time factor to be considered in the use of this machine, but this can be assessed. The projector may be of the type that throws illustrations in books direct to a screen; this is an even more valuable form, obviously.

The epidiascope projects both pictures and lantern-slides. It has the disadvantage of being somewhat costly and cumbersome, but its great value is that it provides an illustration that the whole class can see for as long as is required by the teacher.

(i) Films and Filmstrips

The use of these aids in other subjects is familiar to most teachers. Let us beware of using them merely as entertainment. There are many firms making films and strips, but only a few of these are really worth attention from the artistic and documentary points of view. The magazine *Church and Film* will keep teachers up to date on all matters technical and otherwise concerned with films, and the *Daily Mail Visual Aid Year-book* is completely factual and helpful. As time goes on there will be more films of the Bible story; not many schools have sound projectors, but silent films serve their purpose.

It might be helpful to some teachers not possessing a great deal of technical knowledge, or uncertain of the best educational approach to the film, to indicate a few pointers on method. Be sure to get someone to explain how the machine works; a working knowledge of the projector is absolutely necessary for coping smoothly with its general use and speedily with breakages and accidents.

If you have any doubts about the actual film or if it conflicts in any way with your class teaching, *don't* show it to the children.

It always seems a great pity that the full educational value of a film should be so often lost through failure to treat its use as a real teaching method. In *Principles of Teaching Method,* Pinsent (Harrap), there is a most helpful statement of principles to be observed backed by the soundest possible practical application; the book is strongly recommended on this matter.

In any case, always endeavour to see the film yourself before it is shown to the class, so that you are familiar with its content and ready for questions and explanations, and so able to work out likely exercises based upon its showing. It is always essential to ensure that the purport of the film is clear, so that the children know exactly *why* they are seeing it and *what* they expect to see. There is a warning and true story of a country boy who attended the showing of a film of *Pilgrim's Progress*. It included scenes of Christian dropping his burdens, whilst angelic hosts sang around him. The boy told his mother he had seen a picture "about ladies with wings chasing burglars!"

The *filmstrip* is used more frequently than the film or slides, mainly because it is cheaper to make or hire, as well as lighter to handle. Learn to hold the strip by the edge, keep it free from dust, watch that the sprocket teeth engage the perforations and not the film; if you happen to damage it, repair it—it is lacking in Christian thought and courtesy to pass it on to the next user in a bad state.

Be sure to provide a good screen or paint part of a wall white. Where notes are provided, try to make these your own; amplify and modify to suit the children; don't merely read them frame for frame. Films and filmstrips of familiar stories tend to spoil the child's own mental pictures derived from the lesson in story-telling or dramatising. The best filmstrips seem to be those giving background. From a quarry of strip background it is possible to choose just those frames needed to support a lesson; show each frame sufficiently long for the children to absorb the relevant detail; much questioning may be necessary to direct observation, as for ordinary pictures. Some self-teaching may be done by setting questions on five or six selected frames depicting, e.g., occupations, customs, geographical setting, costumes, etc.

Teachers unable to obtain the filmstrip they really need often make their own. Some firms accept pictures and illustrations for uniform production, and re-issue them with teachers' notes.

Children, too, get a great deal of value, incidental teaching and even fun in making their own filmstrips. Some excellent ones have been made on the Life of Paul. One boy went so far as to build a model cinema, complete with curtains, for the showing of his story, frame by frame carefully turned on a couple of rods.

Before we leave the subject of films and filmstrips here is an account of an interesting experiment in the use of these Visual Aids as an integral part of the syllabus. I am indebted to the Religious Instruction specialist and headmaster of a Devon school for this report on the application of one of the best film series yet produced —"2,000 Years Ago," G.B. Film Division, Perivale, Middlesex.

"When a child enters the school, he is shown the excellent series of films, '2,000 Years Ago,' which forms the Introductory Course. The film 'The Home' is shown at a special Assembly of all first-year forms on the first Wednesday morning of the term. The following Wednesday the filmstrip 'The Home' is shown, with explanations by the R.I. specialist, taken both from the notes supplied with the filmstrip and his own experience. The following Wednesday the second talking film 'The Day's Work' is shown, and this is followed by the filmstrip. . . . So the whole series of films is covered, and the children given a good background for their work in R.I.

"As the main approach to R.I. in this school is dramatic, the teaching is supplemented by the children acting what they have seen. No words are used at this stage, but the scholars act the parts of father, mother, son, elder and younger daughter, and quickly become familiar with the single-roomed flat-roofed house, with its outside steps."

As the children continue to familiarise themselves with the familiar scenes of the Gospels, and the features of Jewish life are drawn and sketched as a secondary method of teaching, there is no doubt that they absorb keenly and intelligently the background against which the remainder of their schooling in Religious Knowledge will take place. This is a fine example of how two aids may be merged and made to play a striking part in the education of boys and girls. It serves to underline the plea that a film or filmstrip is never used just because there is a good film library or—even worse—to amuse; the reason for using it should fit the teaching, the time and the class.

(j) Slides

Lantern-slides fell into disrepute and disuse when movies came along. Now that our sophisticated children are so familiar with tele-

PLATE XIII

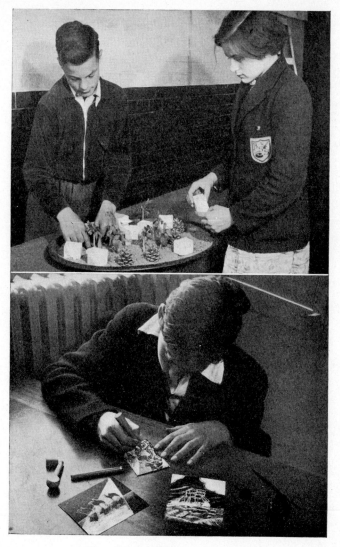

Above: Model Village.   D stream.
Below: Expression work—scraper-board.   A stream.

PLATE XIV

Above: Frieze—the Life of Paul.   A stream.
Below: Time Chart.   All streams.

PLATE XV

Model in household cement.   All streams.

PLATE XVI

Above: Activity—an A stream boy prepares a jigsaw.
Below: Activity—D stream children put it together.

vision, talkies and cinema, the magic lantern of old may appeal with a magic of its own once more. Plain black-and-white slides can be made by writing or scratching on specially prepared blanks. Coloured slides are cheap to make, they last longer than filmstrips, they can be used in any sequence, and they can be used as an adjunct to a film for further examination and discussion. Educationally, of course, they make admirable recapitulation aids, as well as being exceptionally useful as illustrations for story-telling.

Most Missionary Societies possess Lantern Slide Libraries from which excellent sets on almost any subject can be obtained. Also Newton & Co., 72, Wigmore Street, S.W.1, will help.

There is always a certain amount of anxiety in the handling of these sets of slides, probably because of their obvious fragility. Their cost is rather high, too, they are weighty for transport, and often the colouring of the actual slides leaves much to be desired. But there is no doubt that they do serve a great purpose in presenting full-length large-scale shows that are of more educational value than some smaller classroom visual aids.

Children who make their own slides can also rig up a peep-show affair from a long boot-box with one end cut out for the screen and grooves for the slides, the other end being cut for the peephole. Quite a lot of fun is obtained from such home-made affairs, but quite a deal of background knowledge is also developed.

(k) Models

There is much talk about the value of models in teaching, but little actual modelling relevant to the Religious Knowledge lesson seems to be done.

Perhaps it is because of the time it takes. Correlation with the Craft lesson helps, and there really should be more attention to this branch of visual aids. We have to be sure, of course, that the work in hand isn't merely an extra bit of handwork. Its need should arise from a lesson; children should never have to ask, "What's it for?" And don't let it be so complicated that they tire of making it. What shall we consider, then?

Few children can have any idea of the Temple, with its sections and wings and rooms for various worshippers, even from a picture. But with a fair-sized model they can see the Tabernacle, the Holy of Holies, the Women's Court and so on. They can grasp the significance of many of the Psalms and Bible stories when shown the position of the singers and worshippers and beggars at the doors.

They certainly cannot grasp the early Old Testament stories without a knowledge of how the Hebrews regarded the Universe. Their present knowledge of the world conflicts with these early notions, and until a model is before them they cannot understand what were meant by the great deep, the firmament, Sheol, etc. The Bible references—given in the *Teachers' Commentary* and quoted here— are sufficient for the brighter ones to make the model themselves, especially after a diagram has first been drawn. "The world was round and flat and supported on pillars (Job. ix. 6; 1 Sam. ii. 8; Ps. civ. 5). Over it stretched the great solid dome of the firmament held up by mountain pillars (Job xxvi. 11; xxxvii. 18). Above the firmament and under the earth was water, divided by God at the Creation (Gen. i. 6, 7; cf. Ps. xxiv. 2; cxlviii. 4). The floods came up from the 'great deep' below the earth, and the rain came through the windows in the firmament (Gen. vii. 11; viii. 2). The sun, moon, stars, moved across or were fixed in the firmament (Ps. xix. 4, 6). Within the earth lay Sheol, the realm of the dead (Num. xvi. 30‑3; Is. xiv. 9, 15)."

From the resulting model, children can see where and how the crude simplicity of the Creation Story is recognised as being less conflicting with the modern scientific view because they realise the relevance of the two degrees of knowledge. Once more, such a model serves to clarify vague and contradictory notions that are otherwise difficult to eradicate.

Models of Palestine, or selected areas like the Sea of Galilee, are extremely useful. A good physical map of Palestine is needed, and the modelling may be done with clay or pulped paper, or one of the proprietary cements now available. Remember that the Dead Sea is below sea-level, and should be the actual base of the map. The Mediterranean is higher, and the land rises from that layer. Or, perhaps you can gouge out the Dead Sea and have the Mediterranean at sea-level. Where possible, the map should be put on the floor from time to time, so that an aerial view may sometimes be obtained. Making the model on these lines gives the class a surer knowledge of contours and physical features.

Don't overload the map with details; surround it with pictures or notes of Bible incidents, and connect red threads to the spots concerned. In this way, Nazareth, Cana, Bethsaida . . . become alive with background and story.

There are several useful booklets on Bible model-making, illustrating home life—making bread, wine in bottles, mangers, beds, etc. The flat-topped squat house, with its outer staircase and walled courtyard, explains much to children about Eastern homes. It even explains why Peter did not slide off the roof when he had his vision. The interior, with its crude sleeping quarters, stove, lamps, manger, vessels, strawed earthen floor and so on, makes an extremely valuable model. *Bible Model Cut-outs* (N.S.S.U.), giving an Eastern Home, Bedouin Camp, Fishing Scene, Inn, is a useful booklet.

Simple models of tents, ploughs, sheepfolds, fishing-boats and nets appeal to children; cut-out puppet models may be dressed in Eastern costume to represent rich rulers and poor beggars and workmen in the fields.[1] A quite unusual example of model-making is the dressing of a figure representing a Roman soldier, putting on him the Armour of God as detailed in Eph. vi. 13–18.

Water-jars, skins (bottles), walls, wells, may be done in clay, cardboard or Pyruma; with pulped paper there is ample scope for cave homes, villages, Eastern tombs, rocky sheepfolds and Assyrian and Babylonian bas-reliefs.

Young children and backward Seniors enjoy making paper models of such things as fishing-boats, folds, houses, scrolls. A list of models available can be obtained from *Teachers and Taught*, 15, Devonshire Street, Bishopsgate, E.C.2. The Church Mission to the Jews, W.C.2, will loan models and genuine Eastern objects, which can be used as guides for the children's work.

Once they have been made, the more permanent models make useful introductions to future lessons. See that they do not get dusty and knocked about, of course.

In using the article already made, a change of approach is possible and a topic for both teacher and class introduced. Thus, a well scene gives an opening for several well stories, e.g. Joseph, Jacob, Moses and the Daughters of Jethro, Woman of Samaria.

---

[1] I never realised fully the precise significance of "gird up your loins" until seeing a figure in Eastern costume next to another by a plough; I then saw that the ploughman had tied his cloak round his waist to prevent it from trailing and hampering him in his work.

Many of the smaller pieces may be put together in groups representing some Biblical scene, boxed in and lit with transmitted light. When viewed through an aperture or even as set out through glass, the effect is that of a diorama, and makes an attractive model in itself. *Diorama Workbooks* (R.E.P.) are useful guides.

Sand models are often regarded as only suitable for Infants. But Juniors enjoy making them, and backward Seniors find them interesting; the results can be sent to lower classes. Use an old blackboard or side of a tea-chest, and nail an inch-high frame of wood all round it to prevent the sand from slipping off. Use sand to map out a scene, e.g. Sea of Galilee and surrounding countryside. Show villages in clay, paper or cardboard. Coloured chalk dusted over will indicate plains, hills, water; twigs and cut-outs for trees; animals and people can be made in cardboard or plasticine. Quite attractive results can be produced in a very short time. The sand model can be used in the course of the lesson story, or as a recapitulation, in which case any confused ideas will reveal themselves in the expression work being done.

Finally, be careful not to limit model-making to Biblical purposes. Some of the work must cover lives of great people, life in other parts of the world, comparisons of homes then and now; this gives the chance to model African villages, Chinese homes, South Sea coral islands, types of country passed through by the colporteur. Augment with *Study Boxes* on the Church Overseas (E.H.P.). Be on the look-out for models being used in other subjects by your colleagues, and borrow these for your Religious Knowledge lessons whenever you can; and lend relevant models to teachers of other subjects.

(*l*) *Time Charts*

Children have a very vague sense of chronology. This is more hindered than helped if the stories they hear are chosen without some kind of sequence. Moses, Isaiah and Jesus can equally well live together in the same obscure long ago.

A Time Chart that shows in clear colouring, lettering, pictures and drawings, makes for better understanding and clearer appreciation of continuity and time. There are plenty of chronological charts in reference books and also obtainable from publishing firms, but the best one is usually that made by the class. It should begin with a straight line representing the line of time. The first part will be shown as the limbo of forgotten things—and perhaps marked "unknown traditions," or merely "the beginnings."

Using an historical basis, colour a band to represent the periods under Leaders and Judges and Kings to the Division of the Kingdom. Two colours represent the two nations, as far as the Exile. Then follow the periods of the Return, Greek and Roman rule, up to about A.D. 100. Prophets, kings, events, writings and the like should be shown, but great care must be taken that the chart is not lost in a welter of material and details; if it is, it has been a waste of time making it.

A Time Chart of the Growth of the Christian Church is rarely seen in schools. Perhaps the best method is to show a central line passing through periods of darkness and light, persecution and progress, and illustrated by the lives of great men and women of the Faith.

Or you may prefer divisions such as: the Early Church, Persecutions, Spread of the Gospel, Dark Ages, Renaissance, Reformation, Spread of Religion through Missionaries and Evangelism, the Church of the Nineteenth Century, the Present Day.

Quite a simple method is to arrange along one wall of the classroom a series of illustrated sheets of paper, about quarto size, using one for each century.

Economy of space is always a consideration for the teacher, who may have to decide whether to have a horizontal or vertical type of chart. If it cannot be fixed along a wall, arrange the horizontal type of chart in concertina form, so that it opens out like a long booklet. It can be stored in a small place, and opened out when needed. The vertical type need not be larger than two half-imperial sheets.

In all charts, make sure that there is some uniformity. Lettering should be bold and individual—capitals for people, small letters for places, red for kings, black for prophets and so on. Keep to these in all the charts so that the children come to associate forms and colours with historical facts.

On occasion, the sections of the chart may be brought to life, as it were, in costumed tableaux or a procession of representative characters. A complete pageant is a distinct possibility, and might be the subject of a project in its eventual production. There is considerable help in *Practical Book No. 4,* Warr (E.H.P.); pageant work of various kinds is suggested in the *Christian Education Handbooks,* ed. Hamilton (R.E.P.).

Summing up—the lack of some kind of Visual Aid of this type robs children of the sense, and indeed realisation, that Christianity did not end with Christ, but that it went on and is still going on. A chart that shows Aggrey and Gladys Aylward as following in the train of so many pioneers and martyrs of the Faith throughout the centuries, gives just that clarity and enhances just that certainty which children need so much in the busy materialistic twentieth century.

(m) Note-books

No Religious Knowledge syllabus can be followed out successfully without the keeping of some kind of individual record. Children have strange ideas, too, about the importance of a subject, and we cannot afford to let them think that this subject is unimportant because they "don't even have a note-book!" Note-books will be of various kinds. The supply situation will preclude the use of separate books for every suggestion, but ideas may be adapted and even combined, e.g. for general purposes, notes of lessons, exercises, outlines of projects, preparations for lecturettes, findings, points for discussions, Bible diaries and so on.

An old exercise-book may be converted into a useful scrap-book into which pictures, cuttings, drawings and snaps may be pasted. Bible stories, customs, animals, missionary work, great heroes and heroines make a hotch-potch of pleasurable references. Untidy borders can be blacked out and the pages decorated; the cover can be designed to illustrate the content of the book.

Individual collections make note-book work a real joy. Older children especially like to prepare anthologies on such subjects as: Worship, Prayer, Bible Poetry, Great Thoughts. Or there may be Stories of Jesus, Paul's Log, a Roman Diary, Notes of Interviews, Bible Names and Their Meaning, the Story of the Ark, Stories of the Well, Dictionary of Bible Words and Phrases, Biographies, Women of the Bible, Peoples and Tribes, Occupations and Crafts.

Some of these develop to an alarming size, and merit tasteful bindings, jackets and designs; these should be left to the children to be done at home or in the Art lesson.

It is very likely that you will not be able to encourage many of these as part of your actual scheme; that doesn't matter, for the main thing is to get children to take a personal interest in some aspect and to follow it out in their own way, usually in their own time. It might be as well to regard the work as very much their own, in that it need not be collected for marking, although you will have to help here and there in both subject-matter and lay-out, so that they get the best results.

Incidentally, these books should never be allowed to lie about collecting dust and being dog's-eared and torn. Some of the best should be sent—or rather taken by those who made them—to hospitals and welfare centres for small children to look at and treasure.

Some special teaching note-books, mainly for the use of the class, are useful. Apart from the pictorial kind, a file-cover of excerpts and pamphlets for each of a number of specific subjects can be arranged. Under the title of "Self-help Books," with the sub-heading —"If you want to know more about Peter, read here," and so on, these are most attractive additions to school work. These collections become quick reference books, and may be built up by selections from such sources as *Junior Papers* (M.Y.D.), and various Bible-reading Courses.

(n) News-board

This is an idea that may be varied considerably. Some teachers pin up a sheet of sugar-paper and affix cuttings to illustrate texts, altruism, heroism and the like.

A more vivid approach is to have a blank outline map of the world, either on a wall or mounted on a large sheet of paper or on a board. The newspaper cuttings and pictures are then fixed in the spaces round it, and coloured threads are run from these to their locations on the map. In this way, the news-board is centralised.

Such a map may carry news of a new Bible translation, some missionary enterprise, colour-bar questions, disaster and relief measures, excavations in Palestine, discovery of papyri, a canonisation . . . all at the same time. It gives the children an awareness of what may be going on in the world, how far progress and faith are winning ground, and the extent of the influence of Christianity upon people everywhere. Don't forget to include as an item of interest the occasional local event that is relevant to the news-board.

(o) Flannelgraph

This is a type of classroom aid that has become very popular in recent years, particularly with Juniors and backward Seniors. The set-up is simple. All that is needed is a sloping blackboard on which is hung a square of blanket, lint, felt or woollen material. Cut-outs of scenery, figures, properties, etc., are backed with the same material or merely roughened with sand-paper. When they are laid on the board, these things stick with fascinating and magical ease.

Prepare the background—coloured material for sky, water, desert or whatever is needed; as you tell the story and mention the characters, creatures, houses and so on, so you casually place the relevant cut-outs with a sleight of hand that rarely ceases to attract the class. Make sure that the figures are numbered or at least arranged in the required order, so that there are no unnecessary pauses to interrupt the flow of the narration. It is of untold value to rehearse the story and application to ensure smoothness and exactness; it is quite possible, in a crowd scene for instance, to place a figure completely out of focus; and the description of a character might easily be contradicted by the cut-out chosen to represent him.

The use of the flannelgraph should not be overdone, nor should it become mere entertainment just because certain materials are at hand. It is possible, especially with brighter classes, for its magic to fade, but it is certainly a great favourite with some children who can make their own illustrations for class use.

There is a valuable handbook and magazine issued by N.S.S.U., and the *Scripture Flannelgraph Series* (Arnold) may help, too.

(p) *Miscellaneous*

Under this heading are grouped a number of suggestions that may be considered from time to time as interesting adjuncts to lessons.

Crosswords give extra practice in Bible search if references are given in the clues. Those without references tend to be difficult for children, who lose heart if they have no more than a scanty background upon which to fall. Besides, looking up references gives greater pleasure in the solving. Some very good ones are found in the *Christian Herald,* but most religious magazines contain scriptural crosswords at some time or another.

Children find they are not easy to make, but should be encouraged to try their own with small frames of say, 7 × 5 or 11 × 9 squares.

Stained-glass Windows. Very good imitations can be made to cover existing glass in the school windows. The framework of a

A CROSS-WORD PUZZLE

(*Prepared by a boy aged fifteen*)

ACROSS

2. Upon this Rock will I build my Church. Matt. xvi. 18.

5. I — the Way, the Truth, and the Life. John xiv. 6.

8. He rebuilt Jerusalem in 444 B.C.

10. What Adam and Eve did of the Tree of Life.

11. — doth the Lord require of thee? Micah vi. 8.

13. The flowers appear — the earth. Song of Solomon, ii. 12.

15. The wife of Jacob drops an aitch.

17. A book of the Old Testament.

19. Or the pitcher be broken — the fountain. Eccl. xii. 6.

20. A prophet.

DOWN

1. The first miracle was done here. John ii. 1.

3. The "mother" of all. Gen. iii. 20.

4. Paul's letters.

6. Came together.

7. Came to visit Solomon.

9. What Solomon's workers had to do. 2 Chron. ii. 2.

12. He that — ears to hear, let him hear. Luke xiv. 35.

14. Such a good catch, it broke. Luke v. 6.

16. Before.

18. — everyone that thirsteth. Is. iv. 1.

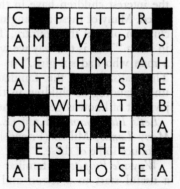

simple design of some Biblical scene, e.g. Noah's Ark, Abraham and Isaac, is made on a sheet of cartridge-paper; irregular shapes similar to those of coloured glass in real windows are then cut out, leaving the pattern somewhat like a fretwork design. The cut-out spaces are then backed with coloured cellophane to imitate the glass fillings; the framework is painted black on the right side, to simulate leading. When the whole is pasted over a window, the effect is remarkably like the genuine thing, especially at a distance.

Jigsaws speak for themselves. These can be made very simply. Choose good pictures in colour, accuracy and design; paste on to plywood; cut into weird shapes, but do not smooth the rough edges, as the roughness makes for a better fit in the re-making. It is a good plan to provide trays or a safe corner where children can leave unfinished puzzles and return to them at odd times. Jigsaws can be made by Senior children in the Handicraft Centre, as gifts to Junior or Infant Departments.

Cards for Christmas, Birthdays, Easter and Get Well cards may be designed and coloured. Simple verses on the subject should be composed and printed in manuscript lettering. Some children might like to attempt Cradle Roll and Baptism Cards for their Sunday-school.

The main idea is that these should all be purposeful and individual in execution.

Games. Various Bible games are described in Chapter XIX, but the interest children have in the Games of Other Lands should be noted. Many of these are singing games, often duplications of games children play in this country. Thus, our "Mulberry Bush" becomes in India "This is the way we wash our clothes," in Iraq "There was a man who had six girls," in Kenya "This is the way we work." The realisation of this familiarity gives a sense of friendship and understanding of children in the lands beyond, apart from the enjoyment of knowledge about these countries.

Let's Play Games, Krall (E.H.P.), and *Children's Games from Many Lands,* Millen (Friendship Press, New York), will help to introduce some of these.

Wayside Pulpits are familiar to most children. Many of them give a useful start to a lesson and may illustrate a Christian precept. Usually short and to the point, often paradoxical, their idea is to prompt thought, to cheer and to exhort. I recall one displayed outside a dilapidated country church during the war—"It's often the last key of the bunch that fits the door"—and have found its recall strangely encouraging ever since. Here is an opportunity for children to coin telling phrases, or to work on favourite texts and pithy sayings.

Wayside pulpits should be done poster size, and displayed in the classroom and school hall; some may eventually get to a local church. The wording should be done in stencilled lettering or manuscript form.

On occasion, a silhouette may be added to add attractiveness and point to the message, e.g. Prayer, Ps. xxiii. A copy of Albert Dürer's famous "Hands in Prayer" would be most effective for the former, whilst "The Lord is my Shepherd" could be silhouetted with a shepherd standing by his sheep, in modern outlines.

Book Jackets. The dust-covers of such books as *The Robe* and *In the Steps of the Master* give an idea of what is possible. Designs may be made for a complete jacket—front and spine—for selected books

By a B stream boy.

in the library or in the possession of the children. These may be pictorial and highly imaginative; some children show a preference for a subtler choice of pattern than an over-all scenic effect, and this should be encouraged as a sign of good taste.

Music has been given thought in the chapter on "School Worship," but there is every reason why music of all kinds should be used in the classroom or Music lesson, as aids to the lesson in Religious Knowledge. Piano illustrations of sacred music, often fitted to words for singing, might be taught and sung, e.g. Bach's "Jesu, Joy of Man's Desiring" and Schubert's "Ave Maria." The gramophone is a great asset. Children can be introduced to the beauties of plainsong, to Tallis, Orlando Gibbons, Palestrina and Purcell. Music by great composers who wrote for the Church, and expressed what the Christian religion meant to them in their music, at least should be brought to the children's notice. Bach, Handel, Elgar, Holst and writers of our own day illustrate this.

Many of the grandest stories of the Bible can be introduced through the great oratorios. These may be introduced to illustrate or start a lesson, but if the opportunity of hearing or attending a full performance locally arises, by all means take it and organise a party of children to enjoy it. Thus, we have Haydn's *Creation*, Mendelssohn's *Elijah*, Handel's *Messiah*, Stainer's *Crucifixion*, whilst there is no good reason to overlook the more difficult *Samson* of Handel, *Belshazzar's Feast* of Walton and Elgar's *Dream of Gerontius*. Perhaps Bach's *Matthew Passion* and the *Requiems* of Verdi and Brahms are even more difficult to appreciate, but some children will find parts of them helpful.

Religious music of other countries often sounds strangely crude and even weird to us, but there is no reason why recordings of such music should not be used. Negro spirituals are, of course, familiar to most children nowadays, but hymns and tunes of many other lands also appeal by their apparent quaintness; I often find myself recalling a Papuan hymn tune I learned as a boy for a Sunday-school Missionary Exhibition. How fascinating we found those tunes, and how remarkable to us the very idea that hymn tunes should come from those far-off lands. Incidentally, it is from the Missionary Societies that the best examples of these tunes are obtained; Warr's *Practical Books* contain some, too.

Rare and ancient instruments have been recorded, and would be found intriguing; an example is the Tutankhamen horn of three thousand years ago.

Stencils of all kinds make for speed of work. They can be for cut-outs, lettering, printing (U.N.O. stencils are the best), outline maps, border designs for Eastern costumes and fabric printing, and for repetitive scenic designs on flats and play properties.

Drawings should be notable for their simplicity. Do not worry about lack of perspective and proportion in children's work; look for imaginative expression. A useful book for yourself and the children is Whanslaw's *Drawing Bible Pictures* (R.E.P.) It is a good plan, especially for backward classes who so often waste a good deal of time in producing indifferent pictures, to cyclostyle or print outlines for colouring. These may be of Biblical scenes, furniture, figures, open Bibles, and all sorts of illustrations relevant to your course. They can so easily be inserted into the children's note-books; a good deal of pleasure is gained in the colouring, and the result is more successful and satisfying often than from the laborious copying of a single example.

Scraper-board designs for texts and imaginative ideas are most effective. The board is of specially prepared material, and is worked with a penknife or pointed instrument that scratches out the black and produces a pleasant and realistic result not unlike a lino-print in black and white. It may be applied to poster-work, too. The disadvantage is the cost of the board, but the best artists should be encouraged and even rewarded by its use.

Lettering gives excellent outlets for expression. Favourite texts, with or without pictorial additions, poems, Psalms, the Decalogue, illuminated capitals, all make pleasing work for classroom display, personal collection or group folio work covering projects and reports of visits. Extremely good results are obtained from the challenge of subjects like: St. Patrick's Breastplate, Housman's Hymn to St. George, the Knight's Prayer, St. Richard's Prayer, especially when done by boys; the material seems to work powerfully upon their imaginations. Nutshell posters of the type "We Thank LISTER for . . . (a list of his discoveries)" are effective, and done on quarto sheets pinned next to one another make a pleasant mural.

The C.S.S.M. print sets of texts for colouring; some of these are useful, especially for younger children or slow seniors.

Poetry. The opportunity of reading to the class excerpts from great religious poets should not be missed. There is much in Donne, Vaughan, Herbert, Milton and Gerard Manley Hopkins that children will enjoy, even though they may not fully appreciate either beauty or worth. It is obvious that both the class and the occasion will need careful choice, and the rendering must be a tribute to the author of the work selected. Given a little guidance, children will produce remarkably good verse on subjects suggested to them by a lesson or a text. To show what is possible to children of twelve and fourteen, here are two poems: "Crucifixion" and "Blindness" (after a lesson on Bartimæus).

Crucifixion of Jesus Christ

Before Pilate He was made to stand,
Then dragged away by Roman band;
But His disciples wept aloud
When He was borne amid the crowd.
Nailed to the Cross—and no one cared
While people just stood there and stared.

On the Cross He hung in vain,
Bearing the cruel nails with pain;
With a crown upon His head
Made of thorns that then were thread.
On the third day He did rise—
But we ne'er saw Him with our eyes.

Boy aged 12

Blindness

Oh, to see the earth's fair loveliness,
　To see the sun again,
To pierce the shroud of emptiness,
　To see the flowers and rain.

To see the beauty of the Spring,
　The whiteness of the snow,
The birds which on the bowers sing
　In the copse where the bluebells grow.

They say they grow so densely there,
But not one have I seen.
Dear God, let me see the earth so fair
And make true all I dream.

Girl aged 14

Week-ends under Youth Hostel Membership may well be spent in a district where you and some of the children can walk or cycle to a famous abbey or some spot renowned for its religious connections. Such a trip should be free of school trappings, but should be planned and treated with intention. An incidental but important part of such visits is the attitude engendered towards other people met in the hostels, as well as the development of courtesy on the road, towards strangers and one another; the extremely practical consideration for others revealed in sharing fairly and doing well the duties entailed, keeping the countryside free from litter, closing gates and so on, is surely an aspect of Christian character-building that can be developed—and if non-existent at the start, can be begun.

Phylacteries are often mentioned by teachers, and even carefully described, but the children are still not clear as to what they are. Drawings or actual models and copies can easily be made, and perhaps placed alongside models of the prayer-wheel. Help is given by the Jewish Museum, Woburn Place, London, but no doubt a local friendly Jew at a nearby synagogue would be most willing to lend some of these.

Costumes. There is always a great desire to provide genuine dresses of all kinds for plays and exhibitions. Too often it is forgotten that these can brighten many a lesson without your waiting for a special event. Meticulous care for accuracy of design and ornament and dress is taken by the Missionary Societies (including the Mission to the Jews), who will provide these costumes at quite reasonable charges. It is also possible to collect pieces of material and make quite good costumes, once an original has been seen. There is an excellent book—*Biblical Costume,* Logan Wright (S.P.C.K.)—for the bookshelf. There is hardly a dress or ornament relevant to Biblical countries of both Old and New Testament history omitted from it.

(q) Library

Perhaps the library is not thought of merely as an aid. It is certainly a necessity. Probably few schools have any semblance of a Religious Knowledge library. In spite of the increased output of literature intended to advance the religious training of our children, there seems still a strange reluctance to provide it. In the recent Institute of Christian Education reports on this matter it was stated that except in a few schools library books for religious instruction were not available. That is a great pity—and the unconscious comparison emphasises the need for attention to the matter. Most of our Secondary Schools depend upon books in these days of search and reference work. If find-out-for-yourself is to be the guiding principle in many of our Religious Knowledge lessons, we must provide our children with the books for it. There should be a nucleus of suitable books for general reading, too, and some for deliberate Christian guidance.

Children ought to be able to refer to modern versions of the Bible; get these into the library. Books treating the Bible archæologically; as literature; geographically; historically; commentaries; biographies of prophets and martyrs, reformers and pioneers; church histories; comparative religion; missionary stories . . . all these should be represented. Of their type, they should be well illustrated, readable and contain plenty of maps. Arthur Mee's *Children's Bible* (Hodder & Stoughton) and *Through the Bible*, Wilson (Collins), are useful. Several books in the style of *In the Steps of the Master*—of *Moses, Paul, St. Francis, The Big Fisherman*, selections from Housman's plays, Yarns, Heroes and Pioneers—all deserve a place. Look out for the additions that read pleasantly and are free from pious sentimentality. Don't forget to cater for the dullest children. This will suggest the buying of many of the Bible in Pictures type of book, but be on your guard against shoddiness of production in colour and presentation. As the need for a certain book arises from a lesson or a discussion, note it and try to get it. The School Librarian (if you have one) usually knows his grant for new books, and should be approached with suggested titles for the Religious Knowledge section—it is so easy to be left out. As the new books arrive, spend time in the classroom with them, explaining their contents and value; of course, there should be no book in this section of the library that you and the children have not considered at some time or another. Obtain a few good Biblical plays, and the kind of book that gives little difficulty for quick reference, such as *A Classical and Biblical Reference Book*, Treble (Murray).

For teacher and children, the series of *Practical Books*, Warr (E.H.P.), are useful for background and "things to do."

(r) Broadcasts

All broadcasts should be considered as part of the syllabus, other-wise they are merely adjuncts to other lessons, and their value is thereby lessened and even wasted. Subject-matter is published in pamphlets well ahead of broadcast times, and this provides ample opportunity for the modifying of a scheme for the term so as to make the broadcasts an integral part of it. Unfortunately there is little direct help for Primary and Secondary Modern Schools in religious teaching. Apart from the Morning Service for Schools and the Sixth Form Talks for Grammar Schools, there is nothing. This is a pity, but we may look forward to a constructive series similar to those for History and Geography and Science. The need is obvious, but the difficulties are many; not the least of these is the provision of broadcasts unbiased in any way—there is always the possibility of offending someone in religious matters. However, some progress is to be expected as time goes on and the hindrances are overcome.

Most tentative attempts at religious broadcasts have revealed that the experts, despite their erudition, often know little of the art of teaching. Success can come only through first-class practising teachers who also have the requisite knowledge. Only when the need for challenge related to the real problems of children is realised will broadcasts be more than just so much innocuous dogma. Boys and girls want to know how to tackle the difficulties in their own lives —often secret difficulties, they feel—and guidance in this is patently lacking.

We may be optimistic of the eventual success of religious broad-casting, perhaps on the lines of the effective interludes now so familiar, plus the vital challenge and the thrown gauntlet. We know that broadcasts can do much that we cannot—but must we fall into the error of regarding them as prefabricated lessons? Broadcasts cannot supersede the teacher at any time, least of all in a lesson in religion. The teacher must, however, regard the use of broadcasts as a means of teaching; if the children are left to sit and listen, the chances are that they will merely sit. The class must be prepared for the topic with helpful illustrations and (if provided) B.B.C. booklets. Then, when the set is tuned correctly, teacher and class should listen *together*. The power of suggestion is strong; a listening teacher makes a listening class. When the broadcast is over, there should be plenty of discussion, some form of summary and the setting of exercises, such as drawing, model-making, dramatic expression, visits, practical service and the like.

Schools may one day be provided with recording and reproducing apparatus, so that teachers can bring back any parts of a broadcast as and when needed. This would meet the present disadvantage of not being able to go back over an important part, and, further, have the advantage of making a Broadcast Library similar to that for film-strips. Teachers could then use a special broadcast entirely for their own benefit at times more educationally effective than the time of the live broadcast.

Certain recordings are obtainable, however, from the School Broadcasting Council, such as—E5—Story of David; E12—Biblical Characters (readings from *Samson Agonistes* and *Daniel Jazz*).

There are always helpful broadcasts in other subjects. Thus, History gives biographies of great folk like Shaftesbury, Wilberforce, Florence Nightingale, Grenfell, Schweitzer, and events like the Crusades as well as the Christmas stories. In Music, there are carols and examples of sacred works; in Science, children may meet Pasteur, Mme Curie; in English, there are Cædmon, Erasmus and the stories of the Renaissance.

At the time of writing there is a Miscellany of Subjects "For the Fourteens," containing the following discussion topics: What is a Lie?; Broken Promises; Tell-tale; Paying a Bus Fare. Such ventures into the realms of "simple" ethics, bringing right down to brass tacks, as it were, the four aspects of Honesty concerned, are exactly right for children due to leave school. Here, if anywhere, they should be able to learn how to face up to some of the most personal —but, alas, most ignored—concerns of their own Christian living. In the same series are two other sections: Working Together and Great Citizens, covering humanitarian aspects of our nation's history. Because they are humanitarian they will also be Christian and worth consideration.

There is great hope of development, especially since the Churches Commission on Broadcasting made recommendations to the British Council of Churches. In these it was urged that the British Broadcasting Corporation should be used "far more extensively as an instrument of evangelism." It was argued that "since the B.B.C. is a public corporation functioning in a Christian country, it is obliged to foster an understanding of the Christian religion," and that "religious broadcasting should be much more controversial." Just as the Religious Broadcasting Department is urged "to cater for listeners outside the range of organised religion rather than for the regular church-goer," so we may hope that in its evangelising policy the B.B.C. may consider providing for the schools broadcasts that will cater for those children who are outside the range of regular Sunday-school attendance.

Before leaving Broadcasting, let us remember that very often there is a talk or a play or a feature with strong religious content and instruction timed for the evening. These should be noted in advance in *TV Times* and *Radio Times*, and brought to the notice of children as worthy of their attention. Children's Hour plays are always suitable, but often, too, the Third Programme has something to offer the thoughtful child; and you should certainly make a point of listening yourself to such a broadcast as that on "Translating the Bible" and similar topics by Biblical scholars.

(s) Television

Just as schools now have radios, so they will be supplied with television sets. Some schools in many parts of the country already treat TV as part of the normal supply of visual aids. By its means dramatic interludes and live talks with a bias towards religious education may be presented with vivid and accurate background. Methods for televising on to the classroom wall are being perfected; by this means a whole school may watch as easily as they now listen.

Meanwhile, we have the B.B.C.'s word for it that "experiments will be made and special attention is being given to the problem of representing the different traditions of worship" (*Church and Film*, Vol. 1, No. 1). This is promising, and progress on these lines will be watched with considerable interest by all concerned with modern equipment and modern aids in the teaching of Religious Knowledge.

CHAPTER XIX

CLASSROOM GAMES

Various quiz and guessing games in Religious Knowledge.

No lessons in Religious Knowledge should be so dull as to give the impression that trying to live the right kind of life is a dreary business. Nor, at the other extreme, should we err on the flippant side. But there is room and reason for relaxation in some of our work, and we consider here a series of educative but pleasant "breaks" from the normal routine of teaching. Some of them are useful for end-of-term periods and odd moments between Assembly and change of lessons. Don't overdo them, and especially beware of falling into the habit of using them as an easy lesson when the class ought to be tackling something a good deal more difficult. Lightness in lessons is necessary, but it must never usurp the real work one has to do.

(i) *Bible Quiz*

(*a*) The Quiz is one of the many forms of testing knowledge that have been popular on the air for some time. Most children enjoy this type of questioning, which gives them a chance of showing their prowess and knowledge. The general idea is a competition between individuals and groups in questions needing factual answers, on the lines of the B.B.C. "Transatlantic Quiz." Two helpful booklets are the *Bible Quiz Book* by Hedges (Pilgrim Press) and *Bible Queries* (Walter).

(*b*) Children like to make their own quiz questions. With a class of forty, making, say, three apiece, it is easy to obtain a useful selection of 100 or so questions. These should be based on the work done plus some on knowledge acquired elsewhere, e.g. home, Sunday-school, radio, reading. Here are a few Bible Quiz Questions compiled by a class of twelve-year-olds:

Name the first miracle done by Jesus.
Who were the three men in the Fiery Furnace?

Name three people who were thrown into prison for their faith.

Name all the disciples.

Who was David's wife; his son; his father?

What was the writing on the wall? What did it mean?

Name the people who were spoken of as: patient; unlucky; doubting.

Name the first and last books of both Testaments.

(c) As a variant, the exercise on a given passage may be made a Group Quiz. The passage is studied first; a few questions are then prepared by each half of the class, and these are used to test the other half, with or without Bibles and the passage. It is important that the half classes change roles of questioners and victims.

(ii) *Bible Alphabet*

This, again, gives the pleasure of competition in factual matters. There are several alternatives.

(a) Children are asked questions on characters or incidents in the Bible, involving answers beginning with initial letters in alphabetical order. Thus:

What name is given to holy books not in the two Testaments?
*A*pocrypha.

Who was the robber released at the trial of Jesus?   *B*arabbas.

What book in the Old Testament tells of the exploits of Kings?
*C*hronicles.

and so on. The fact that the answer begins with the alphabetical initial is a help in the guessing.

(b) Write down the names in alphabetical order of: i, men; ii. women; iii, places, in the Bible, e.g.:

    i. Adam, Benjamin, Caiaphas, David . . .
    ii. Anna, Bathsheba, Candace, Deborah . . .
    iii. Assyria, Bethlehem, Canaan, Dan . . .

It is not likely that complete alphabets will be done at any one time, but eventually complete lists may be made from class suggestions. Some children will delight in preparing more than one set on their own; they should be encouraged to make an Alphabet Book of these for future use.

Some children may even collect a series and write a verse on each, e.g. "A is for Adam . . ." These may be printed and illustrated and passed on to classes in lower streams in booklet or frieze form.

(iii) *Twenty Questions*

This is an adaptation of the popular B.B.C. game, and is too well-known to need more than a reminder. A team is chosen and sent out of the room whilst the class decide upon a subject of Biblical aspect. The team have then to guess the subject in a maximum of twenty questions put to a Question Master, who tells them whether it is Animal, Vegetable, Mineral, Abstract. . . . The usual —"Can you eat it?" "Male or Female?" "Fact or Fiction?" will start the ball rolling.

(iv) *Who's Who?*

Also based on a B.B.C. quiz, this will succeed only with a good A Form, and probably only after much practice. But the eventual enjoyment and incidental knowledge gained will more than compensate your efforts. A good way of preparing the ground is to allow groups to list characters with the same initial, e.g. Samuel, Solomon, Saul, Stephen, Shadrach, Sheba . . . and then deliberately select an S character for the questioning. This saves long, hesitant and dull pauses, and ensures continuity of questioning. Introduce the prepared Who's Who with easy examples and proceed slowly.

The Questions should be framed with rather more subtlety than in the Quiz or Twenty Questions, as the point of the game is for the questioner to "stump" the victim into giving more and more information about himself without revealing exactly who he is. Thus, suppose the victim says, "I am S." The questioner will not say "Are you Solomon?" or even "Were you famed for your wisdom?" But rather, "Did a famous Queen, also an S, visit you?" The answer is then, "I am Solomon, who was visited by the Queen of Sheba."

If the questioner is off the track, however, and says, "Were you the first Christian martyr?" the victim must say, "I am not Stephen who was stoned to death," or words to that effect. Again, "Were you born of very old parents?" "I am not Samuel who was born to Hannah in her old age." If the victim cannot think of the character or selects a wrong one in his reply, he forfeits more information about himself. This might be, "I am male." Or, "I am an Old Testament prophet." This further information obviously helps the questioner, who continues his questionings in the light of this new information. It is wise to set a time-limit.

(v) *What's What?*

This is a variant of Who's Who? in which the victim represents a place. Thus, "I am B." "Are you the village where a famous Babe was born?" "I am not Bethlehem where Jesus was born." "Are you the farthest place (town) in Palestine?" "I am not Beersheba, of 'Dan to Beersheba.'" "Are you renowned as a place of worship?" "I am Bethel." And so on.

(vi) *Famous People*

(*a*) Write down the names of any ten famous men of the Bible that you can think of. Now list them in the order they are mentioned in the Bible. Then list them in order of fame or importance. Be prepared to say why you make this order.

(*b*) Do the same for ten martyrs of the Christian faith.

(*c*) Do the same for ten great Reformers.

(*d*) As for (vi) (*a*) for Famous Women, bearing in mind that in many cases there will be no actual names to write, e.g. the serving-maid of Naaman, the woman at the well, the Syro-Phœnician woman. This should be explained and these accepted, otherwise the list will be ineffective and certainly not fully representative.

(*e*) As for (vi) (*b*) for the famous women of Christian history.

(vii) *Completing Texts*

Fill in the missing word in these well-known texts, e.g.:

I am the Good . . .; the Good . . . giveth His life for the sheep (John x).

Fight the good . . . of Faith (1 Tim. vi).

Thy . . . and Thy . . . they comfort me (Ps. xxiii).

If you cannot do this at once, look up the references. Do so in any case when you have finished, as a check on your answers.

(viii) *Torn Texts*

The teacher should prepare about a dozen texts and divide each into two phrases, mixing them as shown.

The children are then told that they have to find the parts that belong to each other; by pairing off the correct halves they produce the text, which they write down in their books. References are for confirmation.

(a) Blessed are	the whole armour of God (Eph. vi).
(b) Honour thy Father	like a shepherd (Is. xl).
(c) Put on	the pure in heart (Matt. v).
(d) He shall feed His flock	and thy Mother (Ex. xx).

(ix) *Hidden Text*

Children as well as the teacher can devise this useful and interesting game. The initial letters of answers to a set of questions provide the letters of a well-known text. Here is an example:

In which Garden was Jesus captured?	Gethsemane.
Who was the slave lad Paul wrote to Philemon about?	Onesimus
Who was put in a lion's den?	Daniel.
A great Prophet	Isaiah.
What was the name of the Jewish Council?	Sanhedrin.
Who was Jacob's wife?	Leah.
A hill in Palestine	Olives.
The Latin version of the Bible	Vulgate.
Who challenged the priests of Baal?	Elijah.

Hence the text: "GOD IS LOVE."

The popularity of this game is seen in the response of the children who play at it for their own pleasure. There is no doubt of its value in search work and reference finding.

(x) *Who Am I?*

In this exercise, a series of descriptive sentences should be prepared, each capable of a single word answer. These examples will indicate what is needed:

(a) I watched a baby in the rushes	Miriam.
(b) I visited a famous King	Sheba.
(c) I spent my inheritance	Prodigal Son.
(d) I was "the beloved disciple"	John.

(xi) *Who Said?*

This is based on the context of passages read during the term or year. Help may be given by reminding the children of the story in which the speech is to be found, or by the actual Bible references. Here are three examples:

    (*a*) Speak, Lord, for Thy servant heareth (1 Sam. iii).
    (*b*) Hosanna to the Son of David (Matt. xxi).
    (*c*) I find no fault with this man (Luke xxiii).

References should always be checked.

(xii) *Pairs*

Once the idea is put to children, they will think of several "pairs" in the Bible; the mention of one immediately calls to mind the other, e.g. Balaam and his ass, Jacob's ladder. Such pairs can be set out to test general knowledge or use of commentaries and reference books and indexes to these. Here are three more examples:

    (*a*) Widow and her . . .   mite or cruse.
    (*b*) Moses and . . .   bulrushes.
    (*c*) David and his . . .   sling.

(xiii) *Jumbled Names*

Always a popular guessing game, this will give children a zestful exercise in remembering names of great people, both Biblical and of Christian history. Some help will be needed to give children the right line of thought, as seen in these examples:

    (*a*) T R E E P—a disciple   (*c*) N A A L B—a martyr.
    (*b*) V I A D D—a king.   (*d*) G A G Y E R—an African missionary.

(xiv) *Threes*

Children like this exercise intrinsically as a challenge to their factual knowledge and sense of number besides its connection with their Religious Knowledge lesson. Here are examples of what is needed:

    (*a*) Three Bible Maries.   (*c*) Three kings of Israel.
    (*b*) Three prophets.   (*d*) Three Bible trees.

(xv) *Relations*

Relationships in the Bible are not always clear, but some of them are worth recalling and can be set as reminders of studies done. For instance:

(*a*) Father of Absalom.   (*c*) Daughter of Saul.
(*b*) Mother of Samuel.   (*d*) Sister of Moses.

(xvi) *Hidden Names*

Some ingenuity on the part of the teacher is required here. The idea is to plan sentences containing the name of some character or place met with in the Bible or Christian story. Quite ordinary and commonplace sentences can be made, but the nearer to Biblical ideas the better. Here are examples:

(*a*) People:

Martha was busy with her odd jobs about the house	HEROD.
When asked how deep it was, Mark said it was about a fathom as far as he could judge	THOMAS.
Have you a Bible? Yes, the red book is my new one	ESTHER.

(*b*) Places:

This will be the last opportunity of worship	BETHEL.
The Israelites thought their major danger lay from the Philistines	JORDAN.
Paul appealed to Cæsar and Agrippa then sent him to Rome	ATHENS.

(xvii) *Animals*

This is a fairly straightforward piece of reading for the children, who have to find the animals mentioned in the passages given them. Here are a few of such references; others can be found in any good commentary:

Prov. xxi. 31 (horse)	Judges xiv. 5 (lion)
Gen. i. 21 (whale)	Is. xxv. 6 (hart)
Job xxv. 6 (worm)	Lev. xi. 6 (hare)

(xviii) *Picture Story*

This idea is familiar through its use in the Children's Corner of various newspapers. Names of people and places, and short stories, are written in picture form, the test being to interpret the drawings and make sense of the story. They find, for instance, that the word "well" is represented by a drawing of one, and "hear" by an H and a drawing of an ear; and the process of solving the problem is usually very clear from the start.

For backward classes particularly, this is a good exercise to prepare. Choose some of the simpler stories and parables and devise a picture account for the class to decipher. It is rewarding. When they have written their own account, the children should compare it with the Bible one, if that is at all possible. They can certainly be encouraged to use the same method for stories of their own.

(xix) *Puzzle Pictures*

Use drawings or pictures of Biblical and other scenes, and remove all descriptive matter and headings. The children then have to find out what the pictures illustrate, and the reference. Perhaps some of the class can do further examples with pin-men drawings for the rest of the class to track down.

(xx) *Hymns and Texts*

This exercise may be attempted by the children from memory, but in most cases they will need hymn-books. It may well serve as a simple piece of search work. The idea is to list two sets of corresponding hymns and texts, mixing one or the other; the children then have to pair them off correctly. Thus, "Fight the good fight" with "I have fought the good fight of faith." Here are other examples. Pair off correctly the hymn and the text in the following:

"The Lord is my Shepherd"   Christian seek not yet repose.
"Watch and Pray"   Jesus calls us o'er the tumult.
"Follow me"   The King of Love my Shepherd is.

(xxi) *Hymns and Psalms*

A very similar exercise can be prepared in which children learn that certain familiar hymns have been inspired by Psalms. The Scottish metrical versions are obvious. The best approach is to give the Psalm and ask the class to find the hymn related to it.

Here are examples:

Ps. xxiii.	The King of Love.
Ps. lxxii.	Hail to the Lord's Anointed.
Ps. xc.	O God, our Help.
Ps. ciii.	Praise, my soul.
Ps. civ.	O worship the King.
Ps. cxxxvi.	Let us with a gladsome mind.

(xxii) *Hangings*

This gruesome title introduces a most unscriptural game, but children play it with the frenzy of noughts and crosses, so we may as well use it for our own purpose. Left to their own devices in the last Religious Knowledge lesson of the term, two pairs of boys were found busily engaged in hanging one another—metaphorically, and with a great deal of gusto! They were using Biblical names, and proceeded as follows:

Choose a name, e.g. J O N A H. Represent it with five dashes: – – – – –. The victim then calls out letters of the alphabet. Correct letters are inserted in their proper places, and occasionally the whole name is guessed after a few guiding letters have been filled in. Incorrect letters serve in turn to build the body of the victim—torso, arms, legs, head; then the scaffold; finally—the rope! Failure to find the word is thus ignominiously acclaimed.

When reproved for this unseemly game, one of them said, "Why not, sir? It's a jolly good game. We play it for book titles and film stars, too." And another added, "It's better than noughts and crosses, anyway, because you learn something as well—you know, names and places and things"; and, as an afterthought, "in the Bible, of course, sir, *today*." I think that any game that helps them to do that is "jolly good," even if I *was* hanged myself—by Jehu!

(xxiii) *Bible Objects*

(*a*) Children provide objects mentioned in the Bible, e.g. rope, apple, sword, sling, Eastern lamp, pearl, pence, etc. The class then have to guess the significance of each, and tell any text, incident or story that each object brings to mind.

The child producing the object must be able to tell his own story represented by the object.

Here are some examples:

sword	David and Goliath	"The Sword of the Spirit, which is Prayer."
lamp	The Wise and Foolish Virgins	"Thy Word is a lamp unto our feet."
pence	Good Samaritan	"Paying tribute to Cæsar."

(b) A number of objects having been collected, texts can be printed and assigned to the related object.

(c) Give the texts or references, and let the children collect the objects referred to, in a kind of "treasure-hunt"; e.g.:

> "Ye are the salt of the earth."
> "No man lighteth a candle . . ."
> "Thy rod and Thy staff they comfort me."

The objects can be taken to another class and texts fitted to them, as in (b). Care and common sense should be exercised; we don't really want our children to bring sheep and swine to school!

(xxiv) Yes and No

This is a Biblical form of a game probably already known. Names of characters, martyrs, reformers, etc., are printed on slips of paper, and each member of the class has one pinned on his back. He has, then, to guess who he is by asking questions of other members. Only Yes or No may be given in answer. Thus, not "Am I a man or a woman?" But, "Am I a man?" A No will indicate a "woman." Then, on some such lines as, "Am I in the Old Testament?" "Am I a prophet?" "A king?" And so on. The child who guesses his name receives another on his back, and the first one is fixed on his lapel to show he has guessed it. The winner is obviously the one with the most guessed correctly.

(xxv) Odd Man Out

Who or what does not belong in each of these groups?
(a) Luke, John, Paul, Judas.
(b) David, Saul, Herod, Gideon.
(c) Mary, Dorcas, Jezebel, Martha.
(d) Micah, Ecclesiastes, Ecclesiasticus, Psalms.

(xxvi) *Knowing Your History*

Arrange these groups of people, articles, events, in chronological order:

Old Testament:

    (*a*) Micah, Amos, Enoch, Daniel.

    (*b*) Jacob's ladder, rod of Aaron, Isaiah's coal, widow's cruse.

    (*c*) Deaths of Saul, Samson, Uriah, Jacob.

New Testament:

    (*a*) Stephen, Elymas, Felix, John the Baptist.

    (*b*) The snake at Malta, Peter's sword, the five loaves, Paul's letter to Philemon.

    (*c*) Crucifixion, accident to Eutychus, riot at Ephesus, Peter's vision.

Bible:

    (*a*) Paul, Joseph, Delilah, Elisabeth.

    (*b*) David's harp, thirty pieces of silver, Moses' staff, Gideon's fleece.

    (*c*) Burning bush, death of Judas Maccabæus, capture of Israel, Sack of Jerusalem.

(The author hopes to extend and amplify several of these suggestions into a Classroom Games Book.)

CHAPTER XX

ADVANCED COURSES—TOWARDS A CHRISTIAN PHILOSOPHY

The possibilities; teacher and class; Comparative Study of Religions; Set Books; Wisdom Literature; the Four Freedoms; Some "Perennial Problems"; History of Philosophy; Great Philosophers; Philosophy Today; Summing-up.

It is probably safe to say that the majority of panels concerned with the provision of Agreed Syllabuses have taken as their ideal something on the lines of these words in the Spens Report: "There are teachers who believe that religious education, particularly as given to boys and girls who will shortly be leaving school, should deal more directly with the application of Christian principles to the problems —personal and public—with which they will be confronted in adult life. There are others who would probably maintain that the primary purpose of teaching . . . is to attach some significance to the idea of the Christian Faith—the belief that the person and teaching of Christ give an interpretation of life, and the will to act on the assumption that that interpretation is the true one." Herein lies the crux of a Christian philosophy.

Originally, it would certainly seem, the advanced courses suggested in our Syllabuses were meant for the Sixth Forms of Grammar Schools; a course in Religious Knowledge that did not include such material as was suggested in the Syllabuses could not be considered complete. But with the increase of G.C.E. and other academic and technical courses in our Secondary Modern and Secondary Technical Schools and the corresponding extension of school life in such schools, we must not overlook the necessity of providing for these boys and girls courses in Religious Knowledge that will appeal to their steadily growing powers of intellect and increasing interest in life and its complexities. It is obviously not enough to relegate Religious Knowledge to one period per week or to consider the B.B.C. discussions on advanced topics as meeting the problem; for advanced work to be of real value it must be an integral part of the consistent whole approach to religious training. The majority of Agreed Syllabuses devote a chapter to advanced courses in the same spirit in which the bulk of the Syllabus is presented. Even wider freedom, if anything, is extended to the teachers, for it is realised that not only do conditions between school and school vary tremendously, but that also much more depends upon individual teachers. It is felt that so long as religious teaching demands acceptance of a tradition without discussion and question, it is bound to fail; never more so is this true than in the upper forms of our schools. As the *Cambridge Syllabus* says: "For the sixth form (the syllabus) should be designed rather as a springboard, a liberation from a narrow conception of the teacher's task." There is no doubt that this will create in many a teacher a sense of inadequacy, but it is also a wonderful opportunity for him to draw upon the springs of his own faith, his teaching ability and his outlook upon life. Without obtruding his own personality he is required to "lead towards the light without getting in the way of it."

Reverting to the premise of the Spens Report just quoted, it is seen that the teacher has two alternatives—or, perhaps, two needs—to meet. One is to recapitulate, as it were, the work of the previous five years through some closer study of the Scriptures; the other is to develop in his pupils their powers of understanding, analysis and discrimination in such a way that they respond to the beginnings of a philosophy of life that is in effect the Christian attitude towards life itself. It may be possible to do both; but the time factor is as important here as in any other part of the course, and it is probably better that the teacher should decide upon which of the two he shall rest the emphasis of his teaching. Some of his pupils may be with him for a term, others for as long as three years, and this is no small matter to appreciate.

The *Lindsey Syllabus* states that the pupil should have "the opportunity of learning the essential facts of Christianity and also its relevance to life as a whole. This has involved us (the panel) in *a daring venture into the philosophy of religion*." [1] This is bold and refreshing. It is surely possible for this daring venture to be a considered plunge into the fuller study of philosophy as it is related to the Christian faith. Here is a great challenge, not only to teachers of Grammar School Sixths, but also to those who work with the advanced streams of other schools. It is probably true to say that by the time our pupils are faced with their approaching leave-taking, the challenge has come; this, in

[1] The italics are mine.

effect, means that by the time they are fifteen we should already have done much to prepare them with some safeguards of sound argument and clear thinking—which necessity has already been discussed in previous chapters. But we are now on more specific grounds. We are concerned with the pursuit of wisdom. Amongst its many definitions we may perhaps accept that wisdom is the mainspring of conduct— and there is certainly need for guidance in the conduct of life.

This also means the necessary training of adolescents to think for themselves, which is probably what the *Cambridge Syllabus* has in mind when it says that "the general approach . . . should be intellectual rather than devotional." As teachers we need to help these boys and girls to love wisdom and knowledge, so that in acquiring these they may "see life steadily and see it whole." Socrates was asked by Glaucon, "Who are the greatest philosophers?" and he replied, "Those who are lovers of the vision of truth." It is just that vision, however fleeting, that we must try to reveal.

The *Lindsey Syllabus* (q.v.) suggests that our first task should be to clarify by definition the terms we are often likely to use. Philosophy should be explained as the attempt to understand the universe; this in turn leads to a search for a pattern. Our pupils will see the truth of this as they study even briefly the work of the great philosophers. They will see, too, that Religion is the attempt to relate the whole truth of the universe to a way of living; that it is not merely concerned with belief and knowledge, but that acceptance of these must result in active participation in Christian deeds. Theology, on the other hand—and this is often confused with the philosophy of religion—is the reasoned statement of what religion as experienced implies. In the course of their studies pupils will frequently wonder what Science has to say about life and the universe, and what impact upon man's interpretation of the meaning of these it has. They will need to know, therefore, that Science is the study of aspects and facts of the universe by the appropriate methods; they will learn that there is such a thing as scientific truth, but not to the exclusion of all other truths.

The philosophy of religion, therefore, investigates the relation of human life to the universe. Herein lies the answer to Einstein's question, "What is the meaning of human life?"—if we, or indeed any philosopher, could resolve the myriad answers.

We know that in their search for such an answer, the Greeks

brought their philosophy into the street and the market-place; we have to bring ours into the classroom.

Stephen Leacock once wrote of a man who leapt upon a horse and "rode off madly in all directions." Our horse is the philosophy of religion, the rider is the teacher. Unusually good riders will manage this "centrifugal phenomenon" successfully and evolve many diverse and divergent methods simultaneously; but not all of us are good riders, and we may prefer to ride securely and gently along the outskirts, as it were, stumbling along by the light and guidance of one chosen route and perhaps later trying others; there is yet a third group of riders who must eventually (and perforce) dismount and walk, their approaches being the more pedestrian but none the less effective.

Let us, then, turn to the experience of the classroom, the methods to be considered and the practical aspects to be assessed. Again, it is emphasised that not all these ideas will be found of practical value to all teachers; some selection will obviously be necessary, for much depends upon individual interests, ability, leanings, as well as upon the amount of time; and by no means unimportant will be the type of adolescent, his environment and his present attitude towards life. Our main approach is through the Religious Knowledge lesson and, despite the advice that it is to the intellect that we are about to appeal, we ought not to lose sight of the fact that our philosophy is eventually a Christian one, biased towards a love of wisdom to direct the conduct of life and geared to a pursuit of knowledge essential to the application of the principles of this desired conduct. In so doing, we may be able to bring our pupils into the rare atmosphere of a Christian philosophy which designates living as a dedication to the highest service we know.

Much of the work involved, whatever method is applied, will be covered by discussion and debate. It is, of course, possible to discuss at great length for a long time without saying anything of vital importance and without arriving at any firm philosophic decision. The teacher, however, must value freedom of thought and revere independence of mind; he must at all times be as Plato succinctly put it—midwife to his pupils' thoughts.

1. *Comparative Study of Religions*

Religion implies the desire to worship; in worship man accepts a

Supreme Being upon whom depends his existence; he may or may not accept an "other world." By a comparison of the major religions of the world, adolescents may eventually be led to the acceptance of Christianity as the mainspring of their philosophy, and perhaps to that of Irenæus that "the life of man is the vision of God."

The idea underlying the study of world religions is the need to compare and contrast them in such a way that adolescents may see how and why each religion has appealed to peoples all over the world and throughout the ages. They will see that "the practical goodness of Confucius, the valiant devotion of Islam and the contemplative patience of Hinduism or Buddhism all have their place in the revelation of God's character and man's duties shown in the life which was lived among men in Palestine nineteen hundred years ago" (*Durham Syllabus*). When these divergent interpretations of life are presented, they will see that Christianity is the religion *par excellence*, because it meets the needs of all men everywhere—1 Peter iii. 8. To preach this in the classroom is liable to court disaster; its truth has to be discovered by our pupils for themselves. The extent of detail will depend upon their abilities and the amount of time. But for the work to be of any benefit the main features—historical, ethical, theological, sociological, philosophical—must be touched upon.

The following religions should be considered : Judaism (Old Testament); Islam; Hinduism; Buddhism; Confucianism (studied in the Analects); Greek Religion; Zoroastrianism; Christianity (New Testament).

An excellent summary for both teacher and class is the article by Professor F. H. Smith on "The Comparative Study of Religions" given in the *Durham, Middlesex, Lancashire* and *Hertfordshire Syllabuses*. There is a briefer summary in the *L.C.C. Syllabus*. Professor Smith has also prepared a most valuable pamphlet for Discussion Groups (S.P.C.K.—N.S.) that may be used as a basic booklet in class. Other books suitable for reference are somewhat advanced for pupils, but teachers should consider *World Religions and Jesus Christ*, Paton (E.H.P.), *Religions of the World*, Phillips (R.E.P.), *Sacred Books of the World*, Bouquet (Penguin).

Some of the methods of approach already dealt with in the preceding chapters may be tried. The most suitable will obviously be those appealing to the intellect—individual study, answering questions, essays and problems; relevant facts of selected chapters may be collected and collated for individual talks and lecturettes. There will be search work and use of library references. Clarity of expression is absolutely essential and the teacher will be needed for guidance in critical comparison. On occasion he may himself give talks and then provide notes, but if the class do the work themselves, there will be a keener response and a more likely benefit.

The information obtained needs to be tabulated. Here are suggested headings for general guidance:

i. *How did it happen?*

Origins, spread, acceptance/possible persecution, appeal to the individual, to society.

ii. *What effect had it on people?*

Effect upon the emotions of individuals, upon the development of society.

Effect upon the mind, upon behaviour.

How far does each religion take these effects into consideration?

iii. *What did people do about it?*

What made them act as they did?

What was their attitude towards others?

How did it influence "social structure"?

iv. *What kind of a Supreme Being?*

How is He described or indicated?

What is the relation between Him and man?

What things do you consider "good" about this religion?

What things do you consider "bad"? (These answers to be given from the religion itself, without bias of own beliefs and/or Christian attitudes.)

Is it a positive religion?

Is an after-life indicated? If so, what is it like?

Is it a worship based upon fear/love/a philosophy?

v. *What is its conception of Man?*

Is he a slave or a co-partner?

Has he any rights of his own?

Is his belief dictated or from within himself?

vi. *What is its philosophy?*

Is it a negative or a positive approach?

Is anything lacking in it? What? Why?

Could you accept it as a rule of life? Why? Why not?

From these pointers will arise questions that need to be answered in order to ascertain the "value" of each religion to the individual as a mode of living to be followed and a philosophy to be accepted. How far the human personality counts should also be assessed. Healthy and open discussion is necessary, argument and analysis must be developed, pros and cons must be considered; otherwise our pupils will have failed to think for themselves—the essence of the work. Without overriding their views, however, it is the teacher's duty to point the way of Christianity as the supreme philosophy, for it unifies and integrates the life of the individual and society. This should derive from consideration of:

The Christian view of life, immortality, God, Man.

God's omnipotence, His omnipresence; Man's duty to God and his neighbour; prayer; evil; pain; freedom of choice....

Does the Christian base his philosophy on logic or on moral suasion?

Is it a matter of rules and opinions . . . or is it a complete Way of Life?

Had Plato and Aristotle anything to say that might help the Christian?

What views were held by the Stoics and Epicureans?

What did Descartes and Spinoza think about it?

What do "men" say in the twentieth century?

Given sufficient time a class with the ability could dramatise some of Plato's *Dialogues* or produce collections of pungent references from the great philosophers.

Not the least in importance is a kind of summing-up, answers to such questions as—Does each religion find a meaning in human life? If not, to what extent does it help? Can the class list the aspects of human life that reveal the highest good? Are these values personal or social? Discuss Acts xviii. 18, in this light. What was Paul's philosophy? Had it any followers? Has it had any appreciable effect upon life in this country? Does it, today? In this way it is possible to help adolescents realise that the Christian faith is something that demands a decision. This is strengthened by their contact at this age with people from outside the four walls of the classroom—speakers and scholars, distinguished men and women with powerful convictions; now is the time to invite such people to come and speak to and discuss with our pupils who may thus be helped to resolve their doubts and difficulties and diffidences.

2. Set Books

This section is concerned with books on subjects other than Comparative Study of Religions. Set books for study, like all text-books throughout all school courses, are often a temptation and a delusion. They tend to tie the unwary (and lazy) teacher, chapter by chapter to —often—the bitter end. Yet they could, and should, offer many opportunities for adventure. Set books of the "right kind," i.e. both easy enough and yet reliable, are few and far between. These enable a student to confirm or challenge his own views and set him to follow logically a path he may not have travelled before. Teachers should use the set-book method as the author intended; critical guidance and carefully prepared exercises, duly read and assessed and discussed, should be provided. One need hardly say that such a book must be within the range of the class; it should also be of the kind that poses questions without spoon-feeding. One very good book is *God's World*, Yarnold (R.E.P.).

Here, again, the work will be the preparation of material for talks and written exercises. Discussions will arise from these and occasionally a formal debate to be handled precisely and firmly. It is a good thing, too, for the class to ask questions of the teacher—not always a popular procedure with some teachers, who may be afraid of not knowing the answers. But good teachers will regard the poser as an opportunity of "finding out the answer together."

Each book in any suggested list will present its own philosophy, but one particular problem that adolescents imply or "feel" or express clumsily is sure to arise sooner or later, and the set book may well be used to meet it. This is the question that, since Christianity is "played out," what will take its place? (This is a very real question. Even as I write I note the heading of an article in today's "popular press"— "Has Christianity Failed?") Is the answer a code of ethics, some branch of moral philosophy, a series of metaphysical concepts, some "new" creed like Communism . . . "1984"? Adolescents at all intellectual levels, though not always intellectually, will argue fiercely on this.

Here are further books. Others may be noted in educational journals from time to time, and the Bibliography published by the Institute of Christian Education is an excellent source of information. *How Christians Worship*, Fenn (S.C.M.), *The Two Moralities*, Lindsay (Eyre & Spottiswoode), *Why Be Good?* Reid (Hodder &

Stoughton), *Civilisation, Science and Religion,* Ritchie (Penguin), *Personality of Man,* Tyrell (Penguin), *Short History of Mankind,* Somervell (Bell), *Proper Study of Mankind,* Howard (Ginn), *Philosophy of the Good Life,* Gore (Dent), *Philosophy and Religion,* Whitfield (R.E.P.).

If it were not possible to devote time to a set book, which in any case is but one of several approaches to our subject, teachers will find useful information on the *Creed* in their Agreed Syllabuses, e.g. *Durham,* Part II, Ch. 6 (9), and *Cambridge,* 1949 edn., pp. 110–121. Other teachers may care to make good use of Plato's *Phaedo.*

3. *What is Wisdom?*

Philosophy is the love of wisdom, and our duty is to see that adolescents in our care discover to some extent what that wisdom is. One of the best introductions is for the class to turn to Job xxviii. 20, and ponder on the words, "Whence then cometh wisdom and where is the place of understanding?" with the answer in 28, "Behold, the fear of the Lord, that is wisdom; and to depart from evil is understanding" (A.V.). This represents a pre-Christian philosophy, but is not far from Christian philosophy itself. From earliest times philosophers have tried to epitomise experience in some pithy phrase or telling epigram, and many of these are to be found in the Wisdom Literature.

Teachers will need to provide background to these books, to indicate the God-man, man-God relationships that developed from the earliest conception of Yahweh and His divine work as a Creator, down to the Father revealed in Jesus Christ. From the study of religions a class may already have postulated the intelligent working of God or God's agent in creation as Wisdom—the Jewish word for it. Heracleitus first called this shadowy ruler—the "One Being"—by the name "Logos." Philo of Alexandria came near to linking the Jewish "wisdom" with the later Platonic conception of the word "Logos"— the Word that "was made flesh and dwelt among us." In Christ we have moved from this idea to a "proof" of the wisdom of God, for He came to bring Life—and Life everlasting. Teachers will find a most useful chapter on "The Logos" in *The Jews from Cyrus to Herod,* Snaith (R.E.P.).

The study of the Wisdom books, then, will be to some extent within this stream of thought; it provides absorbing and fascinating work.

As the *Hertfordshire Syllabus* says: "It is to little purpose to ask baldly if the Wisdom books are true. The question should be—What are they trying to tell us? How do they interpret human life and conduct, the universe and God? What values are they setting before us? What challenges or assurances do they utter? What are their literary form, historical background, and moral and spiritual meaning?"

The Wisdom literature reflects the strangely earthy and practical philosophy of the Hebrews, evolved it would seem from the prophecies and productive of a system of practical ethics. It was, of course, greatly influenced by the spread of Hellenism and Hellenistic thought after the conquests of Alexander; it is precisely this which distinguishes it from the canonical Old Testament books.

PROVERBS is probably the simplest of the books. Chapters i.–ix. depict Wisdom as an agent of God. Post-Exilic monotheism could not attribute divinity to anyone save to God Himself; this was one reason for the Jewish rejection of Jesus. Divine Wisdom produces for man a philosophy of life that is based upon sound principles of conduct and living. There is freedom of choice; good and evil are in opposition. Pupils can here list the virtues of the man who is wise in experience—humility, honesty, generosity, self-control. The girls may profit from a study of the acrostic poem, Chapter xxxi., called by some "the A.B.C. of the perfect wife." (The boys would probably feel "Elle avait toutes les vertus, et elle était insupportable." But in all fairness, the girls could experience much the same feelings about the ideal man in *Ecclesiasticus*.) This chapter might be compared with I Cor. xi.–xiv. The *Teachers' Commentary* (S.C.M.) recommends ii. 13–iii. 20, sufficient for study. Here are found the blessings of Wisdom; the source is God, Who helps man to recognise and follow the good life as well as to recognise and challenge evil—hence, Wisdom is the supreme prize. (Cf. Job xxviii., Wis. ix. 9, Ecclesus. xxiv., Col. i. 15–18.)

In *ECCLESIASTES* there is bitterness and cynicism enough to challenge any adolescent; here is sheer materialism. God is far away and not interested in the world or the people in it; evil flourishes, all is vanity. Man is the victim of chance and time. Have a good time while the going is good. That is almost a modern outlook for some people, and a small dose of this philosophy is probably quite sufficient for our pupils. A good Commentary will sift the interpolations that some later—rather shocked—writer has inserted to soften the harsh-ness of this philosophy. These might be listed and set alongside the original and their wise counsels discussed.

JOB might be regarded from the angle of undeserved suffering and lead to a study of Lewis's *Problem of Pain* (Centenary Press). The underlying thought might be defined as showing that suffering tests faith, character, personal integrity, personal philosophy. The philo-sopher is concerned how to fit evil and pain into his pattern of the universe; adolescents will find by discussion that evil and pain are not synonymous.

As far as teaching method is concerned, individuals in the class could prepare the arguments of the three friends and Job's answers. An excellent way to bring out the core of the book is to dramatise it. The version given in the *Oxford Shorter Bible*, pp. 234–244, is valu-able. The book should not be left without a comparison with the cruci-fixion of Christ, from which evil and suffering came forth much good. Philosophy says that suffering may be both ennobling (of one's charac-ter) and creative (of other's happiness), but Richard Baxter reminds us that "Christ leads us through no darker rooms than He went through before." This is the Christian philosophy of life. Teachers will find Wheeler Robinson's book, *The Cross in the Old Testament* (S.C.M.), extremely useful in this connection.

In the Apocrypha is *ECCLESIASTICUS*, in which "the Lord created" Wisdom. Here our pupils may glean a delightful set of maxims and wise counsels—"Gather wisdom from thy youth up; so shalt thou find wisdom till thine old age." The main recommenda-tions are Chapters xxxviii. 1–14, 24–34, and xliv. 1–15. Significant words and phrases may be entered in note-books under selected head-ings—Friendship, The Good Life, Good Deeds, etc.

Part of the *WISDOM OF SOLOMON* could be a useful if some-what highly intellectual pursuit if treated as an argument between Jewish and Greek thought about Wisdom. It might be better to dis-cuss striking lines rather than dissipate time over a wider study—e.g., "He that setteth at nought wisdom and discernment is miser-able. . . ." Recommended chapters—iii., iv. 7–10, 13, vii. 22–viii. 21. In vii. 25, we have a link between the Stoic "spirit of Wisdom" and John's "logos" that might be explored. In viii. 7, Wisdom is given as the basis of the four cardinal virtues—self-control, justice, understanding, courage. Some comparison with Stoic philosophy might be made here, too. In verses 19 and 20 are intriguing thoughts, and a class might enjoy arguing, "I was a witty child, and had a good spirit; yea, rather, being good, I came into a body undefiled."

4. *The Four Freedoms*

Rousseau said, "Man was born free and is everywhere in chains."

Some of our children may not even know what the Four Freedoms are, nor when, where and why they were propounded. It will be good for them to discover the philosophy lying behind them, and even before that to find out what lies behind Freedom itself. They may find it to be a dedication of one's personality and life to the accept- ance of an ideal, and they will learn that belief in Freedom urges man to *act*.

These freedoms—Freedom of Worship, Freedom from Fear, Free- dom from Want, Freedom of Speech—may be treated geographically, historically, morally. The best major approach is through the Project (Chapter XVI). The class should divide into four groups, each taking one of the four Freedoms. There will be search work, lecturettes, dis- cussions, talks, visits, essays and the like. Even in the upper forms it is a good thing for expression in Art and Craft, so that discoveries may be shown in friezes, posters and so forth, leading to an exhibition for the school. Social Studies and other normal time-table subjects may usefully be correlated. The guidance on Projects in Chapter XVI will be applicable here.

General aspects of study might follow these lines :

i. *Freedom of Worship*

> What does it mean? Question of creeds, beliefs, rights of others? How many Christian sects? What are they? How did they arise?
>
> Does the thought challenge our sense of values? How and why?
>
> Is refraining from interfering with the various sects the way of preserving Freedom of Worship?
>
> Does it mean anything more positive?
>
> What is tolerance?
>
> What is intolerance? What examples are there historically?
>
> What is religion? What does it entail?
>
> What does it mean to the present class/to the present generation?

ii. *Freedom from Fear*

Of what? Of whom? Of what and of whom are nations afraid?
Look at this from point of view of employer/employee.
Particular fears—parents', teachers', children's, farmers'. . . .
How does it involve loyalties, responsibilities, to God/to others/
to ourselves?
Discuss "Service before Self."
Can fear be met with understanding—wisdom?
What philosophy will meet this "freedom"?

iii. *Freedom from Want*

Difference between "want" and "need."
Employment for all?
Providing and taking opportunities—for what?
Self or country?
Resources of all nations.
Paradox of world gluts and world shortages; supply and demand;
unemployment; waste and famine.
Affording a war *v.* affording a peace. "Guns before butter."
New homes for old.
Provision for the aged and infirm; pensions; the future.
"He that saveth his life . . ." "Take no thought . . ."
"Give us this day . . ." "Am I my brother's keeper?"

iv. *Freedom of Speech*

Without it we lose the power to fight for the other three.
Democracy *v.* totalitarianism.
Propaganda, tabloid thinking, judgment of facts; evaluation of
the "truth." What do *we* think?
Mental *v.* physical "slavery."
Freedom of Education, of Religion, of the Press, to vote.
Democracy and the individual; and citizenship.
Working together for good—for whose good?
When is it legitimate to curb these freedoms?

5. *Some "Perennial Problems"*

By the time adolescents reach the sixth form, even in some cases
the fifth, they have long since accepted with more than a little reluctance the explanations and wise counsels of "authority"—whether
it be teacher or parent. Some of them will have styled themselves
agnostics and materialists, and here and there we meet the scientific
humanist and existentialist in the making. Beating about the bush or
giving patently evasive answers or even "laying down the law" will

not convince such adolescents one way or the other. They have to be given the opportunity of studying and discussing problems as these arise or as they themselves bring them into the open. It is then that the teacher has to provide ways and means of approaching such problems so that the eventual result is satisfying to the questioner, not to himself; and it is to be hoped that such results will satisfy the mind, intellectually, and the spirit. For the teacher must be able to lead his pupils to see that "the holding of Christian convictions is not only consistent with intellectual integrity, but demands it." Jesus said, "Thou shalt love the Lord thy God . . . with heart, soul and *mind*."

By far the best exposition of problems of this kind will be found in the *Hertfordshire Syllabus*, Chapter XVIII. Teachers are strongly recommended to use the guidance given in this valuable chapter, on such topics as The Existence of God, The Creation, Is it True? Miracles, Evil and Pain and The Future Life. Following it (XIX) is a note on the supposed conflict of Science and Religious Knowledge. This might well have been treated also as a "perennial problem." The Science Sixths especially may feel that their knowledge of scientific method is the key to life itself and that the Arts Sixths have no idea of how to use it. With his knowledge of philosophy the teacher needs to come between these to show that the approach of science and religion "is to the same universe, and that they involve needs and capacities belonging to one and the same human creature. We are all religious in some sort and we have all the instincts which, highly developed, make the scientist. . . . The foundations of religion owe nothing to science, though science may help to lay them bare." (*Approach to Religious Education*, Yeaxlee (S.C.M.).)

The teacher's task is a difficult one: he has to resolve this supposed conflict between religion and science. Not the least of his problems will be to help his pupils realise that philosophy has a special claim where the sciences are concerned; she has to review their postulates and harmonise them within the "whole" of which they are but part. But the Christian faith also has a claim to truth and does not accept purely scientific explanations as being sufficient answer to the eternal questions, "What is Man?" and "Why am I here?" A Christian philosophy recognises that both scientific and religious truth—or, reality in terms of quantity and quality—are necessary for a complete grasp of a meaning for life. This apparent conflict is indeed a problem already needing attention in our schools.

6. History of Philosophy

Here is, admittedly, a formidable task, and for adolescents not more than the merest introduction may be envisaged. But again the Arts and Science Sixths might find in this study a much-needed *rapprochement* whereby the cleavage sometimes existing between them may be bridged and a more balanced view of life generally be the result.

A general survey might first be given, so that pupils see what has happened through the ages in which man has sought the secret of life and creation. Something on these lines may be attempted, detail being dependent upon the time allotted and the intellect of the class.

Begins with THALES, Greece, 600 B.C.

i. *Greek Philosophy* 600 B.C.–A.D. 500.

(a) Pre-Socratic —Pythagorus, Democritus; polytheism.
(b) Socratic —development of scientific thinking.
—Heracleitus—"One Being"—Logos.
—Socrates; the climax of monotheism.
—Plato; man's soul proof of God.
—Aristotle; transcendence of God.
(c) Post-Socratic—Epicureans: life of pleasure.
—Stoics: self-sufficiency of man.

(*N.B.* During this period four great religions were forming—Buddhism, Confucianism, Islam, Christianity.)

ii. *Mediæval Philosophy* (Scholasticism) A.D. 500–1600.

Realism *v.* idealism (Anselm).
Nominalism; Rationalism (Abelard).
Return to Aristotelian ideals of transcendence of God (Aquinas).
Opposition to this revival under Scotus.
Growing Christian theology.

iii. *Modern Philosophy* 1600–Present Day.

(a) Pre-Kantian: Descartes ("Cogitur, ergo sum"); Spinoza, Locke, Hume. . . .
(b) German influence: Kant, Fichte, Hegel, Nietzsche. . . .
(c) Positivism and Evolution: Mill, Spencer. . . .

iv. *Contemporary Philosophy*.

Development of thought; impact of scientific progress.
Bergson, Whitehead, Russell, Wittgenstein. . . .

(*N.B.*—Recent thought may be dealt with as a separate aspect, as in No. 8, q.v.)

7. *Great Philosophers*

Again we remember that the greatest question propounded for and by philosophers is the Psalmist's "What is Man?" They continue to ask, "What is the meaning of human life?" Throughout history they have sought a balanced view constructed from the truths discovered by thinkers in all walks of life, and for all of them it has been and still is an endless search for a universally valid answer to an eternal riddle.

Only very advanced pupils can cover a measure of useful work in this section. Study of abstruse theories held by the great philosophers is too difficult for the untrained mind. But it is good for them to have some general idea of the development of philosophical thought, and how man is still searching for a unifying explanation of the universe and a reason for his existence—especially when, as the victims of adolescence, they are certain *they* have the answers to these very questions!

The study may be approached through reading, talks, lecturettes, dramatisation, projects (see relevant chapters), based on aspects of the work of some of these great men and preserving some sense of chronology. Such a course might include—Plato, Socrates, Aquinas, Spinoza, Descartes, Locke, Hegel, Whitehead, Wm. Temple, Russell, Moore, Ryle. . . . On the Third Programme of the B.B.C. there are frequently short and usefully informative talks on certain of the great philosophers; these should be made known to the class in good time. The School Broadcasts on philosophical topics should be used as adjuncts to the course being followed, not as "pre-fabricated lessons" and certainly not instead of or for lack of a prepared school course.

8. *Philosophy Today*

The first thing an adolescent must realise about present-day philosophy is the paradox of man's conquest of space and time. We are no longer in touch with some continental countries and are therefore deprived of some exchange of theories and development of thought; there is undoubtedly a loss in this lack of interchange. Philosophic thought for us is in the main English-speaking philosophy. Here and there we do receive translations of "continentals," however, and it is also fortunate that we have contact still with India, the home of Eastern Philosophy.

In Rusk's *Philosophical Bases of Education* signs are indicated of a healthy return to the basic idealism of Plato, seen further in Joad's

Guide to Philosophy and Green's *Problem of Good*. These men say there is an inner harmony of man's soul and the universe, and that man's mind is in touch with the eternal. There seems to be an endeavour to Christianise Plato, the influence of whose philosophy can be traced in the first chapter of the Fourth Gospel. Canon Spencer Leeson takes this stand in his *Christian Education*. Leonard Hodgson relates Christian thought to ideas in other systems in *Towards a Christian Philosophy*.

But from the continent has come the influence of Wittgenstein, whose main philosophic thought is simple in its profundity—"One is a philosopher because one thinks in a certain way, not because one holds certain opinions." A simple definition for the adolescent until he begins to think about it! Ryle has followed Wittgenstein's theories of language and speech in his *Concept of Mind,* with a somewhat materialistic development. It should be possible to introduce Science Sixths to books on the philosophy of their own subjects; books by Russell and Whitehead are suggested. Brief mention of these men should be sufficient to show the present-day trend.

Summing-up

It is obvious that not all these lines of approach can be undertaken in any one course in any one school; they should be regarded as suggestions, as are all the methods in Part II of this book. But through our endeavours, by whatever means we use in this all-important subject, perhaps our pupils will have a better notion of the Christian interpretation of the meaning of life. Being introduced to philosophical thought at school they may even continue to practise their interest in it long after they have left. The great thing to remember is that the work must be *theirs*—by search, preparation, explanation, drama, brains trusts, question and answer, project, individual study ... NOT the teacher's—by talk and—occasional—chalk.

Plato said that teachers must be philosophers if they are to inspire and guide youth. "And to Socrates we owe the greatest demonstration the world has seen of what it means to be a philosopher—not to use words or hear them without making sure of what they mean, not to allow oneself to be victimised by one set of facts or ideas apart from others with which they are by nature bound up, to think things together and think through them at all costs, and to recognise that 'the spirit of man is the candle of the Lord'." (Yeaxlee, op. cit.)

As Christian teachers, too, we believe that our task is to tackle the problems of the Christian faith in such a way that our boys and girls develop their own powers of constructive thought about life and its meaning. If we do not we are not doing our job. We must see that our pupils leave us with at least the beginnings of a Christian philosophy of life because we ourselves believe that this philosophy is the highest that we can follow.

What is the meaning of human life? This we may not ourselves wholly understand, but we can discover with our pupils how, throughout the ages, man has responded to his Creator, how theories have been evolved, refuted and revived, and how man has continued his search for an answer even to the present moment. And we need to remember with Thomas Traherne that "He knoweth nothing as he ought to know, who thinks he knoweth anything without seeing its place and manner how it relates to God, angels and men, and to all the creatures in earth, heaven and hell, time and eternity."

PART III

SOURCES OF INFORMATION AND GUIDANCE

CHAPTER XXI

THE INSTITUTE OF CHRISTIAN EDUCATION AND SCMS

Its work; subscriptions; value to the practising teacher; SCMS.

In the course of this book I have frequently mentioned the Institute, more familiarly, and indeed, more affectionately, known as the I.C.E., as an organisation available to help practising teachers of Religious Knowledge.

Its Headquarters are at: 46, Gordon Square, London, W.C.1.

Its object is to promote Christian Education at home and overseas.

Its work:

(a) Advice to members on all aspects of teaching the Christian faith.

(b) Organisation of, or assistance in planning, Conferences and Vacation Courses.

(c) Preparation of bibliographies, syllabuses, etc.

(d) Supply of terminal review, *Learning for Living*.

(e) Special assistance to teachers abroad.

(f) Help to Local Associations of Members.

What does all this mean? Just this, that the Institute sets out to give practical and up-to-date guidance on anything and everything you are likely to need in your work as a teacher of Religious Knowledge.

Here are some typical questions asked of and answered by the Institute:

For "suggestions which would assist me to make Religious Instruction more vital and practical to a class of girls aged fourteen and fifteen, who are definitely retarded."

"I have decided to try for the University of London Certificate in Religious Knowledge and would like to be put in touch with some tutor near."

Some ask for information on Bible Archæology, book lists, in-dividual problems, visual aids, vacation courses.

"Can you recommend books of prayers for twelve- and thirteen-year-old girls, and of daily reading?"

"I should like some help with the ordering of books for class use, maps, pictures, etc. The syllabus we use is . . ."

The Institute provides detailed and accurate information on all matters concerning the teaching of the Bible and the Christian faith; syllabuses are devised, books recommended for class and library.

The Study and Research Committee keeps under regular review general and specific problems related to the teaching of Religious Knowledge and the broader issues of Christian Education. It sets up ad hoc groups to study questions concerning Worship, Religious Education in Secondary Modern Schools, Agreed Syllabuses and their Revision, the Relationship between Day and Sunday School Teaching. A close liaison with the various Institutes is maintained, as also with the N.U.T. and the Joint Four, and with S.C.M. in Schools.

An annual residential Vacation Course in Religious Knowledge is organised at which leading Biblical scholars and theologians are secured as lecturers, and experts deal with questions of Method and Presentation. Local Education Authorities recognise the worth of these Courses and give financial aid to teachers attending.

The Institute has an Overseas Appointments Bureau which recruits teachers for secondary schools and training colleges in certain overseas territories, particularly in East and West Africa. Teachers who are practising Christians and well qualified and experienced profession-ally are needed for a variety of subjects. The posts are on short-service contracts of varying length, and superannuation rights in this country may be safeguarded for appointments up to a period of five years. The Overseas Secretary of the Institute will always be glad to supply information about opportunities and conditions in the areas for which the Bureau works.

Included in the annual subscription is the supply each term of *Learning for Living*, containing articles on background, exegesis, methods of religious teaching, book reviews and the like.

This is wonderful value for the annual subscription of thirty shillings. Even this may be reduced, if the subscriber finds it necessary, to a minimum of 10s. without *Learning for Living* or 15s. with it. In some cases the school will pay a subscription on behalf of the teacher, but the reduced contributions are allowed only to personal subscribers. A further advantage to you is that as a member you may purchase booklets at reduced prices, e.g. *The Teaching of Miracles, School Worship, Religious Education* of children at different age ranges, *List of Illustrations, Bibliography for the Use of Teachers of Religious Knowledge, Agreed Syllabuses and their Revision*.

Local Associations of the Institute are established in some sixty centres. There may be one in your town or district which organises conferences, lectures, group studies, etc., and gives you the opportunity of meeting like-minded people for exchange of views and experience.

You need the I.C.E. and it needs you.

The Secretary will send full information; join, and once a member you will appreciate the worth of the Institute more than you may at present believe.

Working in close co-operation with I.C.E. is SCMS. Originally concentrating upon Grammar and similar schools, it has turned its attention to Secondary Modern Schools with considerable success and impact. The Honorary Director of I.C.E. writes, "SCMS goes direct to senior pupils, on the correct assumption that there is much to do that teachers cannot do . . . SCMS specialises in knowing about older pupils, their needs and attitudes and this is a major subject for I.C.E. research at present." (*Learning for Living*, Sept. 1962.)

SCMS does this through several channels. It provides help in the formation and running of Christian groups in schools, organises conferences, supplies discussion material and runs international and inter-denominational holiday and work parties at home and abroad.

Full information as to subscriptions and practical assistance may be obtained from SCMS, Annandale, North End Road, London, N.W.11.

CHAPTER XXII

QUALIFICATIONS

Likely examinations for Diplomas and Certificates; courses of study and conferences.

FROM time to time it has been emphasised that teachers of Religious Knowledge do need special training and qualifications if they are to do their work really well. The specialist in particular should spend time on studying for some kind of Certificate or Diploma, even if he cannot manage a degree; there is already a great demand for the specialist, as can be seen by perusing the vacancies advertised in the various periodicals of the profession, and this is likely to increase as the subject takes its place more and more as one of the utmost importance in schools.

To this end, therefore, here are some of the more likely examinations and courses of study open to the busy teacher; details of these can be obtained from the Secretaries and Registrars of the Examining Boards indicated.

A more detailed list of these may be obtained from the Institute of Christian Education.

(a) *Lambeth Diploma* S.Th. (now open to Men and Women).

Designed for graduate teachers wishing to qualify in Theology. *Greek* essential. Courses under recognised coaches or at approved colleges. Information from: Miss A. E. Fryer, M.A., S.Th., 27, Eaton Court, Guildford.

(b) *London University* B.D. Degree.

Greek and Latin essential.

(c) *King's College Diploma* A.K.C.

Information: King's College, London.

(d) *University of London External Diploma in Theology*

Examination in six subjects, including knowledge of Greek for translation purposes.

Information: External Registrar, University of London, Senate House, W.C.1.

(e) *University of London Extension Diploma in Biblical Studies*

Extension lectures for three years, and a fourth year for two selected subjects.

No Greek.

Information: Director of Dept. of Extra-Mural Studies, Senate House, W.C.1.

(f) *University of London Certificate of Proficiency*

Examination in whole or two parts.

Greek optional.

Information: as (e)

(g) *University of Cambridge Certificate in Religious Knowledge*

Examination may be taken in one or two years, not necessarily consecutively.

No Greek necessary.

Information: Secretary, Syndicate Buildings, Cambridge.

(h) *University of Oxford Diploma in Theology*

For graduates of the University.

Two compulsory and one optional.

Information: Registrar, University Registry, Oxford.

(i) *University of Durham Diploma in Biblical Studies*

Open to graduates; one year full at Durham or Newcastle; or two years part-time Newcastle.

Greek essential.

Information: Registrar, The University, Durham.

(j) *University of Durham Certificate in Biblical Studies*

Open to non-graduates.

Greek not essential.

Information: as (i)

(k) *University of Leeds Diploma in Biblical Studies*

Attendance at classes one evening weekly and on Saturday mornings for two sessions.

No Greek.

Information: Registrar, The University, Leeds.

(l) *University of Leeds Diploma in Religious Education*

Attendance at classes one evening per week, and on Saturday mornings for three sessions.

No Greek.

Information: Secretary, Institute of Education, The University, Leeds, 2.

(m) *University of Manchester Certificate in Theology*
  Attendance at lectures one hour per week for a year.
  Both *Greek* and *Hebrew* required if not offered in (n).
  Information: Registrar, The University, Manchester.

(n) *University of Manchester Certificate in Biblical Knowledge*
  No academic requirements necessary. Three papers.
  No *Greek* or *Hebrew* required. May be offered in preparation
  for (m).
  Information: as for (m).

(o) *University of Sheffield Certificate in Biblical History and
  Literature*
  Two years' part-time study, attendance at two evening lec-
  tures weekly for two terms.
  One *or* both—Elementary *Greek*; Elementary *Hebrew*.
  Information: Registrar, The University, Sheffield.

(p) *University of Glasgow Diploma in Biblical Studies*
  For graduates of Scottish Universities (and others approved by
  Senatus).
  Information: Dr. A. C. Craig, 16 Bank St., Glasgow, W.2.

(q) *University College of North Wales, Bangor, Diploma in
  Theology*
  Open to students of Theological Colleges affiliated to the
  University.
  Information: Registrar, University College of North Wales,
  Bangor.

(r) *Selly Oak Colleges Diploma in Religious Education* [1]
  One-year residential course for Trained Teachers.
  No Greek.
  Information: Registrar, Selly Oak Colleges, Birmingham, 29.

COURSES

Most ordinary Training Colleges now provide supplementary
courses in Divinity and allied aspects of Religious Knowledge, so
that teachers can develop their interests and gain knowledge of both
background and method. No teacher should miss these opportunities

[1] The Selly Oak Course is probably the best course for practising teachers at
present available. Work at a graduate standard is expected, and the qualification
gained is first-rate and highly prized. It would be a generous gesture if Local
Education Authorities released teachers to attend this (or a similar) course, especially
in view of the tremendous interest being taken in the subject since the 1944 Act.

of attending courses, held usually during vacations, but often during term time. The Institute of Christian Education advertises Divinity and other Courses in *Learning for Living* and through correspondence from its headquarters (see p. 244). The Ministry of Education organises regular Courses for secondary and primary teachers; particulars of these are available from L.E.A.'s, or direct from the Ministry's Short Courses Department.

There are others, however, that should not be overlooked; they often have a bias that may appeal especially to you.

Such courses as those run by the *British Drama League* sometimes provide excellent guidance on Stage Production and Playwriting that may stand you in good stead if you are interested in the dramatic aspect of religious teaching.

Information from: 9, Fitzroy Square, London, W.1.

The *Religious Drama Society* runs courses on Religious Drama from time to time, in various parts of the country. These courses give most practical help in all kinds of dramatic expression, including production, music, miming, designing and writing religious drama. The charges for these lectures are usually extremely small.

Information from: Religious Drama Society, 166, Shaftesbury Avenue, W.C.2.

Incidentally, if you never attend such a course you certainly should avail yourself of the excellent quarterly magazine of the Society—*Christian Drama*—in which you will find most useful articles and book and play reviews.

The opportunity to attend *Conferences* arises quite often nowadays, when so much is being done by the various Church Councils for young people. The best of these at present is the one arranged as the British Conference of Christian Youth and organised by the Youth Department of the British Council of Churches. For a week, some hundreds of delegates from churches of all denominations, together with a number from other countries, meet to discuss and listen to lectures based on some over-all theme such as "One God and Father of All." These Conferences are in the "great tradition of the ecumenical youth gatherings at Amsterdam in 1939 and Oslo in 1947", Bangor in 1951, Bristol in 1956 and Bossey in 1958. Try to attend such a Conference if you can; you may even be able to take with you some of your older boys and girls, and so introduce them to the vastness of the Christian faith in this and other lands.

BIBLIOGRAPHY

Bibliographies quickly go out of date, and the books given here are those that have already proved their value and are likely to remain standard works for some time. Some are relatively recent and have made immediate impact upon the work of teaching Religion. For full and detailed books lists, see I.C.E. *Bibliography* and reviews in *Learning for Living*.

BIBLES, ETC.

O.U.P., C.U.P., and Eyre & Spottiswoode, as well as the British and Foreign Bible Society, have various editions and styles; teachers would do well to examine several of these.

MOFFATT : A New Translation. (Hodder & Stoughton.)
PEAKE : Commentary on the Bible. (Nelson.)
MANSON : Companion to the Bible. (Clark.)
Teacher's Commentary. (S.C.M.)
TREBLE : Classical and Bible Reference Book. (Murray.)
Theological Word Book of the Bible. (S.C.M.)
New English Bible. (O.U.P./C.U.P.)
PHILLIPS : New Testament in Modern English. (Bles, Collins.)
WILLIAMS : The New Testament in Plain English. (S.P.C.K.)
NEIL : One Volume Bible Commentary. (Hodder & Stoughton.)
NEIL : Rediscovery of the Bible. (Hodder & Stoughton.)
LOWTHER CLARKE : Concise Bible Commentary. (S.P.C.K.)

BIBLE BACKGROUND

SCHOFIELD : Historical Background to the Bible. (Nelson.)
SCHOFIELD : Religious Background of the Bible. (Nelson.)
OESTERLEY and ROBINSON : History of Israel. (O.U.P.)
RATTEY : Short History of the Hebrews. (O.U.P.)
HEBERT : The Bible from Within. (O.U.P.)
PARMELEE : Guide-book to the Bible. (Eng. Univ. Press.)
ENTWISTLE : Bible Guide-book. (S.C.M.)
Torch Bible Comentaries. (S.C.M.)
WILSON : Through the Bible. (Collins.)
CLOGG : Introduction to New Testament. (U.L.P.)
DEANE : The World Christ Knew. (British Publishers Guild.)

KENYON : Story of the Bible. (Murray.)
HEATON : Everyday Life in Old Testament Times. (Batsford.)
BOUQUET : Everyday Life in New Testament Times. (Batsford.)
SKINNER : Concerning the Bible. (Sampson Low.)
YOUNGMAN : Background to the Bible (4). (Hulton Educnl. Pubns.)

NEW TESTAMENT

HEARD : Introduction to the New Testament. (Black.)
TAYLOR : The Gospels : Short Introduction. (Epworth.)
PATERSON SMYTH : People's Life of Christ. (Hodder & Stoughton.)
MARTIN : Parables of the Gospels. (S.C.M.)
Miracles. (I.C.E.)
HODGSON : Teaching the Christian Faith. (I.C.E.)
GLOVER : Jesus of History. (S.C.M.)
Moffatt's Commentaries on all Gospels. (Hodder & Stoughton.)
HUNTER : Introducing the New Testament. (S.C.M.)
GUY : Study of the Gospels. (Macmillan.)
MANSON : The Servant-Messiah. (C.U.P.)
WILLINK : The Book of the Acts. (R.E.P.)
GUY : The Acts of the Apostles. (Macmillan.)
CULLMANN : Early Christian Worship. (S.C.M.)
CAIRD : The Apostolic Age. (Duckworth.)

STORY OF CHRISTIANITY

SOMERVELL : Short History of our Religion. (Bell.)
WALKER : First Church History. (S.C.M.)
DIAMOND : How the Gospel came to Britain. (O.U.P.)
GARLICK : Pioneers of the Kingdom. (Highway.)
DEARMER : Story of the Prayer Book. (O.U.P.)
HAYES : Yarns Series. (R.E.P.)
Torch Biographies. (S.C.M.)
NEEDHAM : How to Study an Old Church. (Batsford.)
BARKER : Through the Ages. (Church Information Board.)
BEVAN : Christianity. (O.U.P.)
MOORE : Furtherance of the Gospel. (O.U.P.)
SMART : Walking with God. (Hodder & Stoughton.)
YOUNGMAN : Into All the World. (Ed. Arnold.)

METHODS AND AIDS

GILL and PULLEN : Methods of Teaching in Sunday Schools. (N.S.S.U.)
AVERY : Teaching Scripture. (R.E.P.)
HUGHES : Teaching the Bible to Juniors. (Newnes.)

HUGHES: Teaching the Bible to Seniors. (Newnes.)
ARUNDALE: Project Work in Religious Education. (R.E.P.)
ARUNDALE: Religious Education in the Senior School. (Nelson.)
HOLLAND: Self-Teaching Guides. (National Society.)
Religious Education of Pupils, 7–11, 11–16 and 16–19. (I.C.E.)
YEAXLEE: Handbook to Cambridgeshire Syllabus. (S.C.M.)
Handbook of Christian Teaching. (Sheldon Press.)
HAMILTON (ed.): Christian Education Handbooks. (R.E.P.)
WALKER: Paternoster Tales. (S.P.C.K.)
Christian Drama (Quarterly). (R.D.S.)
COLLINS: Christian Play-making. (U.L.P.)
GRAY: Dramatised Bible Reader. (Grant.)
DOWNS: Bible as Drama. (R.E.P.)
SAYERS: Man Born to be King. (Gollancz.)
POLLOCK and GRANTHAM: Men of God. (Gollancz.)
COLLINS: Acting Games. (U.L.P.)
SAUNDERS: Singing Games (S.P.C.K.)
PHILLIPS: A Man Called Jesus. (Bles.)
WHANSLAW: Puppetry Books (various). (R.E.P.)
HIGHAM: Blackboard Drawing. (S.P.C.K.)
RUSSELL: Easy Models. (S.P.C.K.)
Frieze Painting Books. (E.H.P.)
Bible Model Cut-outs. (N.S.S.U.)
Scripture Flannelgraph. (Arnold.)
WHANSLAW: Bible Model Books (various) (R.E.P.)
WHANSLAW: Shadow Play. (Gardner.)
Visual Aid Year-Book. (*Daily Mail*.)
WRIGHT: Biblical Costume. (S.P.C.K.)
WARR: Practical Books, I–V. (E.H.P.)
Westminster Atlas. Library and Class editions. (S.C.M.)
New Scripture Atlas. (S.P.C.K.)
HUGHES: Teaching the Bible Today. (I.C.E.)
GROLLENBERG: Atlas of the Bible. (Nelson.)
BROWN: Storyteller in Religious Education. (R.E.P.)
For guidance on Films and Pictures, apply to the I.C.E.

PSYCHOLOGY AND RELIGION

YEAXLEE: Religion and the Growing Mind. (Nisbet.)
WILSON: Child Psychology and Religious Education. (S.C.M.)
NICHOLL: Child's Personal Religion. (S.P.C.K.)
REED: Eighty Thousand Adolescents. (Allen & Unwin.)
WHEELER: Adventure of Youth. (U.L.P.)

Bompas Smith: Growing Minds. (U.L.P.)
Kenwrick: The Religious Quest. (S.P.C.K.)

Ethics and Doctrine

Osborne: Christian Ethics. (O.U.P.)
Dewar: Outline of New Testament Ethics. (U.L.P.)
Jeffreys: Education, Christian or Pagan? (U.L.P.)
Reeves: Growing up in a Modern Society. (U.L.P.)
Jeffreys: Claucon: Inquiry into Aims of Education. (Pitman.)
Niblett: Christian Education in a Secular Society. (O.U.P.)
Selby Wright: Asking Them Questions (3). (O.U.P.)
Jeffreys: Kingdom of this World. (Mowbray.)
Lewis: Problem of Pain. (Centenary Publications.)
Sandhurst: How Heathen is Britain? (Collins.)
Phillips: Religions of the World. (R.E.P.)
Hodgson: Christian Faith and Practice. (Blackwell.)
Gray: A Theology for Youth. (R.E.P.)
Loukes: Teenage Religion. (S.C.M)
Read: The Christian Faith. (E.U.P.)
Caird: The Truth of the Gospel. (O.U.P.)
Coulson: Science and Christian Belief. (O.U.P.)
Raven: Christianity and Science. (Lutterworth.)
Begin Here! (Discussion topics). (R.E.P.)
Thinking Things Through. (S.C.M.)
Neill: The Christian's God. (Lutterworth.)

Prayer and Worship

Fosdick: Meaning of Prayer. (S.C.M.)
Dewar: Training in Prayer. (Rich & Cowan.)
Martin: Book of Prayers for Schools. (S.C.M.)
Pain: Prayers for Senior Worship. (N.S.S.U.)
Shambrook: Daily Worship. (U.L.P.)
Ferguson: The School Assembly. (R.E.P.)
Ferguson: Prayer Project. (R.E.P.)
Pain: Youth at Worship. (Meth. S.S. Dept.)
Pain: Prayers for Junior Worship. (N.S.S.U.)
Two-Minute Bible Readings. (S.C.M.)
English School Service Book. (U.L.P.)
English School Hymn Book. (U.L.P.)
Prescott: Teacher's Assembly Books. (Blandford Press.)
Religious Education in Secondary Schools. (Nelson.)
Vroom: Introduction to the Prayer Book. (S.P.C.K.)
Winward: Teach Yourself to Pray. (E.U.P.)

SOME USEFUL ADDRESSES

Dr. Barnardo's Homes, Stepney Causeway, E.1.
British and Foreign Bible Society, 146, Queen Victoria Street, E.C.4.
Zenana Missionary Society, 39, Ladbroke Grove, W.11.
International Missionary Council, Edinburgh House, 2, Eaton Gate, S.W.1.
London Missionary Society, Livingstone House, 42, Broadway, S.W.1.
National Institute for the Deaf, 105, Gower Street, W.C.1.
National Institute for the Blind, 224, Gt. Portland Street, W.1.
St. Dunstan's, 191, Marylebone Road, N.W.1.
Salvation Army, Queen Victoria Street, E.C.4.
Society for Propagation of the Gospel, 15, Tufton Street, S.W.1.
Religious Drama Society, 166, Shaftesbury Avenue, W.C.2.
Student Christian Movement, "Annandale," North End Road, N.W.11.
Institute of Christian Education, 46, Gordon Square, W.1.
Methodist Youth Department, 2, Ludgate Circus House, E.C.4.
National Sunday School Union, 104, Newgate Street, E.C.1.
British Museum, W.C.1.
Common Ground, Ltd., 181, High Holborn, W.C.1.
Central Film Library, Government Buildings, Bromyard Avenue, Acton, W.3.
Educational Puppetry Institute, 26, Albert Road, Withington, Manchester, 20.
G.B. Film Library, Aintree Road, Perivale, Middx.
Newton & Co., 72, Wigmore Street, S.W.1.
Youth Hostels Association, Welwyn Garden City, Herts.
Girl Guides' Association, Buckingham Palace Road, S.W.1.
Boy Scouts' Association, Buckingham Palace Road, S.W.1.
Bible Reading Fellowship, 12, Buckingham Palace Gardens, S.W.1.
I.B.R.A., Central Hall Buildings, Durnsford Road, S.W.19.
Scripture Union, 3, Wigmore Street, W.1.
Colonial Department, Institute of Education, University of London.
Hulton Educational Publications, 55/59, Saffron House, E.C.1.
British Council of Churches, 10, Eaton Gate, S.W.1.

(N.B.—The Telephone Directory is a certain source of addresses required.)

INDEX